WAR IN THE WILD EAST

WAR IN THE WILD EAST

The German Army and Soviet Partisans

BEN SHEPHERD

HARVARD UNIVERSITY PRESS
Cambridge, Massachusetts
London, England
2004

Library of Congress Cataloging-in-Publication Data

Shepherd, Ben (Benjamin V.)
    War in the wild East : the German Army and Soviet partisans /
Ben Shepherd.
        p.   cm.
    Includes bibliographical references and index.
    ISBN 0-674-01296-8 (alk. paper)
    1. World War, 1939–1945—Destruction and pillage.   2. World War,
1939–1945—Destruction and pillage—Soviet Union.   3. World War,
1939–1945—Atrocities.   4. World War, 1939–1945—Atrocities—
Soviet Union.   5. Germany. Heer. Security Division, 221st.
6. Germany. Heer—History—World War, 1939–1945.   7. Germany.
Heer—Officers—Attitudes.   8. Soviet Union—History—German
occupation, 1941–1944.   I. Title.

D804.G4S49   2004
940.54′05′0947—dc22   2004047268

Contents

Maps and photographs follow page 128

WAR IN THE WILD EAST

Introduction

The German Army, or Wehrmacht, of World War II enjoys a reputation as probably the most proficient, dogged, and effective fighting force ever to have taken the field of modern combat.[1] At the peak of its efficacy it combined the en masse assembly of first-rate manpower, trained to matchless standards, with a then-unchallenged expertise in armored warfare. Along with the devastatingly effective air support of the German Luftwaffe, it achieved a sequence of successes in the Blitzkrieg campaigns that in three years achieved the conquest of almost the entire landmass between Egypt and the Arctic, the Pyrenees and the Caucasus.

The pinnacle of the Wehrmacht's triumphs were its six-week conquest of the Low Countries and France in spring 1940 and its seizure, in the face of massive logistical problems and a numerically superior enemy, of an enormous tract of European Russia during its eastern campaign of the second half of 1941. From 1943, with the vast size, fearful environmental conditions, and seemingly inexhaustible manpower of the Soviet Union ranged against it in the east, and the economic and military might of the United States increasingly being brought to bear in the Anglo-American war effort in the west, the Wehrmacht executed a fighting retreat of unparalleled tenacity lasting up to the final weeks of the war in 1945. It is scarcely surprising that, even today, the ranks of Wehrmacht veterans, thinning by the week though they are, retain a deep and heartfelt pride in the part they played in such achievements.

Yet this image of military prowess and efficiency, valid though it is, is not the whole truth. For one thing, it ignores manifold problems that increasingly beleaguered the Wehrmacht throughout the war. Chronic defects in manpower and equipment plagued many of its elements. Nor were the higher levels of its officer corps quite the well-oiled machine of popular belief. Flair, efficiency, and resourcefulness were there. Yet so too were organizational chaos, institutional rivalry, operational shortcomings, and strategic ineptitude—and this, contrary to former Wehrmacht generals' postwar claims, *without* Hitler's destructive meddling in military affairs.[2]

Another side of the Wehrmacht's record is far more damning. It transcends narrower issues of military performance to encompass basic issues of moral decency. For the Wehrmacht was also the main sword arm of a barbaric dictatorship. This was a dictatorship that, as well as terrorizing millions of Jews, Communists, and other racial and political "enemies" in its own country, unleashed a war of extermination upon huge swathes of the population of mainland Europe. Merely to eulogize the Wehrmacht's military prowess, then, is to ignore not only its military and organizational failings but also its infinitely darker record of complicity in state-sponsored genocide, terror, and rapacious economic exploitation.

Since antiquity, warfare has been marked by atrocity, brutality, and excess. These may have been born of the "heat of battle" or of the systematic terror tactics that empires such as Assyria, Macedonia, and Rome practiced to spectacular effect. In recent centuries, an emerging fusion of mass industrialization, popular mobilization, technology, ideology, and nationalism has ensured that warfare in its modern, "total" form—waged not just by standing armies, but by entire populations—is marked by killing and destruction on an immeasurably greater scale. Be it the devastation of Spanish villages by Napoleon's troops during the Peninsular War or the mayhem of ethnic cleansing in the 1990s, the main brunt of such carnage has been borne by civilians. The war of extermination that the Wehrmacht waged, then, must be seen against a backdrop of bloodshed and devastation to which dozens of ostensibly cultured and civilized nations have contributed.

But beyond all that, a particularly malignant blend of ideology, careerism, military and organizational failings, pressure of circumstances, and other motivations lent the Wehrmacht's conduct a destructiveness that in many ways exceeded all that had gone before or has come since.

This book is a study of what drove the brutality of the Wehrmacht's war of extermination at the level not of high command, but of prosecution: the officers and soldiers of the lower levels, the "ordinary men" who put it into action. The setting is its antipartisan campaign in the German-occupied Soviet Union.

Revealing and explaining the Wehrmacht's grim record has proven, and continues to prove, an undertaking with severe intellectual, moral, and political complications. Ultimately, however, the undertaking remains necessary. For it illuminates the involvement of an organization to which millions of ordinary men belonged in a criminal enterprise of murderous enormity. As the German historian Wolfram Wette asks: "How was it possible that Germans—members, by their reckoning, of a highly advanced and cultured nation—could perpetrate, know about, or tolerate a war of extermination, a war that trampled the norms of humanity and justice underfoot?"[3]

That said, National Socialist conviction was just one of many influences, albeit a fundamentally important one, that colored the mindset and behavior of ordinary Germans during the Third Reich. The mindset and behavior of Wehrmacht soldiers were shaped also by the attitudes of the institution to which they belonged, of their age cohort, and of the section of society from which they originated; by the dynamics of Third Reich policymaking; and by wartime conditions. Nor, moreover, did the eleven million individuals who made up the Wehrmacht between 1933 and 1945 absorb these influences in the same way or to the same degree. No explanation of their brutality can ignore such diversity, for it was this, ultimately, that determined the propensity for brutality within each unit, indeed each individual. As Theo Schulte, citing the German historian Rolf Elble, wrote in 1989, "what is even meant by 'the Wehrmacht' as a term when applied to a military establishment of more than eleven million personnel? Every single army group? Every single division or even company? Or even every single soldier?"[4]

That said, the overall picture is infinitely darker than that of cozy postwar myth.

Anyone familiar with 1950s war movies will recognize the figure of the "good" German soldier, embodied by the likes of James Mason as Field Marshal Rommel in the 1951 film *The Desert Fox*. There is an abundance of poetic clichés to describe him: the soldier who fought for his country out of a sense of simple patriotic duty, regarded the National Socialist regime with distaste, and remained untainted by the outrages that were perpetrated in its name. The soldier of the "clean" Wehrmacht, a redoubt of decency in the face of the depravities that the SS and other sinister Nazi agencies inflicted upon Jews, prisoners of war, slave workers, and millions of other victims. The soldier for whom, in some especially brave instances, a burgeoning sense of horror at the Nazi regime and the moral and material level to which it had reduced his country ultimately turned to action in the valiant yet doomed attempt to assassinate Hitler in the Bomb Plot of July 1944. The institution to which he belonged, while not completely blemish-free, was essentially an oasis of honor and decency amidst the barbaric apparatus of the Nazi state.

A nationwide denial, within the Federal Republic of Germany, of past collective culpability, and the need to infuse her new federal army, her Bundeswehr, with a sense of history and tradition, ensured that the immediate postwar period saw such imagery perpetuated in the republic's cultural and political life. By the late 1960s, however, historians were amassing evidence that revealed the German Army's senior officer corps as a group whose urge for full-scale rearmament, and recovery of the prestige it had lost after defeat in World War I—prospects dangled enticingly under its nose by the National Socialists—had combined with its infiltration by pro-Nazi elements to secure its support for, and voluntary assimilation into, Hitler's regime. After Hitler's elevation to power in 1933, an event in which the Wehrmacht's predecessor institution, the Reichswehr, was instrumental, the same factors led the senior officer corps to become increasingly embroiled in the regime's ideological radicalism and criminal actions.[5]

In shaping the institutional framework in which all Wehrmacht officers and men would eventually conduct themselves, the motives of different groups of senior officers were crucial. So too was a series of developments that, during the 1930s particularly, channeled those motives in the direction of ever-greater assimilation with both the Nazi regime and the cause of exterminationist warfare. The backdrop created by these complex factors was of fundamental importance to the unfolding campaigns in the east.

Essentially, the Reichswehr officer corps straddled three generations. The eldest, born primarily during the 1870s and 1880s, hailed mainly from conservative, aristocratic stock, the mainstay of the old Prussian officer corps. For the most part, it had filled junior and middle-ranking staff posts in the imperial army during World War I. A second generation, born mainly during the 1890s, originated in the far more numerous, socially diverse "front-line fighters" of that war. A third, born after 1900, had entered the officer corps during the years of the democratic Weimar Republic that succeeded the imperial regime in 1918. The increased social exclusivity that accompanied the vastly diminished state of the army in the wake of defeat in World War I ensured that this generation, unlike that of the frontline fighters, was predominantly aristocratic in origin. But its outlook, reflecting changes in warfare as a whole, was more technocratic than that of its older aristocratic colleagues.[6]

The first motive that fed emergence of support for National Socialism across these officer generations was their shared desire for rearmament and national aggrandizement. The Treaty of Versailles, imposed by the victorious Allies in 1919, had infused this desire with special potency. It had condemned the country to huge war indemnities, loss of overseas colonies, acceptance of all the guilt for causing the war in the first place, and, particularly cruelly for the officer corps, evisceration of Germany's military capability. When Lieutenant Colonel Joachim von Stülpnagel, later chief of the Reichswehr Personnel Office, pilloried the Versailles treaty as "a wrong built on lies," he spoke for virtually all his colleagues.[7]

The officer corps expected little help in overturning the treaty from the new republic's democratically elected politicians. As far as most Reichswehr officers were concerned, the dissemination of timid, febrile democratic ideals had helped erode Germany's fighting spirit and thus contributed directly to its defeat in World War I. The fact that it was the foolish and extreme nature of the German military's own policies that were primarily responsible for losing the war, as well as for helping start it, was conveniently overlooked. Democratic politicians, officers generally felt, were unpatriotic meddlers. They lacked any conception of national defense or of Germany's potential for future greatness. Worse, they had every intention of preventing the Reichswehr from attaining either. General Hans von Seeckt, head of the Troops Office, the vastly scaled-down replacement of the old German general staff, castigated the Social Democratic Party of Germany for seeking to make Germany "defenceless abroad." Stülpnagel wrote that the Reichswehr was being compelled to execute two mutually incompatible duties: "protection of the constitution, of a diseased system, and preparation for the war of liberation, which is prevented by the system."[8] In time, then, the Nazis' advocacy of the overturning of Versailles, of rearmament, and of the abolition of democracy struck a rich seam.

So too did Hitler's call for the seizure of living space (*Lebensraum*) in eastern Europe. Many officers hankered after Lebensraum in part out of desire for national greatness. In part, it was a legacy of the Germans' long-standing urge to "go east." In part, finally, it was a development of the old imperial army's expansionist ambitions of World War I.[9] Not only had eastern expansion been an aim of the Kaiser's army, however; it also had been abruptly reversed, in a cruelly felt blow, when the Versailles Treaty had hived off much of the old kingdom of Prussia to form part of the new state of Poland.[10] Officers might be divided over how much Lebensraum Germany should aspire to seizing, or at whose expense it should be seized,[11] but, true to the "catchall" character of so much of the Nazi program, Lebensraum was a sufficiently broad concept to rally widespread support without close scrutiny of the details.

Rearmament and territorial aggrandizement were not the officer corps' only goals. The interwar years were an era in which economic, technological, and military trends, and the effects of World War I in particular, had created a form of warfare far more technocratic, far more modernized, and therefore far more destructive than before. Thus did the Reichswehr officer corps come to see that only by orientating itself toward efficiency and technology would it be able to wield real power.[12]

The rise of the military technocrat, the "specialist in mass destruction," was an international phenomenon during the interwar years. But for the Reichswehr officer corps, the attraction of gaining expertise in matters of technological mass destruction was heightened by additional factors. Officers of the Weimar generation, too young to have fought in World War I, were anxious for the rapid advancement that the successful prosecution of technological warfare would bring.[13] The overriding obsession across the officer corps, however, was expunging the bitter memory of defeat by being better prepared next time.[14] Thus did the officer corps grow increasingly fixated with narrow, technocratic professionalism, with the organization, specialization, and exercise of mass violence. It was apparent to the Reichswehr that Weimar's democratic regime lacked both the ability and the will to mobilize the nation for a war fought on these lines. It was apparent also, following its failure, in 1932, to rally support for a popular military dictatorship, that the Reichswehr itself lacked the ability. That left National Socialism.[15]

For National Socialism offered more than just rearmament. It also offered an ideology to mobilize not just bodies and materials for the warfare the Reichswehr envisaged but, crucially, minds also. It sought to create a "national community," encompassing the dissolution of all class cleavages and a welding together of the German people in the cause of "the Nation." Officers of all generations came to support this ideal because they believed it would unite the people, in a way more durable than the patriotic ardor of 1914 had done, for the cause of war.[16] General Werner von Blomberg, the minister for war in Hitler's first cabinet, was only one officer among many who perceived the potency of the unifying moral backbone that National Socialism seemed to offer. "A commitment to nationalism is the clear basis of all military activity," he declared a year after the Nazis assumed power. "We must not forget, however, that the ideology which shaped the new State is not only nationalist but national *socialist*. National Socialism derives the basis for its actions from the vital necessities of the whole nation and from the duty of working together for the totality of the nation. It is founded on the idea of the community of blood and fate of all Germans. There is no dispute about the fact that this law is and must remain the basis for the service of the German soldier."[17]

In the age of industrialized, technological warfare, of course, the mobilization would need to be technical also. Yet here too National Socialism seemed the way forward. The technocratic Weimar generation of officers perceived this necessity with particular enthusiasm. Despite their own generally aristocratic background, they happily identified machinery-minded soldiers from industrial areas as the likeliest bearers of the technical excellence needed in the new, mass-destruction-fixated army that was their goal. By mobilizing the minds of such soldiers, the unifying ideology of National Socialism would mobilize their technical abilities also.[18]

Rearmament, careerism, national expansion, and mass mobilization for a war of technocratic, professionalized violence, then, were four key motives that, overall, drew the Reichswehr officer corps into alliance with National Socialism. They did not program it on a straight course toward the exterminationist form of warfare on which it eventually would embark during World War II, but they did lead officers to embrace National Socialism in the first place. They would, moreover, come to play a key role in shaping decisions officers took that did indeed eventually set them, albeit via a less-than-direct route, upon such a course.

In the meantime, there were already additional reasons why many younger officers in particular were drawn to National Socialism. These too would in time come to radicalize and brutalize them fundamentally.

Before World War I, there was already a longing in middle-class circles—the same circles from which the majority of the era's front-line officers came—for a national racial community headed by a strong leader *(Führer)* figure.[19] Such a figure, it was hoped, would provide the national unity, idealism, and dynamism that would release millions of restless young men from the stagnant boredom of Wilhelmine society. For many front-line officers, the comradeship, sacrifice, and sheer intensity of experience they underwent in combat during World War I, particularly in the charnel house of the trenches, were the physical embodiment of those values, and boosted the desire for a leader who would personify them.[20] Among the Weimar officer generation the hankering was to a large extent instilled by right-wing schoolteachers and university professors. These preached a strain of nationalism combining calls for inspirational leadership, hostility to the democratic system, and a veneration of German culture bordering on the spiritual.[21]

The negative side of these ideals was that they combined calls for a vigorous, unified German nation, socially united and culturally superior, with a contemptuous rejection of groups that, because they were deemed inferior, subversive, or both, were seen as a threat to the health of the "national organism": Jews, Bolsheviks, and the races of the lands to Germany's east.

The potential such prejudice held to permeate the officer corps was increased by that fact that, to some extent, older, conservative officers harbored it also. Already during the imperial German period, there were signs that wider societal anti-Semitism—a phenomenon too vast and labyrinthine to address here—was combining with the aristocratic, elitist self-image of the imperial officer corps to provide bountiful ground for distaste toward what many officers regarded as the urban, decadent, and money-minded Jew.[22] Parliamentary legislation according Jews increasingly equal citizens' rights, moreover, caused many to see Jews as synonymous with the onset of those liberal, democratic forces that had sapped Germany's wartime resolve. Thus, toward the end of World War I, Lieutenant Colonel Max Bauer, chief of operations at Army High Command, wrote that the German chancellor, Bethmann Hollweg, had "lost the favour of the parties supporting the state . . . through his servility to the parties fighting against a strong monarchy [Jewish liberalism and social democracy]." Some years later Lieutenant Colonel Werner von Fritsch, who during the 1930s would become the Army's commander-in-chief, wrote that "Ebert [the president of the Weimar Republic], pacifists, Jews, democrats . . . and the French are all the same thing, namely the people who want to destroy Germany."[23]

The unifying reasons for anti-Bolshevism's potency across officer generations originated in the period preceding and following Germany's collapse in 1918. If liberalism, pacifism, and democracy had eroded the dam shielding Germany from impending disaster, officers perceived, then Bolshevism had shattered it. This too was a view shared across officer generations. Spreading disgruntlement, defeatism, and talk of revolution, Bolshevik subversives inspired by the success of their comrades in the Russian Revolution were seen to have engineered a hemorrhaging of discipline and morale. This had led, successively, to disintegration on the home front in 1917–18, mutiny in the armed forces—via the insidious influence of the soldiers' councils, the "bastard offspring of the Bolshevik-influenced revolution"[24]—and near-collapse of the established order.

Anti-Slavism completed the infernal trinity. This too was a prejudice to which older officers were receptive also. Anti-Slavism was, after all, rooted both in centuries-old russophobia, common to the West in general, and in Germanic notions of racial superiority over eastern neighbors. In the eighteenth and nineteenth centuries, writers such as Friedrich Forster, Johann Reitemeier, and Heinrich von Treitschke had vilified the "Sarmatian brutality" and "notorious uncleanliness" of Germany's eastern neighbors, celebrated Germany's "pitiless racial struggle" against them, and preached the virtues of Germany's mission to civilize them.[25]

Yet it was younger officers who harbored these prejudices with most conviction. For one thing, they were integral to the "conservative revolutionary" nationalism to which the Weimar officer generation was subjected in its youth. But it was among many former frontline officers that such prejudices displayed their hardest edge and most frightening potential. The cause lay in the intensity of the experiences these officers had undergone during World War I and immediately after.[26]

Ernst Jünger conveys how World War I brutalized men. "The turmoil of our feelings was called forth by rage, alcohol, and the thirst for blood," he wrote. "As we advanced heavily but irresistibly toward the enemy lines, I was boiling over with a fury which gripped me—it gripped us all—in an inexplicable way. The overpowering desire to kill gave me wings. Rage squeezed bitter tears from my eyes . . . Only the spell of primeval instinct remained."[27] The prejudices of many former front-liners, then, were combined with a strong propensity for violence.

For officers who had served on the Eastern Front during World War I, radicalization also came from another direction: the direct, violent encounter, at a formative time in their lives, with the "backward east."[28] Hermann Hoth, one of Germany's leading Panzer generals of World War II, described the "bestial cruelty" the Russians had meted out during their invasion of East Prussia in 1914, and Gottard Heinrici, another leading World War II field commander, wrote that the Russians had perpetrated acts of "blind destruction and mindless annihilation of a kind we never would have thought possible."[29] This was gross oversimplification, but it testifies both to the strength of anti-Slavic prejudice and how the intensity of wartime conditions radicalized it. The backwardness of Russian living conditions also made a deeply negative impression. One officer serving in Russia in 1918 described it as a "lumbering, living corpse, riddled with every kind of disease."[30] Given that this aversion often was combined with a Germanic zeal to civilize, the failure of the High Command in the East, OberOst, to "rationalize, germanise, and civilize" its occupied regions during World War I was taken as a lost opportunity, a bitter blow, and a spur to subjugate the east thoroughly when future opportunity arose.[31]

Toward the end of the war, of course, the "backward east" became the cradle not only of Slavism but also of the "dangerous, subversive" creed of Bolshevism. In turn, the fact that many prominent Bolsheviks were Jews caused some officers to develop a view of the enemy in which Jew and Bolshevik shared the same face.[32] Such, for instance, were the sentiments expressed in the diary of Major Bothmer, a German staff officer stationed in Russia in 1918. Bothmer singled out the Jews as the source of all Bolshevik infection there, and detailed with gratuitous relish how he would "just love to see a few hundred of these Jew-boys strung up from the walls of the Kremlin, dying as slowly as possible so's to enhance the effect."[33] Even older, conservative officers, of an often far-from-radical disposition, drew similar connections. Karl-Heinrich von Stülpnagel, regarding the Soviet Union in 1935, wrote that the "devious machinations of the mainly Jewish [Soviet] commissars recall the nightmare beginnings of the Communist regime."[34]

After all the undeniable hardships and sacrifices they had both undergone and witnessed during World War I, many officers, though front-line officers particularly, found defeat in 1918 and the humiliation heaped upon army and nation in its wake awful if not impossible to bear. Consequently the odium with which they regarded the "guilty" parties—democrats, Bolsheviks, and the Jews with whom they associated both—was particularly poisonous. It assumed particularly violent form during the "Time of Struggle."

"Time of Struggle" was the overly poetic label for the period of gore-spattered havoc that engulfed both Germany's cities and its eastern borders in the wake of the country's military defeat. Within Germany, it saw Marxist-inspired uprisings apparently mushroom all over the country, and a panic-stricken appeal by the new republican government both to the regular Reichswehr and to right-wing vigilante Free Corps units, composed largely of monarchist and nationalist ex-soldiers, to suppress them. Together, the Reichswehr and Free Corps crushed the uprisings wherever they sprang up—Berlin, Munich, the Ruhr—and restored order. The period also saw Free Corps and Reichswehr units take on Polish separatists in Silesia and Posen, and the Free Corps itself take on a succession of enemies in the Baltic region: pro-Bolshevik Latvians, nationalist Baltic armies, and Bolshevik forces in the Russian civil war.

Anti-Bolshevism, anti-Semitism, antidemocracy, anti-Slavism, eastward expansion of Germany's realm, and a brute desire, forged in war, for extreme violence all inspired different Free Corps men to different degrees. Overall, however, there is no doubt that many officers, whether they continued in the Reichswehr or were readmitted only with the military expansion of the 1930s, were marked indelibly by the Time of Struggle.[35] For the forces that inspired officers during its course were in turn intensified by it. "Someone wants to hand part of our land over to barbarians!" wrote Heinz Guderian—who in later years would play a pivotal role in developing Germany's Panzer force and leading it into action—to his wife during the height of the Free Corps campaign; "the Poles, Lithuanians and Latvians are halfway to wild animals. Shabby, dirty, devious, incompetent, and gone to the dogs!" In Mitau in the Baltic, he wrote, "the Bolsheviks lord it all over the place and cavort like beasts."[36]

The legacy of the Time of Struggle was not the main reason why the Reichswehr officer corps as a whole was attracted to National Socialism. It did, however, ensure that many officers who were attracted to it were attracted for reasons that National Socialist doctrine fused and intensified to shape their conception and prosecution of the "eastern crusade" during World War II. Even before that, the ideological mindset prevalent among the Reichswehr officer corps' increasingly predominant younger sections ensured that much of the officer corps supported National Socialism not only from the head—founded on the perception that National Socialism offered opportunities to reassert and extend its military and political power—but also from the heart.

Thus did a panoply of motivations—militaristic, imperialist, technocratic, careerist, and ideological—generate a huge measure of approval of National Socialism within the Reichswehr officer corps. The approval was not universal. Many older, conservative Reichswehr officers were appalled by the doctrine of thuggery and upheaval espoused by Ernst Röhm and the populist rabble-rousers of the Nazis' paramilitary organization, the SA (Sturmabteilung, or Storm Section). They also were intensely unsettled by the desire these elements harbored for a "Brown Revolution" to "sweep away the forces of privilege and reaction" in German society. Increasingly, however, they went along with the course their more preponderant younger, radical colleagues were setting. Hitler helped ensure conservative officers' widespread approval of his passage to power by directing at them a "flood of lip service to nationalism, tradition, the Prussian spirit, Western values, or the spirit of the front-line soldier, ostentatious displays of respect for the person of the Reich President, and stress upon decency, morality, order, Christianity, and all those concepts which went with a conservative idea of the state." For the most part, reservations that remained once Hitler was in power were further eroded by a "policy of friendly gestures and marks of favour."[37]

But the fact that certain elements of the officer corps needed more convincing than others needs to be recognized. It shows that the officer corps' brutalization under the Third Reich was not inevitable and that, even as it was taking place, there were limits to its penetration of the officer corps.

Generally speaking, however, people and events conspired to ensure that such elements could do little between 1933 and 1941 to halt the new Wehrmacht's slide down this slope.

During the Third Reich's early years, most senior officers, through whatever combination of calculation and zeal, cooperated with the regime approvingly.[38] In the Night of the Long Knives of June 1934, which with the murder of the SA leaders removed its main rival as the nation's would-be sole bearer of arms, the officer corps was thoroughly implicated. This was followed two months later by the introduction of what Blomberg saw as something essential to demonstrating that the Wehrmacht merited the trust Hitler had invested in it: an oath of allegiance to Hitler personally. By chiming closely with soldiers' traditional notions of honor and loyalty toward the head of state, this fastened the officer corps further to Hitler by a simple yet powerful expedient.

The cause of fastening the Wehrmacht to the national community led, over the next three years, to the remodeling of the new, expanded Wehrmacht as the embodiment of the "national racial community," the increasingly systematic exclusion of all political and racial elements for whom that community held no place, and the intensifying ideological instruction, *by the Wehrmacht itself*, of the rank and file. Within the officer corps, no noticeable opposition to any of these steps emerged.

Indeed, in both composition and outlook the officer corps itself already was starting to change fundamentally. Expansion of the Wehrmacht combined with meritocratic National Socialist principles— albeit meritocratic principles applicable only to those of the right race, political persuasion, and so on—to subject the officer corps to a process of enlargement, upheaval, and social diversification. As well as recruiting new, young, and politically impressionable officers en masse from a social spectrum much wider than the officer corps' traditional base, the Wehrmacht reactivated many ex-officers of the front-line generation. Thus for many did the Wehrmacht provide a longed-for "return to arms," recovery of personal prestige, and an end to the perilous economic existence to which they had been condemned as civilians in the circumstances of hyperinflation, mass unemployment, and pandemic bankruptcy that blighted the Weimar Republic throughout so much of its existence.[39] Meanwhile, many former front-line officers who had continued to serve in the Reichswehr found new opportunities for advancement at the highest levels.

All this created an officer corps markedly more middle class and above all more nazified than its predecessor. And it was a self-imposed process.

An additional, albeit less centrally important, motivation for the officer corps to bind itself closely to the regime came from the very nature of Third Reich policymaking. Third Reich policy development was shaped not just by direction from Hitler, but also by the initiatives of rival power blocs jockeying for position.[40] The military aspirations of other Reich elites threatened the Wehrmacht's status as "sole bearer of arms." Hitler had disposed of the leadership of the SA, the officer corps' main rival during the regime's early years, because he knew that the SA never would have provided the rigorous professionalism that the foundation and training of his new national army required. Once these were assured with the Wehrmacht, however, he placed no checks on the military aspirations of the SS. The growth of the combat wing of the SS, the Waffen-SS, was a reminder, if any was needed, of the senior officer corps' need to keep ideological pace with the regime if it was to prevent further erosion of its power.

More decisive in smoothing the senior officer corps' path to criminality, however, was the outcome of its own internal power struggles. Some more conservative officers, though supportive of National Socialism in principle, were anxious that the Wehrmacht work in a spirit of partnership with the regime, but not one of total assimilation. Moreover, although virtually all senior officers favored aggressive war of some kind, some were growing thoroughly alarmed at the accelerated pace toward and likely scope of a war for which they felt Germany was not ready.

But numerous factors ensured that, in 1938, this "opposition" was overruled and outmaneuvered by both Hitler and its more numerous younger, radical colleagues. It did not oppose National Socialism in principle; indeed Blomberg, whose nerve failed over the acceleration toward war that year, had been one of National Socialism's most zealous advocates from the start. It was rent by division itself— Blomberg and Fritsch, the army commander-in-chief, having always been at loggerheads over how far the Wehrmacht should assimilate with the regime—which Hitler and the officer corps' more nazified elements exploited. Finally, it lacked the ruthlessness of its opponents; in the event, both Blomberg and Fritsch fell from office when unsubstantiated tales about their private lives "happened" to come to light.

Thus was Hitler able to purge the conservatives and speed the Wehrmacht's assimilation with both the regime and its increasingly radical agenda. He fired doubters from key positions, replaced them with fawning yes-men, and set up his own personal military office, the Armed Forces High Command, as a rival and officially superior organization to the existing Army High Command. Disquiet remained, but it remained muted. Indeed, the new command setup ensured this near-silence. Hitler, assisted by the conscientious yet toadying General Wilhelm Keitel at the Armed Forces High Command, appointed himself commander-in-chief of all the armed forces. Fritsch's successor as commander-in-chief of the army, General Walther von Brauchitsch, was a man whom Gerhard Weinberg describes as "an anatomical marvel, a man totally without a backbone." And it was his slavish devotion to Hitler, and consequent failure to check the increasing military recklessness and moral degeneration that characterized the Wehrmacht over the following years, that was "perhaps the single most important factor in the internal German military situation before the war and during its first critical years."[41]

Developments throughout Europe that year further stifled dissent within the officer corps. For one thing, both Hitler and many generals believed that Germany's rearmament program, which the officer corps had promoted ardently, had unleashed an arms race that Germany must lose unless she swiftly attained the conquests she sought. For another, the peaceful incorporation into the Reich of Austria in the spring, and of the predominantly German-populated Sudetenland region of Czechoslovakia in the autumn, propelled Hitler's star to new heights in the eyes of the German people. At the same time, Hitler's fury at himself for having settled, in the face of international pressure, for peaceful incorporation of the Sudetenland rather than smashing the whole of Czechoslovakia in war made him determined never to repeat such a "mistake," and determined also to fire any officer who counseled otherwise.[42]

Together, the officer corps' various motives for supporting National Socialism, power rivalries in the Third Reich, the erosion of internal opposition, and the dynamics of the international situation had combined to bind the Wehrmacht even more tightly to a course of assimilation with the regime and pursuit of aggressive war. The invasion of Poland in 1939 would see not only the outbreak of World War II, but the first stages in the evolution of that so brutal form of warfare in which the Wehrmacht would become increasingly enmeshed.

Hitler's determination to smash Poland in 1939 is well documented. Well documented also is how readily the Wehrmacht's senior officer corps viewed the prospect of a reckoning with a country it saw as racially backward, as the bastard spawn of the postwar peace settlement that had eviscerated Germany's eastern territory, and as a source of Lebensraum. Indeed, the prospect of Lebensraum at Poland's expense was a cause around which all elements of the officer corps, including those against war with the Soviet Union, could rally.[43]

Nor did Hitler make any secret of his desire that the Polish campaign be fought with special harshness. For the Germans were going in to Poland not merely to defeat it, but to subjugate it utterly so that it could not "be taken into account as a political factor for the next few decades." Thus, as Poland's antiquated and outnumbered forces were swept aside in the Blitzkrieg campaign that followed, SS task forces or Einsatzgruppen, charged with liquidating all possible sources of opposition to future German administration, followed on the heels of the advancing armies. They rounded up and murdered members of the Polish ruling and administrative classes, the clergy, and the intelligentsia. They also killed around 7,000 Jews, and expelled many more into Soviet-occupied eastern Poland. By December 1939 the full tally of their victims had reached 50,000.[44]

Yet such elements of sanity and restraint as the Wehrmacht's senior officer corps retained failed to arrest the increasingly radical, brutal course on which the corps was set.[45]

At least one officer, General Johannes Blaskowitz, was outraged by events, and showed a prescient feel for the likely long-term consequences. "When high officials of the SS and the police call for atrocities and brutalities and publicly praise them," he asserted, "then within the shortest spell of time only the brutal will rule. With astonishing speed men of the same sick leanings and character will come together, in order to give full vent to their beastly and pathological instincts."[46] Far more commonly, however, officers "protested" not in strong moral terms, but in milder practical ones: against SS units "exceeding their authorization," creating unrest among the occupied populace, or damaging the discipline of Wehrmacht troops who had witnessed the killings.

The reasons why protests not only were relatively muted but also relatively infrequent were, first, that Hitler refused to rein in the SS—indeed the Reichsführer-SS, Heinrich Himmler, made clear in March 1940 that Hitler himself had ordered the killings—and, second that, some halfhearted attempts notwithstanding, Brauchitsch failed to mount any significant higher-level protest.[47] More generally, however, field officers were culpable also: some may have protested about "excesses," but all too many approved of the motives. They stopped short of sanctioning the wholesale murder of innocent civilians, but such by now was the officer corps' collective mindframe that the aims of expelling Jews from German-occupied Poland, flushing out all forms of potential resistance, and terrorizing the "inferior" population into acquiescence all met with their extensive accord. Indeed, a number of commanders actively assisted the SS in all these respects, and when it came to what those commanders perceived to be the needs of security, they were quite prepared to use murderous violence themselves.

The moral degeneration the Wehrmacht underwent in Poland set it even more firmly on course for damning collusion in a war of conquest, plunder, subjugation, and mass violence in the Soviet Union. For in acquiescing, indeed colluding in mass murder during this campaign, it became more inured to it in the future.

Then came the Wehrmacht's triumph, inside six weeks, against the

Low Countries and France in the spring of 1940. In the wake of this campaign, Hitler, who as commander-in-chief of the armed forces had actually shown some strategic flair during its course, was praised by Keitel as "the greatest warlord of all time."[48] The result was that his stock with both people and generals rose to its zenith.

It was in this context, on 31 July 1940, that Hitler decided to invade the Soviet Union.

> And so we National Socialists consciously draw a line beneath the foreign policy tendency of our pre-war period. We take up where we broke off six hundred years ago. We stop the endless German movement towards the south and west of Europe, and turn our gaze towards the lands of the east. At long last we put a stop to the colonial and commercial policy of pre-war days and pass over to the territorial policy of the future. But when we speak of new territory in Europe today we must think principally of Russia and her border vassal states. Destiny itself seems to wish to point out the way to us here . . . This colossal Empire in the east is ripe for dissolution, and the end of the Jewish domination in Russia will also be the end of Russia as a state.[49]

So proclaimed Adolf Hitler in *Mein Kampf*, the Nazi "bible" he penned during the 1920s. The ten months that preceded Hitler's decision actually to invade the Soviet Union had seen German arms subdue Poland, Scandinavia, the Low Countries, and France in a succession of triumphant campaigns. The only prominent enemy, stubborn yet isolated, that still defied the Third Reich was Britain and her empire. The timing of Barbarossa was influenced by Hitler's strategically based desire to break Britain's ongoing will to resist by depriving her of potential allies. But the invasion itself was an ambition Hitler had nursed for decades.[50] And the fate he and the Nazi elites had reserved for the Soviet Union was determined by the ideological and economic imperatives of National Socialist imperialism.

The country's retrograde, barbaric Communist system, principal bastion of "Judeo-Bolshevism," was to be destroyed utterly, the backward Slavic peoples of the east subjugated and enslaved, and the country's vast economic potential ruthlessly exploited to feed and supply a Nazi-dominated Europe. "The war against Russia," as Hitler himself said, "will be such that it cannot be conducted in a chivalrous fashion. This struggle is one of ideologies and racial differences and will have to be conducted with unprecedented, merciless, and unrelenting harshness."[51] The fact that the Reich had in August 1939 signed a nonaggression pact with the Soviet Union was forgotten.

The war against the Soviet Union and its horrific consequences were the crowning phase in the Wehrmacht's embroilment in the criminal enormities of the National Socialist regime. It is worth reflecting here on how far the Wehrmacht leadership had in this respect come since Hitler's assumption of power. Indeed, in one sense Wehrmacht leadership is a misnomer. The dwindling portion of the officer corps that still was not thoroughly in thrall to National Socialism, confined mainly to a rump conservative clique, could hope for little in the way of leadership from Field Marshal von Brauchitsch. The portion that was enjoyed a far greater preponderance than it had before the Wehrmacht had remodeled itself as a "people's army," been purged of conservatives from senior positions, dirtied itself in Poland, and basked in the glory of Blitzkrieg triumph.

It is unsurprising, then, that on ideological, imperialist, and careerist grounds, the prospect of a conquered Soviet Union now enticed many officers just as much as, if not more than, the prospect of a conquered Poland.[52] Not only was the Soviet Union the cradle of Germany's ancient racial enemies, the Slavs. It was also the bastion of Bolshevism. And, with the associations many drew between Bolshevism and Jews, the invasion held out the prospect of the ultimate reckoning not only with one dangerous foe, but with three. Colonel-General Hoepner, commander of the Fourth Panzer Group, spoke for many senior officers straining at the leash. "The war against the Soviet Union," he wrote early in May 1941, "is an essential component of the German people's struggle for existence. It is the old struggle of the Germans against the Slavs, the defense of European culture against the Muscovite-Asiatic flood, and the repulsion of Judeo-Bolshevism."[53]

Victory, moreover, promised an extreme "annexationist peace," exceeding Germany's aims for the east in World War I, that would deliver land and resources on a scale far greater than what victory against Poland had delivered. Alfred Rosenberg, Reich minister for the Occupied Eastern Territories, conveyed the magnitude of the prize awaiting: "This 'crusade' against Bolshevism is not just to save the 'poor little Russians' from it for all time, but to drive Germany's global policy and safeguard the German Reich."[54] Moreover, the favor of the regime which the campaign's successful prosecution would bestow upon the officer corps would assure it, collectively and individually, of its position not just in the Reich itself but in German-dominated Europe.[55]

Some older, more cautious officers may not have been quite so mesmerized, but their undoubted propensity for anti-Semitism and anti-Bolshevism helped win them round.[56] Further compulsion came from a set of hard, practical calculations. On the economic front, memories of the last war gave the Wehrmacht leadership more reason than most to fear the consequences of wartime food shortages in the Reich. An immediate benefit of seizing the Soviet Union's foodstuffs would be to prevent a repetition of the erosion of civilian morale that had blighted Germany during World War I.[57] Its economic resources as a whole, meanwhile, would equip Germany for future challenges, against both the British Empire and the United States, for global supremacy.[58]

Of more immediate concern was the current military situation. Some generals did have misgivings about the wider strategic wisdom of a campaign that, with Britain still in the reckoning, would be creating a two-front war. But with the invasion of Britain called off and a strategy to attack her Mediterranean and Middle Eastern holdings insufficiently viable, invading the Soviet Union seemed the only feasible means for the Wehrmacht to demonstrate its prowess in the foreseeable future. This narrow operational consideration overwhelmed such strategic misgivings as some generals felt. It seemed to promise rapid advances across flat terrain, against a Red Army whose officer corps had just been devastated in Stalin's purges and whose combat effectiveness, if its performance in the 1939–40 war against Finland was any guide, was simply shoddy. This, of course, was reckless overconfidence; it reflected a wider institutional failure to appreciate the importance of reliable intelligence and effective logistics. Both led the Wehrmacht's planners to underestimate the capacity of the Red Army to fight defensively and replenish its manpower, and to overestimate their own ability to supply troops expected to advance rapidly across an area that, flat though it was, possessed a truly dire transport infrastructure.[59] But the generals' willful neglect of these considerations undoubtedly strengthened their resolve to attack.

As the buildup to invasion began, moreover, officers persuaded themselves that the Soviets had designs on Finland and Rumania—the latter being a crucial source of the Reich's oil and grain. They also persuaded themselves, in a textbook example of the self-fulfilling prophecy, that Soviet protests against threatening German troop movements were evidence of the Soviets' aggressive intentions.[60]

The sense of urgency created by all these motives, suffused with ideological conviction, determined what was effectively the entire senior officer corps not only to take on the Soviet Union, but to do so with unprecedented ruthlessness. The generals considered the vastness of both the Soviet Union and, whatever else they thought about it, the Red Army, and their own still relatively limited military resources. They concluded that the rigorous exercise of terror against possible resistance from the population and the ruthless prosecution of combat would make a crucial contribution to the campaign's outcome. The fact that such brutal methods chimed not only with Hitler's intentions but also with many officers' ruthless inclinations strengthened the incentive to use them.

The exercise of extreme severity required the troops to have the right attitude. Thus did the officer corps massively step up the indoctrination of its troops, readying them for a crusade against Judeo-Bolshevism and Slavic subhumanity, during the buildup to the invasion. The Wehrmacht leadership also was involved actively and readily in formulating a succession of directives saturated in Nazi ideological language and aimed at spurring the soldiery to the singularly ruthless execution of warfare. The aim of the entire effort was to condition the troops to regard the enemy with brutal disdain and to fight accordingly, to retaliate with ferocious collective reprisals against the slightest resistance from the occupied population, and directly and readily to hand over "suspect elements," particularly Communist functionaries and Jews, to the SS. On this last point particularly, the contrast with the degree of reticence the Wehrmacht had displayed in Poland was startling; but it is worth remembering that both Wehrmacht implication in SS brutality during that campaign and post-Blitzkrieg euphoria had diluted its moral inhibitions considerably.

This does not mean that the Wehrmacht leadership contemplated a *protracted* race war. More-fanatical officers may have harbored this aim, but the majority, if only out of concern for the discipline of their own troops, instead saw the campaign as a necessary but hopefully brief "stretch of dirt." Thus, Wehrmacht laws against soldiers who committed "excesses" against civilians would be suspended only for the duration of the campaign.[61] But the directives the Wehrmacht leadership formulated still indicate a readiness, indeed enthusiasm, for enormous ruthlessness. When the stretch of dirt extended far beyond its expectations, that ruthlessness would intensify.

Yet by accepting the arguments both for invading the Soviet Union and for conducting it so ruthlessly, the Wehrmacht leadership *already* countenanced a far greater scale of *mass* death. Testimony to this was the Army High Command's involvement in plans for the troops to "live off the land" during the advance. This, it held, was the only means of ensuring that its troops would be supplied adequately during the necessarily rapid advance. The desire to safeguard domestic tranquillity in the Reich by ensuring that the troops' needs were not met at the German population's expense hardened the logic even further. Thus the Wehrmacht leadership readily accepted a plan guaranteed to cause the starvation of millions of Soviet prisoners of war and civilians in the occupied areas, something Reich Marshal Göring readily foresaw as "the biggest mass death in Europe since the Thirty Years' War."[62]

The Wehrmacht had expected to destroy the Soviet Union's ramshackle military and political structure in a lightning campaign. It found instead, soon after unleashing the invasion, codenamed Operation Barbarossa, in June 1941, that it had underestimated both the strength of the Red Army and the difficulty of supplying its advancing troops across a region of such vast distance, dire infrastructure and grueling terrain. The soon horribly apparent reality, and the prospect of a lengthy campaign which it augured, created new dynamics in the Wehrmacht's behavior.

Part of its response showed that nazification of the Wehrmacht had not been so wholesale as to extinguish sanity and restraint completely. For some senior officers, the pressures of occupation and combat in the east prompted a more sensible appraisal of how the population should be treated. The new situation did prompt a number of them to recommend watering down the ruthlessness of the corpus of directives that had been issued in 1941. A lengthy campaign, they reasoned, could be won only with the help of the native population itself—as functionaries of occupation administration, as sowers and gatherers of the harvest, and as manpower deployed against their countrymen in the partisans and Red Army. Winning the population over through *viable* occupation policies that did not simply terrorize and exploit it, but offered it something in return, had, they reasoned, assumed new importance.

The miseries Stalin's regime had inflicted upon millions of Soviet citizens would give German calls for cooperation some potential for success—but only if the population was prevented from starving and was engaged by genuinely effective "hearts and minds" measures. Thus some senior officers regulated rationing to try to mitigate the devastating effects of the Wehrmacht's demands on the population's food supply, appealed to prisoners of war to "come over" and take up arms in German service, and, in time, proposed an array of economic, social, and political reforms to try to win over the occupied population for the long term.

In the event, however, the much more brutalizing dynamic that the new circumstances also created increasingly hamstrung the effectiveness of such measures. The Third Reich had not invaded the Soviet Union to curry favor with its population. It had done so in order to subject it to a program of ruthless terror, subjugation, and exploitation. The intensified pressures of a protracted and increasingly difficult campaign, and its wider implications for a war in which Germany now faced not only Britain and the Soviet Union but also, from December 1941, the United States, drove the Nazi elites even more ruthlessly in pursuit of that aim. For in it they now saw not just the fulfillment of their original agendas, but the means by which the occupied territories could be subjugated and exploited as pitilessly as possible in the cause of final victory.

The retirement, forced or otherwise, of almost an entire generation of older generals and field marshals during the winter of 1941–42 bolstered ruthlessness among senior officers; it led to the rise to highest field command of a new cohort of even more harshly inclined officers drawn from the former front-liners of World War I.[63] Thus did the Wehrmacht often meet the mounting challenge of securing the occupied Soviet Union, and exploiting it for the ever more voracious, desperate demands of the Reich's war effort, with intensified terroristic oppression and economic exploitation. Sometimes it relinquished responsibility for "security" and economic exploitation to the SS. Thus did it enable that agency to exploit the occupation for its own aims of destroying the Jewish population in the east and culling the Slavic one.

The results overall left the population half-starved and bereft of millions lost to the demands of compulsory labor service in the Reich. A microcosm of this terrible dynamic was the intensification of the antipartisan campaign. In the central German-occupied Soviet Union, it is estimated to have spawned the destruction of more than 5,000 villages and the killing of up to 300,000 mainly civilian Soviet citizens.[64] Not for nothing does the historian Alexander Werth maintain that the butchery and upheaval inflicted upon "allegedly pro-partisan peasants and their families must rank among the worst atrocities committed by the Germans and their stooges, and that is saying something."[65]

No explanation of the Wehrmacht's intensifying ruthlessness during the war in the east should omit the role of the often provocatively ruthless measures of Stalin's regime itself, and those of its partisans especially. Indeed, as will be seen, the fact that another brutal dictator proved so ready to fling the gloves off in his efforts to drive the "fascist beasts" from Soviet soil was a key factor in the spiral of terror that came to characterize the Russo-German War.[66] Wehrmacht obduracy almost certainly was reinforced, moreover, by the cold, depersonalized nature of modern industrialized warfare—symptomatic of which, lest it be forgotten, were the annihilation of Dresden and Tokyo by Allied fire-bombers and the dropping of the atomic bombs during the same war.[67]

But the overall balance sheet of terror and rapacity, and the decades-long role the motives of the Wehrmacht senior officer corps played in eventually bringing them about, make for a singularly damning picture overall.

The crucial point, however, is this. However condemnatory the picture presented so far, it has focused on the Wehrmacht's behavior as an institution, and on the senior officer corps that shaped it. But the "ordinary" men and women who, in standing by, facilitating, or killing, converted the Third Reich's "higher goals" into reality, were just as essential to the Nazi machine as the elites whose maneuverings shaped those goals in the first place.

Daniel Goldhagen's *Hitler's Willing Executioners* is only one controversial instance of a study that asks "how it was possible" of the middle-ranking desk-bound bureaucrats who processed the Third Reich's criminal decrees, of the lowly functionaries who pulled the trigger or worked the gas chamber, or of the millions who stood by and allowed it all to happen.[68] Because of what they imply for judgment both of an entire generation of Germans *and* of the wider, modern society that produced them, the issues are pressing.

Nowhere are they more pressing, save over the unprecedented phenomenon that was the Holocaust of European Jewry, than over the conduct of the Wehrmacht. For such was its size and importance that the Wehrmacht was the single institution that, more than any other, shaped the lives and actions of ordinary Germans between 1933 and 1945. The Wehrmacht was enormous both in its size and in the diversity of its personnel, of the influences that shaped them, and of the concrete conditions that beset them. A nuanced, differentiated view of the levels below the senior officer corps, of the extent of their brutality and of what caused it, is therefore particularly crucial.

It was not just the doctrines of National Socialism and German military thinking that shaped the attitudes of these men. So too did the influences they had imbibed from the civil society to which most of them, particularly those from older age groups, had belonged for lengthy periods of their adult lives. And, while the doctrines of National Socialism and German military thinking may have reinforced each other to brutal effect in shaping soldiers' behavior, the civilian influences soldiers brought with them into the Wehrmacht did not necessarily work in the same way. Germany's civil society, historians have shown, did not embrace National Socialist values as readily or as extensively as did Germany's military leadership.[69]

Not that Nazi values didn't resonate widely. A great middle-class swathe of small businessmen, small farmers and landowners, white-collar workers and professionals, together with the increasingly "bourgeoisified" workers of the skilled, nonunionized blue-collar sector, proved a receptive audience. All saw the social and economic changes German society was undergoing under Weimar—the economic development of the cities at the expense of the countryside, the mounting power of both organized labor and big business—as a dire threat to their own status and security. And when Germany went into the throes of political and economic chaos after 1929, it was not just personal interests, but the stability of society, politics, and the economy in their entirety that seemed in peril.[70]

Thus did Nazi promises of a "national community," ordered and stable, and devoid of the conflicts generated by class antagonisms and the wranglings of democratic politicians, assume even more urgent appeal. And even when, after the Nazi assumption of power in 1933, the social and economic policies ostensibly designed to bring the national community about assumed often-disappointing substance, the Nazis were able to orchestrate it, in appearance if nothing else, to placate enough members of enough socioeconomic groups enough of the time. Indeed, even this is to underestimate both the depth and broadness of National Socialism's appeal; the impression made by economic policies that, if nothing else, restored full employment to a population ravaged by mass unemployment only a few years previously, was enormous.[71]

The *ideological* dimension of the concept of a national community, with its rejection of certain groups, also resonated with many ordinary Germans. The middle-class aversion to Bolshevism, with the threat to private property and established order it was seen to carry, is explained most easily. Yet anti-Semitism too found fertile ground. Well before 1933, such things as resentment at the perceived concentration of Jewish economic power (fueled, perhaps, by personal avarice) and prejudice against the "alien" Jewish refugees who had emigrated to Germany from eastern Europe were fueling the belief that Jews should be "removed," albeit via economic and legal rather than genocidal means, from the mainstream of German society.[72] All this gave National Socialist anti-Semitism something on which to build.

Attitudes toward eastern races also were susceptible to National Socialism. OberOst's failure to put the occupied east in order during World War I was blamed, quite unjustifiably, on the slothfulness, backwardness, and ingratitude of its Slavic subjects. Literary, academic, and cultural circles therefore became increasingly fixated not only on the collective "primitiveness" of the east, but also on the potential for its development under harsh, efficient German mastery.[73]

Militarism, moreover, enjoyed a particularly pronounced flowering in German culture and society between the wars. The enormous proliferation of veterans' associations and, in the literary world, novels and memoirs that glorified the sacrifice of German soldiers during World War I testifies to this trend.[74]

On the other hand, much of German society remained unimpressed by the Nazis before 1933. Even the national elections of July 1932, the peak of Nazi electoral success under Weimar, delivered them only 37 percent of the vote. It took the "backstairs intrigue" of Germany's conservative elites to lever Hitler into the chancellorship, with the tragically misplaced hope of "taming" him within the confines of respectable office, to get the Nazis into power. Even under the Third Reich itself, amid a welter of National Socialist propaganda and education, the German people did not absorb such spirit to anything like a complete degree. The enduring strength of such forces as class consciousness, religious and moral sensibilities, youthful rebelliousness, and basic disgruntlement at the regime's inability to deliver the state of bounteous egalitarianism it had pledged seriously restricted Nazism's ability to break down all the social and intellectual barriers that confronted it.

None of these reservations converted into widespread, open rebelliousness—though there were scattered forms of rebellion.[75] Their existence, however, does show that the mindset of German society was differentiated, nuanced, and complex. This manner of mindset has obvious implications for any investigation of the conduct of the people's army that emerged from that society.

Coming full circle, finally, it must be recognized that not all the influences officers imbibed from the Wehrmacht itself were necessarily brutalizing. Most if not all of the senior officer corps had gone along with Nazism, in very many cases with enthusiasm, to a very great extent. But officers at all command levels, and not just those of the officer corps' dwindling conservative clique, had their limits. The stress upon such things as decency, morality, and Christianity, with which Hitler had to assuage certain more dubious sections of the officer corps before his assumption of power, shows that certain values that were in reality anathema to National Socialism still were harbored.[76] How far they survived the onslaught of nazification that the Wehrmacht underwent is highly debatable. Certainly, subsequent research now makes Alexander Dallin's assertion that, during the war itself, certain types of officer, "having earned their ranks in earlier days . . . had higher standards of judgement and . . . did not mind reporting to home in terms that ran counter to accepted stereotype" look rather rosy.[77] But as will be seen, the suggestion that this description held truer of some officers than many of their colleagues should not be dismissed. Ultimately, "doubters" might be moved to heroic resistance; the officers who were moved, ultimately, to try to assassinate Hitler are the crowning and sadly all-too-rare example.[78] Generally speaking, an individual with some kind of barrier to the full-scale inculcation of National Socialist ruthlessness was still unlikely to resist the regime openly and heroically. But if the extent and causes of Wehrmacht brutality are to be investigated properly, then nuance is important.[79]

This work focuses on the motives and conduct of field officers of the Wehrmacht's "middle level." Such officers were pivotally important figures. The intermediate command positions they held, and the freedom of action they enjoyed, meant that the orders they issued were a vital cog in the machinery that converted the ideological, military, and economic imperatives of the Third Reich's war of extermination into action. It was these officers, moreover, who generated what is by far the most comprehensive source base available for studying the Wehrmacht in the field: the official paperwork of its field formations.

Armed with this paperwork, the historian is able to analyze orders, conditions, and conduct at the level of the basic administrative unit into which the Wehrmacht was organized, the division. The most comprehensive collections of divisional files also contain material on divisions' subordinate regiments, and below them battalions, as well as on the garrisons of small towns and villages. They also shed light, albeit less directly, on the mass of noncommissioned officers (NCOs) and rank-and-file soldiers. For both divisions and their subordinate units constituted a command level whose decisions affected the mass of Wehrmacht soldiery more directly than those of Hitler and his generals far from the front.[80]

The specific focus is on the officers of the security formations of the Ostheer, the German Eastern Army, that prosecuted the antipartisan campaign in the Soviet Union. The units that constituted the campaign's backbone—the security divisions, and the regiments, battalions, and other units they commanded in turn—are examined within the setting of the central army group's rear area. The unit that is the book's main focus, the 221st Security Division, was one of five such divisions that operated in the Army Group Center Rear Area, which covered much of present-day Belarus, at different times between 1941 and 1943.[81]

Chapter 1 considers the longer-standing military and ideological forces that shaped the antiguerrilla doctrine the Eastern Army took with it into the Soviet Union in 1941. Some of these forces shaped the prosecution of antiguerrilla warfare as a whole during the nineteenth and early twentieth centuries. The influences that conditioned German military thinking on antiguerrilla warfare were particularly brutalizing well before the advent of National Socialism. The National Socialist conception of antiguerrilla warfare that the Wehrmacht took into Poland in 1939 and, particularly, the Soviet Union synthesized and intensified those influences to terrible effect.

Chapters 2 and 3 analyze in depth the unfolding, increasingly radical brutality of the Eastern Army's security campaign during the final six months of 1941. They show that initially it was Jews and Communists who bore the brunt of the Wehrmacht's pitiless, nazified attitude to the business of rear-area security. In time, however, the mounting duration and arduousness both of rear-area security and the entire war in the east piled the pressure on the Wehrmacht's underresourced, inferior security units. The result, an unsurprising one among officers and units already hardened by ruthless doctrine, was the intensification of *indiscriminate* brutality. And all this despite the fact that, at this stage, the Germans faced no genuine partisan threat to speak of.

Chapters 4 through 7 examine the campaign in the field during 1942 and 1943. This period saw the Nazi occupation respond to Germany's deteriorating strategic situation by intensifying terror and exploitation in the occupied rear, with increasingly ruthless economic calculation driving the mass requisitioning of native livestock, the razing of native villages, and above all mass killing in large-scale mobile operations. The regiments, battalions, and garrisons that were subordinate to the security divisions experienced antipartisan warfare most intensely and directly and often lashed out particularly brutally. Yet even during this period, many elements of the Eastern Army realized that, with no quick end to the war in sight, cultivating rather than terrorizing the population was a more viable long-term means of achieving German goals. The Eastern Army's antipartisan campaign thus responded to a burgeoning and increasingly effective partisan movement with a confused and ultimately self-defeating mix of terror and cultivation.

No security division files for the Army Group Center Rear Area survive beyond the end of the summer of 1943. Yet the period on which the book focuses does illuminate the changing, often brutalizing, yet always complex and nuanced impact of the array of personal influences and particular conditions that were brought to bear upon the Wehrmacht's prosecution of the antipartisan campaign in the Soviet Union. Intricate though the issues are, however, no attempt to explain or quantify the brutality of the Wehrmacht as a whole during the Third Reich should lose sight of the sheer dreadfulness of so much of its conduct or of the volume of human misery and destruction that conduct caused.

I

"Success Comes Only through Terror"

THE GERMAN EXPERIENCE OF ANTIGUERRILLA WARFARE

During the nineteenth and early twentieth centuries, as the scale of warfare grew and its stakes were raised, combatant nations often no longer satisfied themselves with merely defeating their adversaries on the field. They sought instead to conquer, subjugate, and exploit. This development, combined with the rise of nation states and the solidifying national and ethnic self-awareness that accompanied it, was a colossal impetus to the emergence of guerrilla warfare.[1] Since then, the use of military invasion as a tool of international power relations has subsided, but both military occupations and guerrilla movements are, for various reasons, still prevalent.

The guerrilla movements that have arisen on all six continents have been united by modes of fighting—determined by their technological or numerical inferiority, the traditions of their peoples, or the character of the terrain—that are a universe away from what conventional practitioners of modern warfare were once used to. By definition, the "war of the flea" is not about open combat with the occupying enemy's armies. It is about covert operations to sabotage his communication and supply lines and disrupt all his efforts to administer and economically exploit his newly conquered territory. Most fearfully for his men in the field, it is about terrorizing his troops with merciless hit-and-run strikes at individual soldiers and detachments. Guerrilla fighting methods, employed not by recognizable uniformed combatants, but by fighters so attired as to be indistinguishable from the wider population, include the forest ambush, the bomb on the rail line, the piano wire across the road, and the knife across the throat at dead of night.

And just as guerrillas feel compelled, for whatever reason, to shun conventional methods of warfare, so too do the security forces committed to combating them. If a guerrilla force is to be effective, it must be able to operate in often-difficult environmental conditions and rough, extensive, and/or inaccessible terrain. Moreover, if it is to obtain the shelter, provisions, and intelligence essential to its survival and success, it must gain a significant measure of support from the wider population. If it enjoys these conditions, an occupier who deploys purely conventional military tactics against it, however numerically superior his own troops, is unlikely to prevail. The Red Army in Afghanistan is just one oft-cited latterday example of an occupation regime that, at the gravest cost, failed to heed this lesson.

An occupation regime with enough sense—the British in Malaya during the 1950s, the ruthlessness of some of their conduct notwithstanding, are a textbook example—will try to master the situation by combining selective ruthlessness against the guerrillas themselves, carried out by sufficient numbers of specialist antiguerrilla troops, with a comprehensive array of "hearts and minds" measures. Propaganda, enlightened occupation policies to win over a majority of the population, and leniency toward guerrilla deserters are the essence of such measures.

These measures not only make for more effective antiguerrilla warfare. They are also the most effective means by which antiguerrilla warfare can help the wider occupation administration to achieve and balance its essential aims. These may be threefold: *engagement* of popular cooperation; *pacification*, or defeating the guerrillas themselves militarily; and, in the case of conquering as opposed to peacekeeping regimes, *exploitation* of the occupied area's economic resources. Given limits on manpower, the size of the occupied region, and the difference a cooperative population can make to the smooth running of occupation, the first is very often an essential precondition of the other two. Even when pursuing engagement, the regime needs to maintain some kind of armed presence, if only to remind the population of the possible consequences of noncooperation. But an occupation regime that genuinely works to engage the population's support, and prosecutes its antiguerrilla campaign on that basis, finds that its need to inflict such consequences is greatly diminished.

Many times, however, the dread and revulsion whipped up by the ruthless, underhand, "dirty fighting" that guerrillas employ, the inability of the often-overstretched occupation troops to punish or even identify those guerrillas, the rigors of environment and vastness of space in the occupied country, lack of understanding, indeed feelings of contempt, for the native population from which the guerrillas stem, and the ruthless, exploitative dictates of wider occupation policy have conspired to stunt the effectiveness of such efforts. What they have inspired instead are vastly more ruthless methods such as mass execution of "pro-guerrilla" civilians, burning of villages, and seizure of the population's food supply in order to deprive the guerrillas of its benefit. Such methods may have been driven by the perceived dictates of cruel necessity, or by brutalized, ultimately self-destructive frustration. But regardless of what has motivated them, they have invariably fortified the cycle of dehumanizing terror that so often characterizes guerrilla and antiguerrilla warfare. Ultimately, they usually have been self-defeating. Alienating the population, rather than cultivating it, is rarely a recipe for success in antiguerrilla warfare.

This conflict of approaches was clear in the entire course of antiguerrilla warfare from the Napoleonic Wars.

Bonaparte's army in the Peninsular War of 1808–1813 is a clear case of the "unsophisticated counterterrorism" of most eighteenth- and nineteenth-century antiguerrilla warfare.[2] During the years in which the French occupied Spain, up to 50,000 Spaniards ardently responded to their government's call to "attack and despoil . . . French soldiers, seize the provisions which are earmarked for them, and in short do them as much harm as possible." Taking to the mountains by the thousands, they wrought inestimable havoc upon the occupiers. The guerrilla movement, the French ambassador declared, was "an evil which demands a special treatment, and which will not be destroyed until it is attacked everywhere by units set up for this sort of service." The terror and repugnance the guerrillas inspired in the French soldiery ensured that "special treatment" often meant brutal reprisal, with guerrillas actual or suspected hanged from the nearest tree and endemic destruction of allegedly pro-guerrilla villages. "Only ruins can now be seen where Algodonales once stood," wrote Marshal Nicolas Soult of one Andalusian village. "A strong band of inhabitants of Grazalema has tempted once more the fate of war," he wrote of another. "But it has been destroyed."[3]

In nineteenth- and early twentieth-century European colonial campaigns, ingrained racist beliefs that the lash and the Gatling gun were by far the best remedy for rebellious "darkies" often ensured that insurgencies by nonwhite peoples invited a retaliation even more vicious. A 1906 revolt in Britain's southern African colony of Zululand, which saw twelve white settlers killed, spurred the colonial forces to slaughter "at least 3,000 pitifully ill-armed men" on the native side. These "were shot down by the colonial forces, most of them hunted down like animals in the Nkandla forests . . . or flushed out of their lairs in the scrubby hills." "The lash," moreover, "was applied to the backs of prisoners."[4] Similarly, when the Italians conquered Libya in 1911–12, continued resistance there prompted them to initiate a campaign of summary executions that claimed hundreds if not thousands of Arab lives.[5]

White troops in colonial campaigns learned particularly to appreciate the trials of terrain and environment. Against Cuban insurgents between 1868 and 1878, the Spanish lost 30,000 troops to disease. During the Anglo-Boer War of 1899–1902, the British lost nearly twice as many troops to disease as to battling the Boers themselves. The vast expanses of nigh-on-impenetrable terrain that native insurgents usually favored also presented daunting challenges: the need to take the high ground in mountain warfare, to move along single tracks in the jungle, or to fire clearing volleys in the African bush.

The fact that the insurgents themselves knew the terrain so well made these challenges more arduous still.[6]

When European armies enjoyed only a slight technological edge, or none at all, over their opponents, the damage firearms-equipped colonial insurgents wrought on occupying forces also could drive those forces to great harshness. During the Anglo-Boer War of 1899–1902, the technological gap between British occupier and Boer insurgent was narrow at most. The British commander, General Horatio Kitchener, believed that part of the solution was to hit the insurgents in the stomach. He ordered "deliberate, thorough, wholesale destruction of farms: all buildings burned to the ground, all crops set alight, all animals slaughtered, hundreds of square miles turned into a wasteland" in order to starve the Boers' mounted guerrilla force into capitulation. British columns scoured the veld burning Boer farmsteads and, by herding Boer women and children into concentration camps, deprived the guerrillas of all other forms of civilian assistance. Up to 30,000 farms may have been burned during this campaign, and 3.6 million sheep slaughtered. One British soldier wrote that "our course through the country is marked as in prehistoric ages by pillars of smoke by day and fire by night. We usually burn from six to twelve farms a day." Neither the volume of devastation, nor the fact that the teeming and insanitary concentration camps became death traps for up to a third of their inmates, perturbed Kitchener in the slightest.[7]

During the late nineteenth and early twentieth centuries, sincere international efforts were made to "regulate and civilize" the prosecution of guerrilla and antiguerrilla warfare. But the messy reality in the field and the fundamental incompatibility of each side's aims complicated such efforts tremendously.[8] That said, developments in antiguerrilla warfare during the decades before and immediately after World War I did suggest that some commanders were adopting a more constructive approach, one that recognized the importance of winning the population's hearts and minds as well as defeating actual guerrillas militarily. General Joseph Gallieni, as a commander in

French North Africa during the early twentieth century, articulated the rationale behind this approach particularly clearly:

> The best means for achieving pacification . . . is provided by combined application of force and politics . . . We must always treat the country and its inhabitants with consideration, since the former is destined to receive our future colonial enterprises and the latter will be our main agents and collaborators in the development of our enterprises. Every time that the necessities of war force one of our colonial officers to take action against a village or inhabited center, his first concern, once submission of the inhabitants has been achieved, should be reconstruction of the village, creation of a market, and establishment of a school. It is by combined use of politics and force that pacification of a country and its future organization will be achieved. *Political action is by far the most important.* It derives its greater power from the organization of the country and its inhabitants.[9]

Commanders in the decades before and after Gallieni was writing put various aspects of this conception into practice.[10] Generals Nelson Miles and Elwell Otis clearly saw the importance of winning over occupied populations: the former established an Indian school in Pennsylvania in 1879, while the latter initiated the building of schools and public works to improve communications and health among the population of the U.S.-occupied Philippines at the turn of the last century. British interwar commanders in India and the Middle East, meanwhile, sought an approach that genuinely integrated the use of politics and force. Sir Charles Gwynn's 1934 manual *Imperial Policing* advocated primary reliance not upon military force, but upon effective local police forces, who would cooperate fully with the military when necessary. It also advised that, although military force should be used as a guarantor of native compliance, and be implemented swiftly and firmly when necessary, it should not be relied upon excessively. Hugh Simson's *British Rule and Rebellion,* written in 1937 and focusing particularly on the 1936–1939 Palestinian revolt, urged that local police be stationed in guerrilla-friendly villages on a permanent basis. For Simson, effective military force meant small patrols of specialist counterinsurgency troops, benefiting from specialist clothing, equipment, and training, superior mobility, and the ability to operate in the same conditions as the guerrillas themselves. This force, too, could be used in a measured way, because it was by nature equipped to combat guerrillas themselves, rather than terrorize a potentially guerrilla-friendly population.

Numerous lessons can be drawn from these accounts. To the extent that an occupation regime recognizes the population's desire to continue its daily existence without fear of terror or excessive exploitation; seeks actively to improve that existence; teaches its troops, while reminding the population that the alternative of force exists, to approach the population in a spirit of cooperation; possesses human and material resources sufficient for pacifying and administering an often vast and inhospitable area effectively; and employs specialist antiguerrilla units to seek, locate, and attack insurgents *specifically*, without recourse to terrorizing the population, it maximizes its ability to execute precisely the kind of antiguerrilla campaign that is most likely to succeed. It is an outcome well worth the extra resources of manpower, equipment, administrative acumen, and general effort and patience this approach requires.

To weaken any of these preconditions is to reduce the chance of success and to increase the likelihood that troops will resort instead, through fear and frustration, to indiscriminate, alienating brutality. To weaken them all is a recipe for enormous bloodletting. To *negate* them all, through occupation policies whose whole purpose is subjugation, extermination, and exploitation, through troops schooled in an ideology preaching the racial inferiority of the occupied, and through a security force condemned to inadequacy through lack of sufficient manpower, equipment, and administrative means, is to unleash consequences as horrific as they are self-defeating.

A necessarily differentiated view demands recognition that Wehrmacht antipartisan warfare was not such a wholesale negation in all its forms. But taken as a whole, it came nearer to that state than many other campaigns did. And it was not just the dynamics of National Socialist ideology or the pressures of wartime that infused it with such ferocious potential, but also destructive forces of longer historical standing.

The old Prussian officer corps' aversion to guerrilla warfare was apparent as early as Prussia's national struggle against Napoleon in 1813—even though, on that occasion, the Prussian officer corps was advocating precisely that kind of warfare itself. As a conservative elite, it regarded the notion of citizens in arms, with all their potential for mounting a revolutionary challenge to the established order, with horror. It was prepared to stomach such an abomination only for the sake of national liberation. And even then, it ensured that the mass levy that it raised for the purpose was kept on a leash. Thus the people's army, or Landssturm, which it raised in 1813, was to be disbanded as soon as the war was over, and bound by an oath as long as the war went on. "Any attack on, robbery or looting of, property in friendly territory," the oath ran, "without orders from commanding generals and military governors, any attempt to evade taxes, duties, compulsory labour, or due obedience to local authorities resulting from or aided by, the arming or mobilization of the Landssturm, will be mercilessly punished by death."[11]

During the Franco-Prussian War of 1870–71, abhorrence to armed civilians on political grounds was joined by abhorrence on military grounds. The average Prussian officer saw the essence of a warfare that was, in his eyes, clean, decent, and proper, as well as effective, as residing in superior tactics and technology employed by coordinated, uniformed field armies in open combat. Of course, his fondness for this style of warfare came with the comforting knowledge that, in 1870, the Prussian Army was the incomparable master of it.

When the Prussians invaded France, destroyed Emperor Napoleon III's armies at the Battle of Sedan, and occupied a vast chunk of the country in an effort to compel the rest of it to surrender, the

French started displaying a strong proclivity for guerrilla warfare. With French government officials urging their citizens to form up into irregular forces and "cut off convoys, harass the enemy and hang from trees all the enemies they can take well and truly by the neck, after having mutilated them," it is perhaps even less surprising that the Prussian Army swiftly perceived guerrilla warfare as the appalling antithesis of its own doctrine.[12]

In the event, the toll the French guerrillas, or *francs-tireurs*, exacted upon Prussian supply, communications, and manpower was less than alarming. But the toll they took of a personal sense of security among the Prussian troops was indeed alarming. An incensed Crown Prince Frederick described how "single shots are fired, generally in a cunning, cowardly fashion, on patrols, so that nothing is left for us to do but to adopt retaliatory measures by burning down the house from which the shots came or else by the help of the lash and forced contributions." "We are hunting them down," wrote Bismarck. "They are not soldiers: we are treating them as murderers."[13] In the event, the Prussian response to the *francs-tireurs*, horrific exceptions aside, relied more on fines and imprisonment than on fire and sword. But if the views of Frederick and Bismarck are any guide, the experience scarred the army's institutional mentality.

This may be one reason why, in its quelling of nonwhite native uprisings in African and Asian colonies, the army of the German empire founded in 1871 displayed a ferocity surpassing even that of the racially brutalized campaigns of its imperialist peers. For callous, systematic ruthlessness, no colonial campaign against nonwhite insurgents came close to matching General Lothar von Trotha's "genocidal repression" of the 1904–1905 Herero uprising in German South West Africa.

"The tribes of Africa," wrote Trotha, "respond [only] to force. It was and is my policy to use force with terrorism and even brutality. I shall annihilate the revolting tribes with streams of blood and streams of gold."[14] In the campaign's most terrible episode, Trotha combined a devastating artillery bombardment of trapped Herero forces in the Waterberg area, women and children among them, with the ruse of leaving them an eastward exit through which to "escape." Yet when 8,000 Herero fighters, with twice as many women and children in tow, did flee the field, they found that the route Trotha had left them had plunged them into a waterless 2,000 square miles of wilderness. Trotha ordered all the water supplies poisoned and the entire desert cordoned off.

He then issued an "extermination order." "Within the German boundaries," Trotha declared, "every Herero, whether found armed or unarmed, with or without cattle, will be shot. I shall not accept any more women or children. I shall drive them back to their people—otherwise I shall order shots to be fired at them."[15] Those Herero who survived this fearful trial eventually died in droves in labor camps. By 1911, 65,000 of the original 80,000-strong Herero population had perished.[16]

Trotha's actions earned the congratulations of his military chiefs in Berlin. This does not mean that a straight line linked the brutal suppression of the Herero rebellion with the ferocity of Wehrmacht antipartisan warfare. Yet the practice of extreme brutality in an anti-guerrilla campaign against an "inferior" colored race, according to John Horne and Alan Kramer, further loosened the German military's inhibitions about the use of such brutality generally.[17]

During the German advance into Belgium and northern France in August 1914, less than a month into World War I, isolated potshots taken at a German officer in Louvain spurred the Germans into subjecting that Belgian city to an orgy of killing, pillage, and pyromania. Horne and Kramer describe "a fusillade all over the town, with soldiers breaking into houses and firing down into the streets. Men were dragged out of these houses in front of their terrified families; some were beaten and shot immediately, others were taken to the railway station. Hubert David-Fischbach, for example, a man of 83, who had had German officers quartered in his house, was tied up and made to watch his house burn, beaten with bayonets, and finally shot. Others were killed during the night as they fled from their burning houses."[18]

Yet this was only the most dramatic case of much wider bloodletting that summer. It was a bloodletting in which the advancing German armies, responding to an almost entirely imagined popular uprising against them, killed 6,500 Belgian and French citizens.[19] The German military's aversion to guerrilla warfare that the Napoleonic and Franco-Prussian Wars had nurtured was only one of the forces that fueled it.

Some of the vicious impetus did come from the troops themselves. These were troops compelled by the dictates of Germany's Schlieffen Plan, a plan for a lightning campaign to beat France in six weeks, before her Russian allies could mobilize on Germany's eastern frontier, to march enormous distances *on foot* within an utterly unrealistic time limit. The state of frustration, exhaustion, and jumpiness to which this pressure reduced them was almost guaranteed to increase their propensity to "lash out" at the slightest provocation. In tandem with this, the gossip, rumormongering, and emergent hysteria generated by the few incidents of genuine resistance seem to have created a mindset akin to that of a seventeenth-century witch craze.[20]

But the officer corps' institutional mentality was crucial also. With a victory of superior firepower and maneuverability, of a kind the officer corps always had idolized, being hindered by the Allied armies, the specter of a people's uprising both stoked officers' frustration *and* gave them an excuse to inspire a new, harder spirit in their troops by issuing terroristic directives for treatment of the population. This specter also fed off a paranoid worldview that many officers shared with the same pan-German movement that would eventually spawn the Nazi Party. The officer corps saw French and Belgian guerrillas not just as external enemies, but as external enemies with the same characteristics as many of the Reich's internal enemies: Catholic, working-class, and, like the inhabitants of Alsace-Lorraine, provinces France had been forced to relinquish to the German empire in 1871, pro-French.[21] It was not just colonial races, then, who were marked for ideological contempt—another harbinger of future practice.

Just as important to later developments, finally, was the German reaction to the international condemnations heaped upon these actions. "The hypersensitivity of the German military to the accusation of wrongdoing in 1914," Horne and Kramer assert, "reaffirmed its doctrine of the illegality of enemy irregular warfare during Weimar. This provided one strand of its descent into lawlessness and barbarity during the Third Reich."[22]

The German military's remarkable propensity for brutality in antiguerrilla warfare was complemented perfectly by officers' growing preoccupation, both during and after World War I, with the mastery and application of violence. The officer corps' subscription to National Socialist ideology intensified the destructive potential of this combination.

In Hitler's eyes, the first principle of occupation security was the enforcement of submission through fear. In a December 1942 conversation with General Alfred Jodl, his Wehrmacht chief of operations, Hitler postulated the following scenario: "What should you do: the swine have barricaded themselves in a house in which there are also women and children. Should the soldier set fire to the house or not? If he sets fire to it, the innocent are burned. There shouldn't be any doubt about this! He must burn it down!"[23] Many officers were more than amenable to such an attitude; General Lothar Rendulic was far from the only high-ranking Wehrmacht field officer who subscribed to the maxim that, when it came to rear-area security, "success comes only through terror."[24]

National Socialist ideology influenced the violence of the German military's antiguerrilla doctrine in two ways. In the first place, as Hitler's assertion to Jodl shows, it advocated violence if anything even more enthusiastically. Second, during the campaign in the Soviet Union particularly, it would incite antiguerrilla violence against new ideological enemies—Jews, Bolsheviks and "eastern races"—to replace the French fifth columnists, working-class agitators, and Catholic subversives with whom the *francs-tireurs* of 1914 had been associated. In both senses, of course, it already had a strong base on which to build.

The vicious brutalization that the fusion of these elements brought about did not happen straightaway. The Polish campaign pushed the process forward. For one thing, guerrillaphobia, proclivity for organized violence, and prejudice toward eastern races were all heightened by what officers and men actually experienced of civilians during the campaign. Civilian resistance to the German invasion, in contrast to the invasion of Belgium a quarter-century earlier, was fierce and widespread. Meanwhile, men already poorly disposed toward Poles on cultural grounds found "legitimacy" for their views in their experience of the often extreme poverty of rural Poles. Eastern Jews earned similar opprobrium; among other things, some blamed their corruption and avarice for the dire rural conditions.[25]

The campaign of violence that this combination of outrage and contempt fuelled far outbrutalized the imperial army's conduct in Belgium; by the time of Poland's surrender in early October, the Wehrmacht had executed 16,000 civilians. General Max von Schenckendorff, who decided, independently of higher command, on a rota of ten hostages shot for every German killed, was just one officer who subscribed to unprecedentedly harsh antiguerrilla doctrine with thoroughness and enthusiasm.[26]

Wehrmacht ruthlessness, in the cause of "security," toward the population of Poland was not nearly as systematic or wholesale as the form it would take in the Soviet Union. But it was a dress rehearsal, one that not only eroded inhibitions further, but also convinced its participants that the brutality was entirely justified. The fact that Wehrmacht reprisals in the west, both during and after the 1940 Blitzkrieg, were much more restrained, did not detract from their potential ferocity during any future campaign in the east.[27] For reprisals in the west were not directed against what in Nazi terms were racially inferior peoples.

The criminal orders that preceded the invasion of the Soviet Union intensified, refined, and systematized antiguerrilla brutality on a new level.

The duties of the Eastern Army security units, the principal formations assigned the task of securing the occupied Soviet Union, receive a dry, technical description in the "Guidelines for the Training of Security Divisions" that the Army High Command issued in

March 1941. They encompassed guarding supply points and transport routes, securing airports and supply dumps, overseeing and transporting prisoners of war, and regulating traffic. From the start, however, "all leaders of security forces," rather than restricting themselves to defensive duties, were expected also "to strive to fulfill their tasks through offensive action against the partisans."[28]

But official expectations, in line with the general ruthlessness with which the Wehrmacht leadership intended to prosecute the war, contributed to a singularly pitiless conception of how pacification should be implemented.[29]

A "practical" dimension that bolstered the brutal impetus was the perceived need to "square the circle" between the vastness of the region to be occupied and the meagerness and inferiority of the forces the Wehrmacht leadership had committed to the task. It was not that the Wehrmacht leadership, despite its traditional neglect of intelligence and logistics, had spectacularly underestimated the obstacles to rear-area security. Rather, it suffered from an "over by Christmas" attitude to the campaign as a whole: prioritizing front-line units at the expense of those in the rear would hasten the Soviet Union's expected swift collapse; this in turn would erode resistance in the rear, relax the situation at the front automatically, and release large numbers of front-line troops for long-term occupation under the new administrative setup of the civilian-administered Reich commissariats.[30] With its ideological proclivities and long-standing advocacy of terroristic antiguerrilla warfare, the Wehrmacht leadership believed that terrorizing the population into acquiescence would go a considerable way to overcoming such resistance as its security forces would face in the brief initial period. "In the East," Hitler himself maintained, "harshness today means lenience in the future."[31]

The woeful misjudgment about the ease of "blowing Russia over" and the nonappearance of such generous reinforcements ensured that even while rear-area troops employed terror, they were unable to master their situation. The resulting frustration would cause many to prosecute terror even more vociferously.

The security forces' handicaps, then, were crucial both to the original high-level decision to put the security effort on a savagely terroristic footing and to the further expansion of that terror. We shall see these effects upon the 221st Security Division.

The concept, shared by Hitler and the Reich's elites, of a vast eastern hinterland subverted to the "greater good" of a German-dominated Europe, envisaged its eventual division into a cluster of civilian-administered Reich commissariats. Until the military campaign was won, however, the Eastern Army was to administer much of the occupied Soviet Union itself. Its jurisdiction would stretch from the front farthest east, westward through the Army Rear Areas administered by individual infantry and Panzer armies. It would culminate west of these in three enormous jurisdictions, each administered by one of the three army groups. These Army Group Rear Areas would form by far the largest sector of Eastern Army jurisdiction. It was within them that the Eastern Army's security divisions were to be deployed primarily.

The nine divisions, three of which were allocated to each Army Group Rear Area, fell far short of the yardstick of military excellence with which the Wehrmacht is so widely associated. For one thing, they were significantly smaller than the Wehrmacht's normally 15,000- to 18,000-strong infantry divisions; infantry divisions contained three regiments, security divisions only two.[32] And their diminutive size was not compensated for by their quality.

The 221st Security Division, which with the 286th and 403d Security Divisions was committed to the rear area of Army Group Center, typified the Eastern Army security divisions of 1941. It had been newly established that spring as a mixture of already-active reservists and recently raised territorial defense troops (*Landesschützen*). Aside from the divisional commander, the operations officer, and a small number of others, most security division officers were reservists also. These were men who, almost by definition, had exhausted their best military potential and were no longer deemed young or dynamic enough for the rigors of front-line combat. The 221st's commander, General Johann Pflugbeil, was a fifty-nine-year-old veteran of the trenches who also had served in the Reichswehr during the interwar years. The only other full-time regular officer in charge of a division-level department, that of the Operations Office (Ia), responsible for general security matters and planning particular antipartisan operations, was thirty-two-year-old Captain Karl Haupt, who had joined the Reichswehr in 1928.[33]

The other three departments that would hold significant responsibility for antipartisan warfare, relations with the population, or both, were all commanded by reservists. The Intelligence Section (Ic), concerned with the population's mood, propaganda, and matters pertaining to the troops' leisure activities and "spiritual well-being," was commanded by Lieutenant Helmut Beck. Major Kurt Graf, as divisional quartermaster (Ib), was responsible for gathering reports generated by various divisional subsections, including the divisional court, the military police, and transport, supply, and administrative offices. Hans Wieder, the principal official in charge of Section VII (occupation administration) was charged with ordering the economic life of the division's jurisdiction and with recruiting the population for tasks such as the overseeing of the harvest and day-to-day administration.[34]

The 221st's mobile combat troops consisted of a "Category Three" infantry regiment, the 350th, commanded by Colonel Hellmuth Koch. Its men were mainly reservists aged over thirty. Because they had originally been garrison troops, they were far less mechanized than their colleagues in full-time regiments. And, instead of the two years of training the Wehrmacht's regular peacetime troops had received, they had received only three months of training.[35] Some had already seen action in earlier Blitzkrieg campaigns. These Category Three reservists were the only divisional troops deemed fit for front-line duty.[36]

Although the preparation these troops undertook for their duties as a mobile force executing "active" security operations fell well short of thorough, they looked considerably more formidable than their comrades in the security divisions' territorial and guard battalions. These static security troops were charged with guarding supply points, transport routes, and prisoners of war in the rear.[37] Their men, grouped in the 221st Security Division's case under the 45th Territorial Regiment, were even older, even more poorly trained and equipped, than their Category Three comrades.[38]

Also subordinate to security divisions, and similarly wanting in quality, were the Feld- and Ortskommandanturen, charged with garrisoning particular towns and villages. These static units would be responsible, as far as practicable, for overseeing day-to-day occupation administration and organizing/coercing the population into co-operating with German antipartisan efforts on the local level. From the start, the effectiveness of the Kommandanturen would be stymied by the dearth of properly qualified German personnel and the sheer size of the occupied territory. In time, direct responsibility for day-to-day social, political, and economic administration in this overwhelmingly rural region would fall increasingly to German-appointed native civilian officials. These too would prove to be of extremely uneven quality.[39]

But the principal difficulty the Eastern Army's security administrators faced was that their inadequacies increased their reliance not just on active collaborators, but on the cooperation of the wider populace also. Without this, basic tasks such as maintaining public order, gathering crops, and regulating transport—essential to smooth administration and economic exploitation—would be nigh-on impossible. In turn, the need for such a degree of popular cooperation made an effective hearts-and-minds campaign to win civilians over even more essential.

Such a campaign, as indicated earlier, did actually have potential, particularly in the especially anti-Soviet Baltic states and the Ukraine. And beyond even these regions, much of the rural population of the areas the Germans would come to occupy held the Stalinist system, particularly the collective farming policy that had unleashed famine and untold misery upon it during the 1930s, in bitter contempt. Their initial readiness to see the Germans as liberators generated a degree of potential support that a more far-sighted occupation regime might have harnessed to great effect. Ultimately, however, the very nature of the Reich's agenda for the occupied Soviet

Union, merciless and rapacious as it was, not to mention the general character of the Wehrmacht's antipartisan campaign itself, would cripple the effectiveness of such methods. For the security divisions, the whole spectrum of occupation tasks would grow ever more intractable.

Admittedly, security divisions could call on support from other types of units. Artillery, engineers, and a company of military police were at each division's disposal. So too was extensive assistance from Himmler's Order Police and the Wehrmacht's own Secret Field Police. This latter agency held extensive responsibility for intelligence gathering and other security duties, particularly the "screening" of "suspect elements."[40]

But even if the Eastern Army's security forces had been twice as numerous and combat-worthy, the size and environment of the region in which they were to operate still would have intimidated them.

The site of the 221st Security Division's occupation was the Army Group Center Rear Area. During the first two years of the eastern campaign, this jurisdiction was commanded by General von Schenckendorff, the same General von Schenckendorff who had carved out such a brutal reputation for himself in Poland. It eventually would cover an area of roughly 145,000 square kilometers. By the end of July 1941 the 221st Security Division's jurisdiction alone covered 35,000 square kilometers.[41] Moreover, all three regions the area would encompass during 1941—eastern Poland and western Belorussia, which had been overrun by the Soviets in 1939, and eastern Belorussia—shared a geography ideal for partisan warfare.

The character of the region was overwhelmingly rural, with over four-fifths of its population engaged in agriculture.[42] This population was scattered across the land in such a way that the task of administering it, harnessing it in the cause of economic exploitation, and marshaling its cooperation, by whatever means, was a hugely problematic one. And not only was the terrain rural; much of it was impenetrable. Two million hectares of Belorussia were covered by swampy, forested terrain, affording the kind of cover and inaccessibility that were a boon to partisans and a bane to occupying troops.[43] The Germans, according to General Halder after the war, "were confronted with the fact that the Russian was able to move about in these impenetrable forests and treacherous swamps with the certain instinct and sense of security of an animal . . . Even the most thorough training applied to troops from the West cannot replace the natural instinct peculiar to eastern Europeans who were born and raised in a region of forests and swamps."[44]

This, then, was the array of circumstances facing the security divisions, which the spirit and practice of the ferocious directives they received before the invasion were intended to overcome.

The three blanket security-related decrees the Wehrmacht leadership issued immediately before the invasion are known as the "criminal orders." In reality, they were less orders than a set of brutal *guidelines* intended to infuse the troops' conduct with an ideologically driven ruthlessness well beyond what international convention deemed permissible. By allowing certain freedom of action, moreover, the orders provided opportunity, through a demonstrated capacity for harsh and effective action, for personal promotion.[45]

In other words, the criminal orders embodied the National Socialist "leadership principle." This principle, by combining the motive power of ideological conviction and careerist ambition, was central to the radicalization of National Socialist policy. The key to personal advancement, the leadership principle held, was to be seen to implement the Führer's will more "radically" than one's rivals. Achieving this necessitated the display of ideological belief and the application, resourcefulness, and above all ruthlessness necessary to put it into practice.[46] In this policy as with antiguerrilla doctrine, the Wehrmacht had a doctrinal base on which to build. For the German military had long stressed not only the technical aspects of military prowess but also hardy character and resourcefulness.[47]

The Barbarossa Decree of 13 May 1941 ordered that all attempts by "enemy civilians" to "interfere" with the smooth running of military operations be countered with the utmost severity. It denied civilians the protection of military courts. It gave officers holding the position of battalion commander or higher the right to execute reprisals against any village from which German troops had been fired upon. It declared, in a passage of particularly cold-blooded ruthlessness, that "acts committed by Wehrmacht personnel or followers against enemy civilians, even if the act is a military crime or offense, may go unpunished."[48] This was prescribing a policy that, over reprisals particularly, gave harshness in the name of security a new definition.[49]

But even the Barbarossa Decree did not go as far in its brazen renunciation of international norms as the Commissar Order. This particularly unequivocal piece of "ideological" military thinking, issued on 6 June 1941, ordered Eastern Army units to collude in the eradication of the proclaimed principal carriers of Bolshevik infection within the Red Army's ranks: the Soviet commissars responsible for the political instruction of its troops. These, in the language of the Commissar Order, were the "originators of the barbaric, Asiatic fighting methods" that the enemy practiced.[50] Denied combatant status by the terms of the order, the commissars were to be either shot by the troops themselves or turned over to the SS to suffer the same fate. To liquidate a category of persons not because of any particular crime they had committed, but because of their function in a political system, was an especially murderous assertion of the ideological imperatives that underpinned the conduct of Germany's eastern war.[51]

Yet it was the undemonstratively titled "Guidelines for the Conduct of the Troops in Russia," issued six days after the Barbarossa Decree, that were designed to have the widest, most fundamental effect on soldiers' conduct. For the Guidelines sought to foster the mentality that could justify such cruel measures. "Bolshevism is the mortal enemy of the National Socialist German people," they proclaimed. "It is against this subversive worldview and its carriers that Germany is fighting. This battle demands ruthless and energetic measures against Bolshevik agitators, irregulars, saboteurs, and Jews, and the total eradication of any active or passive resistance."[52]

In addition to being issued with the criminal orders, the security divisions were instructed to give material and logistical support to Einsatzkommando and Sonderkommando units of the SS Einsatz-gruppen.[53] The background to this lay in an arrangement regulating the activities of the SS in the occupied areas that the Army High Command reached with the SS in April 1941.[54] The Einsatzgruppen were assigned a similarly central role in "cleansing" the occupied rear of "suspect elements." They would enable Himmler and his ambitious SS technocrats not only to participate fully in the "ideological crusade" in the east, but also to use the security campaign to advance themselves and the bureaucratic power and grip of the SS as a whole.

To an extent, the same motive prompted Himmler to draft a number of Order Police battalions for security purposes. This militarized police force had been drawn from various branches of the civilian police, schooled in National Socialist indoctrination, and readied for extensive security service in the east. The strength of its National Socialist conviction varied. Many units though, particularly the "300-number" battalions, contained large contingents of relatively young, ruthless, and ambitious men with a strong propensity both for National Socialist thought and, something they would demonstrate to often horrific effect, for the most brutal forms of National Socialist action.[55]

Detailed instructions about the assistance the troops were expected to render the SS were issued in the Army Group Center Rear Area on 24 June, two days after Barbarossa had been launched, by the area's Operations Section.[56] They show that the Wehrmacht was ready to collude with the SS and Order Police to the hilt—ghetto-izing and marking Jews out, rounding up and interning "suspects," transporting them to areas preparatory to "processing," and providing the manpower to cordon those areas off. Gone was the reticence of the Polish campaign; in the wake of such SS-Wehrmacht friction as that campaign had seen, the declaration that the massacres had been the will of the Führer, and its renewed enthusiasm for the regime after the Blitzkrieg in the west, the Wehrmacht leadership was anxious to build bridges.[57] More practical was a quid pro quo consideration. The Wehrmacht leadership recognized that even the "hard, resourceful character" expected from its own security personnel would not meet even short-term security needs unless those same SS and police units provided additional manpower when the Wehrmacht itself needed it.[58]

Together, then, the Barbarossa Decree, the Commissar Order, the "Guidelines for the Conduct of the Troops," and the provisions for Wehrmacht-SS cooperation sought to foster a mentality of harsh conviction among officers and men, to detail specific measures for the brutal conduct of reprisals and security measures generally, and to single out two groups, Jews and Communists, who, by virtue not of their actions but simply of their identity, warranted especially ruthless treatment.

The third of these aims merits a closer look. On the surface, it seems a measure that was both purely ideological and a diversion of attention and scant resources from the task of genuine pacification. But the readings of various historians suggest that it was in fact a brutalizing fusion of genuine ideological contempt, widely held across officer generations since 1918, and some ruthless interrelated calculations.

One related particularly closely to the ideological dimension: victimizing Jews and Communists explicitly could enable the troops, on top of the massive indoctrination they had undergone prior to the invasion, to project their ideological ardor onto special hate figures. The campaign to kill the Red Army commissars, for example, should, in General Jodl's words, be "set up from the start as a revenge action."[59] Certainly, the barrage of ideological propaganda to which the troops were being subjected formed a strong basis of preparation for this.[60]

Second, it was Communists, of course, who ran and made up the political elite, intelligentsia, and security personnel of the Soviet regime. Jews also were seen as being inordinately represented in these groups.[61] And indeed, though Nazi ideological paranoia did exaggerate Jewish preponderance, it was certainly considerable. This fact is hardly surprising; in those areas of the Soviet Union and its occupied territories with a tradition of anti-Semitism—in other words, most of them—a career in Communist activism or officialdom was often the only way for Jews to secure any prospects in life.[62]

In German eyes, of course, Jews in these positions constituted not just a confirmation of the equation between Jew and Bolshevik, but also a possible nucleus of future resistance. The murder the SS had unleashed upon such "nuclei" in Poland had pointed the way to how their perceived equivalents in the Soviet Union would be treated.[63] Granted, some Wehrmacht officers had balked at the killings in Poland. But the very different ideological, military, and economic factors shaping their prosecution of the campaign against the Soviet Union meant they were bound to support the removal of the "bacillus" here.[64] As Colonel-General Georg von Küchler, commander of the Eighteenth Army, put it, "the political commissars and GPU [Soviet security police] people are criminals. These are the people who tyrannize the population . . . They are to be put on the spot before a field court and sentenced on the basis of the testimony of the inhabitants . . . This will save us German blood and we will advance faster."[65]

Finally, given that the security forces lacked the manpower to terrorize all the population all of the time, victimizing Jews and Communists could at least impress the population with the German *capacity* for terror. Terrified into acquiescence at the spectacle of Jews and Communists being arrested for subversion or shot as reprisal victims, with the clear message that others would be next if they stepped out of line, the population would be less likely, or so it was believed, to make trouble.[66] Related to this mindset, albeit in the most pitiless form, was a certain awareness of local sensibilities. Local anti-Semitism and anticommunism, particularly prevalent in the Baltic states, the Ukraine, and Soviet-occupied eastern Poland, meant that victimizing Jews and Communists might also contribute to a divide-and-rule policy. Non-Jewish and noncommunist civilians not only would be in fear of German terror, not only would feel relieved that such terror was not being visited upon them, but also would positively approve of the Germans' choice of target. The

Army High Command rushed out an additional directive urging such a course when, three weeks into the campaign, it started seeing its potential.[67] Gruesome evidence of the virulence of anti-Semitism in these regions was the ease with which the Einsatzgruppen, during the opening weeks of occupation, incited the populations of eastern Poland, the Ukraine, and the Baltic states to unleash horrendous anti-Semitic pogroms.[68]

The criminal orders, then, were the culmination of a process that had begun with the raising of the Prussian Landssturm in 1813. This process, founded on the brutalizing potential of antiguerrilla warfare as a whole, acquired particularly ferocious potential in its German incarnation. By the early twentieth century no other military establishment in the world stood so ready, and with such moral certitude, to terrorize civilian populations in the name of antiguerrilla doctrine. Such readiness, together with the officer corps' wider ideological attitudes and its ambition to attain the most effective and ruthless mastery of violence, made for an immensely destructive brew. The adoption of National Socialist ideology synthesized these ingredients and intensified their potency. The Polish campaign eroded moral inhibitions further. Finally, the particular combination of ideological, imperialist, and ruthlessly pragmatic precepts that underpinned the invasion and occupation of the Soviet Union invested this synthesis with a motivating power still more destructive.

Such was the context of the campaign the 221st Security Division commenced after the invasion of 22 June 1941.

2

"Jew-Bolsheviks," Civilians, and Partisans

Compared with the destruction it would later unleash, the Eastern Army's security campaign appeared to start quietly in the early summer of 1941. But this tranquil image is entirely superficial.

The seeds of brutality were sown from two directions. Some were sown by the fusion of nazified security doctrine, ruthless pragmatism, and careerist ambition that the criminal orders embodied and promoted. The security divisions gave brutal expression to this in their involvement in a campaign of persecution and, already, killing of Jews and Communist functionaries.

Other seeds, however, were sown primarily on an altogether different wind: frustration, already mounting, at the intractability of pacifying and administering a vast, inhospitable region with mainly understrength, second-rate formations. The difficulties went beyond anything the Wehrmacht planners, in their sanguine self-assurance, had anticipated. In their turn, they generated new dynamics of destructiveness. Destructive potential was increased by the fact that, as became clear very quickly, the campaign against the Soviet Union would not be over swiftly after all, and that therefore reinforcements would not be forthcoming.

The course of military events in the eastern war's opening phase was unprecedentedly dramatic.[1] Arrayed along the Soviet frontier on midsummer's eve 1941 was a force of three million German soldiers and 180 divisions, distributed across the three main army groups of North, Center, and South. Each army group had been assigned objectives of key strategic importance in the coming campaign. North was to advance through the Baltic states toward Leningrad, South to seize the "Ukrainian breadbasket." Center, in what was to prove the pivotal effort, was to drive for Moscow. The final point, a front line at the Ural Mountains, beyond which German bombers would be able to penetrate and assault Soviet industry further east, was to be reached before winter descended.

The scale and strength of the German attack that broke all along the frontier in the small hours of 22 June was historically unparalleled. The bulk of the Red Air Force was blitzed on the ground before it had time to take off. Army Groups North and South achieved spectacular advances, but the achievements of the vanguard of Army Group Center, Colonel-General Guderian's Second Panzer Group, were particularly awe-inspiring. On the central front, Soviet armies around Bialystok, Minsk, and then Smolensk were encircled and destroyed and more than 600,000 prisoners taken. During August and September, as Hitler placed new importance on the drives on Leningrad and the Ukrainian breadbasket, much of Army Group Center's armored force was diverted to the flanks. But superlative achievements were accomplished here also, particularly in the south. There, the destruction of the Kiev pocket in September sent 665,000 more Soviet troops into captivity.

Yet no amount of tactical success and prisoners bagged could conceal the fact that the Germans had committed themselves to a fearsome undertaking—one drastically underestimated by a command culture that had downgraded the importance of credible intelligence and logistical planning. Within weeks, the tenacity of Red Army resistance, the apparently inexhaustible well of manpower upon which it could draw, and the challenge of supplying German forces across immense distances via dirt tracks and uncovered railway cars were snarling up the advance and inflicting fearful losses. None of this is even to mention the toll taken of men, machinery, and horses—still a major staple of Wehrmacht transportation—by wilting temperatures, stifling humidity, swampy terrain, or the dust clouds billowed up by the columns of troops advancing along the country's decrepit road system that summer.

As early as July, then, the High Command was revising its predictions about how long the campaign was likely to last. Though the effect upon the security effort, both crippling and brutalizing, would take some months to become obvious, ill omens were gathering already.

Initially, however, the task that confronted the security divisions seemed less daunting. It helped that, during this earliest period of the eastern war, there was no actual partisan movement to speak of. The effect this had upon the security divisions' execution of their tasks was important.

In the central sector, the first leap forward in the German advance took it across the River Bug into eastern Poland. Poland itself had been split down the middle under the terms of the Nazi-Soviet pact of August 1939. Its eastern half had been overrun swiftly by the Red Army early that autumn, while its own ill-prepared army had had its back turned in the doomed struggle against the Wehrmacht further west.

The eastern Polish population had two years of Stalinist oppression behind it and, as yet, little inkling of the far worse terror and exploitation that lay in store under its new Nazi masters. It therefore felt a strong, widespread inclination to extend an at least cautious welcome to the Eastern Army and to turn over fugitive Communist functionaries and Red Army soldiers to it. The 221st Security Division's own war diary records that, on the first day of the invasion, the population "greeted our troops as liberators with flowers, salt, and bread."[2] Well into August, Einsatzgruppe B still described the Poles' "enduring joy at their liberation from the Soviet yoke."[3] Popular unrest, let alone meaningful partisan activity, seemed far from likely.

Initially, then, the security divisions accustomed themselves to their duties with some ease. The 221st Security Division's first tasks —following an initial phase, together with most other security divisions, on the front line—were simply to secure two major highways and to pacify the area around Bialystok and the Bialovieza forest so that Reich Marshal Göring could convert it into a game park.[4]

Hardly did Army Group Center and its subordinate security divisions pause for breath before the advance drew them eastward into Belorussia. Already, on 20 July, the 221st Security Division's jurisdiction was extended eastward to encompass an area of 35,000 square kilometers.[5] Yet the Poles and White Russians who made up this region's ethnically diverse population, subdued by the Red Army two years previously as they too had been, shared a similar loathing of the Soviet regime and a readiness to greet the Germans as liberators. "Everywhere, as far east as Vitebsk, Orscha, and Mogilev," Einsatzgruppe B reported in early August, "the popular mood is pro-German. Everywhere there is antipathy to the Bolshevik regime."[6]

The absence of any pronounced pro-Soviet feeling among the populations of these regions was not the only thing that plagued all initial Soviet attempts to establish effective resistance in the German rear. During the 1930s Soviet military planners had, extremely unwisely, discarded a potent, 130-year-old tradition of Russian irregular warfare. The tradition had originated when armed Russian peasants had combined in their thousands with regular tsarist armies and the ravages of the Russian winter to destroy Napoleon's invading armies in 1812. The planners' dismissal of irregular warfare had also caused them to ignore the successes it had achieved, less than twenty years previously, in the name of their own party and state: partisan units had harried anti-Bolshevik armies during the four-year civil war that followed the birth of the Soviet Union in 1917. In the fearful atmosphere induced by Stalin's murderous purges of the 1930s, however, allaying the dictator's suspicions took urgent priority over military sense. Advocating guerrilla warfare in the event of invasion was a sure way of arousing such suspicions, for inherent in it was the "treasonous" notion that the Red Army might not be *able* to repel an invasion on the Soviet Union's borders. Moreover, the civil war partisans had hardly been a model of political reliability. They had included anarchist and social revolutionary elements with a notorious disregard for higher-level orders. Partisans establishing themselves in different regions of the Soviet Union in any future war might, it was feared, prove just as much a political headache. They might even, in defiance of Stalin's tyrannical, centralizing regime, provide a focal point for resistance to the Soviet state itself.[7]

In their disregard for the lessons of history, Soviet military planners failed utterly to lay the groundwork for effective partisan warfare in 1941. In the western regions in particular, such frantic attempts as were made to throw some kind of effective effort together were thwarted by the speed and suddenness of the German advance. Virtually all the regional authorities were able to offer up were "destruction battalions," small territorial defense units composed of loyal officials and party members, whose duties were hastily diverted to the task of sabotaging German supply and communications. Certainly, there was little hope at this stage of utilizing the innumerable bands of fugitive Red Army soldiers cut off by the German advance. Most of these men were dispersed, disorganized, and, more to the point, unarmed. They were hiding in the vast swamps and forests of the expanding German rear not from some patriotic urge to fight on, but mainly from fear of the bullet that probably awaited them if they surrendered.[8] "The mass of partisans," reported the 339th Infantry Division, "are convinced that, were they to be taken prisoner, they would be shot anyway."[9] With German field units, mindful of the danger to their own troops' discipline posed by the arbitrary killing of prisoners, already warning their units that "bumping off Russians already taken prisoner is unworthy of the German soldier," such fears certainly were warranted.[10]

The Eastern Army, then, faced nothing remotely approaching a genuine partisan threat during the early summer of 1941. The initial effect of this lack of resistance is a salutary reminder that nothing in history is preordained. For on the whole, the absence of serious resistance *greatly reduced* the scale of harshness and violence to which the criminal orders, that culmination of decades of institutional brutalization, had incited the troops.

Many individual field officers appraised the situation quite differently. In their judgment, there was little purpose in trying to counter a potent, ruthless partisan enemy with vicious oppression, butchery of civilians, and burning of farmsteads if no such enemy yet existed. They recognized that in such benign circumstances they could forge unofficial pacts of sorts with villagers and townsfolk. The German Second Army, for example, declared in mid-July that "while the troops must conduct themselves in the east as masters, they must also avoid any actions that might damage the trust the population places in the German Wehrmacht."[11] Such were conditions at this stage that such hopes were not entirely naïve.

Manpower restraints, of course, restricted the divisions' scope for indiscriminate terror in any case: one of the motives for the particular stress the criminal orders had placed on the extensive targeting, as "examples" to the population, of Jews and Communists. Even so, the criminal orders also had urged a considerable degree of *general* terror. The almost complete absence of such terror during the campaign's early weeks, even in retaliation for such resistance as the Wehrmacht did face, therefore was even more pronounced than the Wehrmacht's planners had anticipated. This is not to say that officers and men felt did not feel contempt and distrust for the "inferior" eastern peoples with whom they were coming into contact; as will be seen, they very often did. Clearly, though, such contempt and distrust, even though the criminal orders had sought systematically to foster it, needed conditions considerably more intractable than those the security divisions faced at the outset if they were to be hardened to the extent of greater indiscriminate brutality.

In any case, would-be Wehrmacht apologists should resist feeling smug. For of *victimizing* terror there was plenty. Driven by whatever combination of ideological belief in the Jew-Bolshevik threat, the objective fact that some Communist functionaries were indeed Jews, and the aims of firing up the troops, dividing and ruling, or using Jews and Communists in order to impress the population with the German *capacity* for terror, the practice of systematically victimizing Jews and Communists was widespread. The ideological conviction that underpinned it has been detailed already. One of the major calculations that underpinned it was alluded to most clearly by Karl-Heinrich von Stülpnagel, now commanding the Seventeenth Army in the Ukraine. "Collective reprisals," he decreed, "should not be indiscriminate. As long as there is no firm evidence that the Ukrainian population is responsible for an attack, the village headmen should in the first instance be required to select Jewish and Communist inhabitants [for reprisal] . . . Jewish members of the Young Communists should be singled out particularly as culprits for all sabotage acts and bandit activity." Part of Stülpnagel's calculation of the likely effect on the populace was the "population's widespread dislike of Jews."[12]

Thus did victimization of Jews and Communists, whether in handing them over to the SS, targeting them as reprisal victims, or subjecting them to degrading measures such as ghettoizing and forced labor, proceed apace during the early weeks. The case of the 221st Security Division affords a more detailed examination of one unit's motives for such actions.

At the start of September 1941, Lieutenant Beck, the 221st Security Division's intelligence officer, proclaimed that his division had done "everything in its power to pacify its jurisdiction." An essential precondition had been "the *complete* removal of the treacherous, subversive, and rabble-rousing Jews."[13]

The first stage in the process encompassed a raft of measures of segregation, discrimination, and exploitation. In the Army Group Center Rear Area, it was the military administrators on the spot, and not just General von Schenckendorff himself, who took the lead in ghettoizing Jews, coercing them to wear the Star of David in public, confiscating their property, and dragooning them into hard labor.[14] Such was the announcement of the Wehrmacht field commander in Minsk: "as of this date, a Jewish residential district is created in Minsk . . . The entire Jewish population must resettle immediately in the Jewish residential district . . . After resettlement, the Jewish district is to be closed off by walls from the rest of the city . . . It is forbidden for Jews in work columns to remain outside the residential district assigned to them . . . A forced loan . . . is imposed on the Jewish Council to carry out the administrative measures resulting from resettlement."[15]

The 221st Security Division's files recount many such measures. Some of the specifics are detailed coldly in documents generated by Feldkommandantur 528 (V). Among this unit's duties was the framing of "Jew laws" including supervision of "Jewish councils, marking the Jews out, banning ritual slaughter, putting the Jews to work, criminal penalties [for Jews], confiscation of Jewish property," and "accommodation of Jews in special areas."[16] The 221st also pressganged Jews into forced labor. In early July, for instance, Jews from evacuated villages north of Bialoviza were made to toil in the midsummer heat improving roads.[17] The division's Administrative Section looked on approvingly and, late in July, issued its own orders for forced labor: "Able-bodied [Jewish] males between fourteen and sixty years old, females between sixteen and fifty. Use mayors' registration cards to gather them into labor gangs."[18]

Captain Hermann Kremp, a staff officer whose unit, the 2d Security Regiment, was temporarily attached to the 221st that summer, provides a vivid glimpse of the ordeal the Jews were undergoing: "The place is crawling with Jews. We're rounding them all up for work, some to sweep the streets, some to mend them. We've got girls washing and darning and boys to clean our boots. For the last couple of days we've been forcing them all to wear the yellow star. Mind you, to get them to do any of this we had to set an example first, for the Jew elder had insisted the job mustn't be rushed. He refused our demand to hurry it up, so we had to shoot him. That got the bastards moving!"[19]

General Pflugbeil, the divisional commander, and Captain Haupt, the operations officer, also entwined anti-Jewish persecution with the wider security effort. Such was the clarion call Haupt issued on 8 July—just two days after the division assumed its security duties, and well before any genuine challenge to German authority in the rear existed—to the 221st's troops. "It has been firmly established," Haupt proclaimed, "that wherever Jews live, the cleansing of the area encounters difficulties. For the Jews support the training of partisan groups and the destabilizing of the area by escaped Russian soldiers. Immediate and complete evacuation of all male Jews from the villages north of Bialoviza has therefore been ordered."[20] On 18 July General Pflugbeil, not to be left out, ordered "the seizure of Jews in the Bialystok area as hostages, to be shot at the slightest sign of troublemaking."[21]

There is also no indication, in either the divisional files or the Einsatzgruppen reports, that the 221st supplied anything but the fullest cooperation, as did its fellow security divisions, in the liquidation of "dangerous elements"—mainly Soviet commissars and "suspect" Jews—by the Einsatzgruppen.[22] Arthur Nebe, commander of Einsatzgruppe B, the main Einsatzgruppe operating in the Army Group Center area, described his unit's relationship with the Eastern Army's military administrative offices in the rear as "good without exception."[23]

At a level as operationally low as a division, *precise* motives for such conduct can be hard to decipher.[24] Some of the motivations that underpinned these measures may indeed have been of the ruthlessly pragmatic type alluded to above. And the whole enterprise, of course, would play well with superiors. But what the files reveal about the 221st Security Division is that none of these motives can be separated from the genuine, *heartfelt* anti-Semitism of prominent division-level officers. The first days of the campaign provide the blood-spattered Exhibit A.

Toward the end of June 1941, following a fierce engagement during its brief spell as a front-line formation, the 221st Security Division captured the city of Bialystok. On 27 June, with Bialystok almost completely in German hands, 2,000 to 3,000 Jewish men, women, and children were massacred by Reserve Police Battalion 309 of the Order Police. The battalion, which the 221st had charged with cleansing the city of escapees and "potentially subversive elements," committed the massacre in full view of the division.

Peter Longerich, using official documents and postwar judicial testimony, provides a glimpse of the slaughterhouse into which the city streets were transformed that day. Reserve Police Battalion 309 was one of a number of Order Police battalions composed largely of younger, ambitious volunteers. Among its personnel were numerous fanatical Jew-haters.[25] "Late in the morning," Longerich writes, "battalion commander Weis gave the order to comb the synagogue quarter and arrest all men old enough to use a weapon." Many of the policemen of the battalion's third company, fervent in their anti-Semitism and drunk on triumph and liquor after the city's fall, promptly rampaged. They "blew up any door not immediately opened to them with hand grenades, set Jews' beards alight and forced them, at gunpoint, to dance in front of them with arms outstretched shouting, 'I'm Jesus Christ.'" But the blood the battalion's first company shed eclipsed even the indiscriminate killing that accompanied these outrages. It was that company's commander, Captain Behrens, who now ordered Jews to be arrested en masse: "The arrested were taken to the market place, where Behrens separated out the orthodox Jews and ordered them shot a dozen at a time." General Pflugbeil saw fit to object to the killings only once they were taking place literally outside his own headquarters.

Then came the crescendo. The policemen herded another 500 to 700 Jews into the synagogue, "among the last of whom were women and children . . . [A]fter setting fire to the synagogue with the aid of gasoline and a bundle of hand grenades thrown through the window, battalion personnel gunned down anyone trying to escape. A group of men who had managed to break the synagogue door down were shot. Later, some Jewish men appeared at the windows, holding up children and pleading with the Germans to spare them at least. But the policemen standing guard fired on the women and children also."[26]

No other Order Police or SS unit was murdering Jews on such a scale so early in the eastern campaign. And the atavistic delight shown by many of the battalion's men resembled less the clinical mass executions those agencies would later carry out than the savage abandon of the pogroms already being perpetrated, with a nod and a wink from the newly arrived SS authorities, by native anti-Semitic extremists in the Baltic states, the Ukraine, and elsewhere in Poland.[27]

The 221st Security Division responded to this unbridled bloodletting by covering up the burning of the synagogue with the excuse, recorded in the Operations Section's divisional war diary, that "the synagogue was set alight because shots were fired from it."[28] Indeed, anyone reading the 221st's files in isolation could be forgiven for thinking that no massacre had taken place at all.

General Pflugbeil apparently was morally unmoved by this revolting episode. Yet he also failed to protest on pragmatic grounds—against the disintegrating effect such a barbaric spectacle might have on the discipline and mental well-being of his own men. He might, at the very least, have asked the Order Police to carry out the killings "down a back alley" instead of in full view of the 221st's troops.

This concern, pragmatically rather than ethically motivated though it was, haunted Wehrmacht officers in the Soviet Union as it had in Poland. Field Marshal Gerd von Rundstedt, commander-in-chief of Army Group South, was just one officer who forbade individual Wehrmacht troops to, as he saw it, "take matters into their own hands, participate in the excesses of the Ukrainian population against the Jews . . . watch or photograph the measures being taken by the Sonderkommandos."[29] Many officers might well have wanted to "harden" their troops for the "ideological crusade" in the east, but assaulting their discipline and mental balance was hardly compatible with such an aim.

If Rundstedt expressed grave concern about the impact a more clinical Einsatzgruppe killing might have on his men, one might expect that Pflugbeil and Haupt, faced with an unbridled, bestial massacre, at least would have voiced disquiet. Indeed, not only could they have registered some form of disapproval without fear of repercussion; they might even have been able to intervene. Granted, while the Order Police battalions were under the security divisions' tactical command, they were in reality "on loan" from the Higher SS and Order Police leaders attached to the various army groups under which the battalions were operating. This meant, presumably, that ultimate power for reprimand and discipline lay not with General Pflugbeil but with the regional Higher SS and police leader.[30] Yet, though the drunken revelers of the police battalion's third company may well have been too far gone to have been halted by anything less than armed force by the 221st itself, Pflugbeil might have been able to impose upon Captain Behrens, if only for the sake of the discipline and mental well-being of the 221st's own troops, to halt or at the very least "relocate" his portion of the killing.

Instead, there was not so much as a murmur of disapproval. This silence, especially given some officers' clear disapproval of Wehrmacht units being present at more "disciplined" Einsatzgruppe killings, is significant. It indicates a level of agreement with the police battalion's actions that was incompatible not only with morality, but with pragmatic considerations also. Such agreement in turn indicates very strongly that, whatever else drove the anti-Semitic measures carried out by Pflugbeil and Haupt, no explanation is complete without genuine, virulent, *ideological* hatred.

Ideology was probably also a genuine motive for the Intelligence Section. Alongside Lieutenant Beck's description of "treacherous, subversive, and rabble-rousing Jews" were his remarks in a summary compiled at the end of July for units about to take over the western parts of the 221st's old jurisdiction. "The tensions between the two population groups [Poles and Russians]," he reported, "were exploited by the Jews for their own ends. They [the Jews] are now getting the payback for all their swaggering and oppression."[31] Perhaps Beck was not giving vent to genuine, ideologically founded contempt so much as calculatingly, albeit ruthlessly, furthering the cause of divide and rule to which Förster alludes. Or he may simply have wished to impress his superiors, along the lines the leadership principle encouraged, with a show of ideological intensity. There are other times, however, when his genuine loathing of the Bolshevik system—and probably, by extension, the Jews who were seen as its principal upholders—is unmistakable. His venomous description of the prisoners the division took after Bialystok is shot through with a gratuitous venom beyond what would have been needed to impress the superiors who read the report:

> It is a tattered, ragged, almighty mish-mash of European and Asiatic races. Only a few wear boots where the leg isn't made out of leather . . . This, then, is the Red Army soldier of the Soviet paradise. Two worlds are colliding, one of cleanliness and order, the other filthy and chaotic in every respect. [The prisoners] are fearful and suspicious, taught for decades as they have been to distrust both outsiders and their own relatives. The senses of many seem completely dulled. Horror propaganda, fear, and then the sudden release of tension after the battle have reduced them almost to the state of wild animals.[32]

In summer 1943, moreover—by which time it would have had no practical benefit—Beck would be admixing anti-Semitic and anti-Bolshevik diatribe in the propaganda he was disseminating to potential partisan deserters.

All this points to one conclusion. Collectively, the ideological convictions of the 221st's division-level officers were genuine. Their readiness to inject harsh, indeed murderous anti-Semitism into their "security" effort, and probably anti-Bolshevism also, may have been calculated to some extent, but it certainly was heartfelt as well.

The security campaign conducted by the 221st Security Division's subordinate units, its regiments, battalions, and Kommandantur garrisons, initially presents an equally nauseating spectacle. Not only did they assent to ideologically saturated directives received from divisional command and above; they also took the lead themselves.

At Bialystok, units of the 350th Infantry Regiment and Guard Battalion 701 subjected those Jews who had escaped the bloodlust of Police Battalion 309 to a degrading public ordeal. In what was a wider debasing practice favored by Eastern Army units during 1941, they set them to work toppling monuments to Lenin and Stalin in full view of the town's population.[33] A letter from Gunner Heinz

Backe to his parents jovially describes similar events in the Baltic
town of Liepaja:

> All the town Jews were got together and put in a room the
> Bolsheviks had used for their conferences. This room was
> stuffed full of oversized portraits and busts of Stalin and co., and
> all sorts of Soviet symbols and paraphernalia. The Jews had
> to carry the lot out and walk in procession through the town
> streets to the River Windau, where a pyre was lit, and the Jews,
> naturally, were made to feed the flames with all the stuff they'd
> been carting.
>
> Today we had half a dozen Jewesses peeling potatoes for us—
> another job we don't have to bother ourselves with any more![34]

More pitiless even than this was the proposal that Colonel Koch,
commander of the 350th Infantry Regiment, forwarded in mid-August. He urged that the "Jewish question . . . be tackled far more radically. I suggest that all Jews living in rural areas be put under guard
in labor camps. Suspect elements must be eliminated."[35] At that particular time, the idea of interning *all* rural Jews in actual labor camps
went beyond even what divisional command itself felt ready to approve, and overall, Koch's proposal seems to have been interpreted
at divisional level as a call for the scale of "elimination" that Eastern
Army units were still keen to avoid dirtying their own hands with,
preferring instead to leave it to the Einsatzgruppen and Order Police.[36] Sometimes, moreover, lower-level units also went beyond the
strict dictates of the Commissar Order; as well as handing them over
to the Sonderkommandos, they shot commissars themselves.[37]
Several motives, including the "pragmatic" ones of example setting, dividing and ruling, and firing up the troops, may have been
at work here also.[38] Koch, moreover, may well have been seeking,
again along the lines the National Socialist leadership principle encouraged, to impress superiors with his ruthless zeal. Indeed, his

overzealousness on this occasion did not bar him from promotion soon after. Again, though, any explanation that neglects genuine ideological conviction does not look plausible. It was not just the fact that conceiving and implementing such measures would have been easier for an officer of anti-Semitic and anti-Bolshevik bent. For ideologically based hatreds—anti-Bolshevism directly but also probably anti-Semitism—almost certainly were exacerbated by what officers and men experienced of *Soviet* brutality.

Much of the murderous account sheet the Soviet side was accumulating may well have been retaliation for the gathering catalogue of German atrocities against commissars and prisoners of war. But on German field units, pressured by their situation and already influenced by ideological contempt as they may well have been, such subtleties were likely to be lost.

For one thing, Red Army commissars, who could expect a bullet if captured, had the strongest possible incentive to resist the Germans with all their fury, and to cajole and terrorize their troops into doing likewise. It is no surprise, then, that the Germans frequently clashed with Red Army units that resisted them with animal-like ferocity.[39] A directive issued early in the campaign to units of the German Fourth Army, the 221st and 286th Security Divisions among them, declared that "the main reason why the Russian never surrenders is that, dim-witted half-Asiatic that he is, he fully believes the notion, drummed into him by his commissars, that he will be shot if captured."[40] Perhaps still more provocative of anti-Bolshevism was experience of Soviet atrocities. Killing of German prisoners was rife, and reports that they also had been tortured and mutilated were no rarity.[41] Egon Niemann, an NCO in the 6th Infantry Division, recalled the discovery of twelve members of his company, "bestially murdered or mutilated so badly after being killed that they were no longer recognizable."[42]

There was also murder, such as the NKVD's massacre of political prisoners in Lemberg just before the Germans entered the city, on the grand scale.[43] The officers and men of the 221st Security Division didn't need to be on the scene themselves to learn of it. Accounts of Soviet barbarism probably came to them, perhaps with some lurid embellishment, from Polish civilians. Heinz Hagemann, another 6th Infantry Division NCO, wrote that "everywhere in this region we've been warmly greeted, sometimes even with swastika banners, by happy faces and people relieved, finally, to have escaped the Bolshevik yoke and terror! These people were almost completely cleaned out by the Bolsheviks, and they suffered atrocities—the political prisoners especially—that are almost beyond comprehension: mutilation, burning alive, the lot!"[44]

German security policy, in particular, was radicalized further by the speech Stalin made to the Soviet people on 3 July. He commanded them to rise up in the fascist invader's rear, disrupt his communication and supply lines, and use all manner of ruthless, clandestine measures against him. The Germans must be thrown out of the Russian motherland in a struggle for the liberation not just of the Soviet Union itself, but of Nazi-controlled Europe. "Partisan detachments must be formed," he ordered, "be they mounted or on foot, in all those places the enemy has occupied. Anywhere and everywhere, diversion groups must fight the enemy's units, and support the partisan effort by blowing up bridges and roads, destroying telephone and telegraph communications, and burning forests, depots, and trains. For the enemy, as indeed for all his accomplices and collaborators, conditions in the occupied areas must be made unbearable . . . he must be hunted down and exterminated, and all his plans foiled."[45]

Of course, this language bore no resemblance to the pathetic reality of Soviet partisan efforts at this very early stage. But it was ominous enough for Hitler and the High Command, in an endeavor to harden conduct to the degree the criminal orders originally had envisaged, to exploit to the hilt the fear it induced. "Ten days later," writes Jürgen Förster, Hitler "openly declared that the partisan war behind the front offered the possibility of 'exterminating all that stands against us.' To pacify such a vast area as quickly as possible, 'anyone who even looks at us askance' was to be shot."[46]

Higher command bodies followed Hitler's lead. On 23 July, the

Armed Forces High Command issued Directive Number 33. This declared that "resistance in the occupied East should be broken not through the 'judicial punishment of the guilty,' but by inflicting such terror that the population would lose 'all inclination to resist.'" On 25 July Field Marshal von Brauchitsch responded to the discovery of Soviet directives ordering the formation of sabotage groups in the German rear, and to what he viewed as the troops' failure to conduct themselves with the necessary severity. Nothing, he declared, was as important as the security of the German soldier himself. The only means of ensuring this was the vigorous practice of harshness, the only "proper" response to partisan attacks summary executions and destruction of villages. Brauchitsch, too, made particular play of Bolshevik bestiality.[47]

The Wehrmacht's propaganda departments, via the millions of leaflets, papers, and placards they distributed to the troops, took up the theme with fervor. Such were the sentiments of one leaflet: "Anyone who has ever looked at the face of a Red commissar knows what the Bolsheviks are like . . . We would insult the animals if we described these mostly Jewish men as beasts. They are the embodiment of Satanic and insane hatred against the whole of noble humanity . . . The masses, whom they have sent to their deaths by making use of all means at their disposal such as ice-cold terror and insane incitement, would have brought to an end all meaningful life, had this eruption not been dammed at the last moment."[48]

Soviet ruthlessness, then, was one rationale the Germans could use to respond to the pressures they faced and to bolster their ideological convictions with intensified brutality. But brutalization, at both divisional and subdivisional levels, also could come from a different direction. This source had ramifications not just for Jews and Communists, but for the wider population also.

Of genuine, significant partisan activity there might as yet be no sign in the early summer of 1941. But even in these relatively benign circumstances, garrisoning towns and villages, guarding supply routes, prison camps and prisoner-of-war columns, *and* executing active security operations across an enormous area, with forces seriously wanting in both quality and quantity, were tasks guaranteed to provoke frustration. No longer was this a situation confined to the map room. It was one that, for the officers and men charged with its implementation, was now unpleasantly real. Equally real was the fear of the depravities an unseen enemy *might* be capable of. In such circumstances, of course, the militaristic and ideological harshness of the criminal orders stood to inflame the brutalization even further. But the hardening effects of frustration and fear, irrespective of the criminal orders, were already considerable. Accordingly, units that failed to locate and combat partisans might vent their frustrated anger on the population.[49] Units that felt—often rightly—that they stood little chance of victory even if they did locate any partisans might persuade themselves that terrorizing the population, and thus deterring it from aiding and abetting partisans, was another means of making an impact. After all, it wasn't as though the Wehrmacht's antiguerrilla tradition discouraged such notions.[50] Third, units that had enjoyed no antipartisan success for long periods might want to convey a deceitfully dynamic image to their superiors by concealing their failure with impressive-looking body counts.[51] On all three counts, the butchers' mentality that drove such conduct might be buttressed by uncertainty as to where native civilian loyalties lay. Even before the population had its illusions about the Germans shattered and supported the partisans in ever-greater numbers, German troops on the ground often had no idea who was a loyal civilian, who a partisan accomplice, and who, indeed, an actual partisan. Discovery of enemy agents, "sometimes in positions of considerable trust . . . made the occupation personnel jittery and aware of being surrounded, watched, and exposed to constant dangers." The cumulative, brutalizing effect is summarized by Alexander Dallin, Ralph Mavrogorduto, and Wilhelm Moll:

In the latter part of the war, German soldiers would not stray from the main arteries of communication or walk singly even in the most strongly garrisoned towns. The feeling of isolation and danger was particularly pronounced among the thinly manned outposts and strongpoints which dotted the country-side . . . The feeling of insecurity and nervousness that was created among the German occupation personnel probably had a far-reaching psychological impact on the individual German. It is a common phenomenon that individuals with a pronounced inferiority complex will go to considerable lengths to disguise their feeling of insecurity by an outward show of superiority and aggressiveness.[52]

As the war continued, the increasingly extreme conditions the Eastern Army's security forces faced could brutalize even men who actually held relatively little truck with the anti-Slavism, guerrilla-phobia, capacity for professionalized violence, and careerism which colored the Wehrmacht as an institution and which the criminal orders sought to enshrine. Most certainly, this institutional ruthlessness legitimized and encouraged brutality. Often, however, the combination of fear, frustration, physical hardship, and unremitting pressure from above for results was enough to render antipartisan units immune to the sufferings their actions were inflicting on innocent civilians, and to eclipse the normal notions of good sense and humanity they might otherwise have displayed.

Though all this lay in the future in the early summer of 1941, the difficulties that would come to plague the security divisions' efforts, and contribute to brutalizing them, were already becoming apparent.

Third-rate mobility, to start with, was a curse on the security divisions even before the campaign started. Once the campaign was under way, the effects were swiftly apparent. The 286th Security Division, for instance, reported at the start of August that 65 percent of its trucks were of foreign make, with insufficient replacement parts, and liable to break down on bad roads.[53] The 221st Security Division, blessed as it was with the presence, till early September, of a major motorized element in the shape of Police Battalion 309, was relatively fortunate.[54]

But the 221st's other subordinate units were suffering. In mid-August the commander of the 350th Infantry Regiment's second battalion reported that the long marches his troops had to undertake to their operational area often completely wore them out even before they had arrived.[55] The territorial battalions were even worse off: they possessed no motorized transport of any kind.

Problems of mobility were heightened, of course, by the distances security units had to traverse. But the primitive environment of European Russia was not only vast; it also could be thoroughly unpleasant. "The biggest hardships we face," wrote Erwin Jost, an NCO in the 44th Construction Battalion, "are the dreadful heat, the lack of water . . . and the awful sandy tracks." "This place is indescribably miserable," wrote Major von Schönerer of the 7th Panzer Division. "The only signs of settlement are the famous Russian huts, between them badly tended fields and those awful forests, crisscrossed by pathways that, depending on the weather, resemble either a sandstorm or a swamp."[56]

Not to feel frustrated by such conditions would have required saintly patience indeed. And, though frustration had yet to harden to the point where it directly fueled brutality, already this process was starting. For one thing, frustration bred a sense of helplessness. This, in turn, made subordinate units more susceptible to another influence of brutalizing potency—fear. The sense of oppressiveness exuded by the wooded, swampy areas covering such enormous tracts of the Army Group Center Rear Area could only exacerbate such fear. A vivid illustration of the mindset this was likely to create is provided in a letter from Corporal Hans Brüning:

[The forests are teeming with danger.] Any snipers who fall into our hands are of course shot; their bodies lie everywhere. Sadly, though, many of our own comrades have been lost to their dirty methods. We're losing more men to the bandits than in the fighting itself.

Hardly any sleep to be had. We're awake and alert almost every night; you have to be in case they attack suddenly. If the sentry drops his guard just once then it could be over for all of us. Traveling alone is out of the question.[57]

Fear of partisans, real or imagined, was exacerbated by higher-level directives seeking to harden attitudes to irregular warfare further. The commander of VII Corps, to which the 221st Security Division was subordinate during the opening week of the campaign, ordered his divisions to regard "any civilian carrying a weapon, even if it's only a razor blade in his boot," as an irregular to be shot accordingly.[58] Developments in the 221st's jurisdiction could only heighten the tension. On 14 July Captain Haupt informed the 350th Infantry Regiment and the 45th Territorial Regiment that, despite strict orders to the contrary, many civilians, some of whom were "obviously" Red Army soldiers in disguise, had been caught wandering on the road from Bialystok to Baranovichi.[59] On 19 July, Haupt's office stressed that, explosives-laden Soviet paratroops having landed in the area of Bereza Kartuska, the division must brace itself for an increase in attacks and sabotage.[60]

Such incidents were likely, even this early on, to cause fear of partisans to generalize into distrust of the entire population. For some officers, such distrust may well have been buttressed by older notions of the Germans' natural superiority over their eastern neighbors. This was something by which the security divisions, raised from regions with a violent legacy of centuries-long confrontation with "the East," may have been particularly affected.[61]

In turn, firsthand impressions of Russians themselves, beginning with the "tattered, ragged, almighty mishmash of European and Asiatic races" taken prisoner during the very first days, might nourish anti-Slavism further.[62] Upon many officers and men, encounters with the living conditions of the Russian peasantry imprinted themselves forcefully. Heinz Hagemann wrote of "a primitiveness you can't comprehend. A landscape almost devoid of people stretches into the distance. There's the odd settlement here and there, but the houses are made out of branches and the gaps are filled in with earth and moss. Many have got only the one room, or two at the most, where the women, kids, poultry, and pigs are all thrown in together. One bed, perhaps, made out of a couple of grubby furs. Often it's impossible to breathe. But there are kids of all shades and sizes, many suffering from rickets. Plenty of pregnant women as well, from barely mature girls to older women. Often not a father in sight." Blunter still were the views of Major Hans Schär of Pioneer Battalion 652. "These Russians are beasts," he asserted. "With their animal-like expressions, they look like the niggers we fought in the French war."[63] Anyone who described the population in these terms clearly held other races in contempt anyway. But upon men who perhaps had never left Germany before, the undeniably backward living conditions of the east were almost certain to make some kind of impression. Lieutenant Beck reported that, from the moment the 221st Security Division had crossed the old Polish-Russian border in July, the spectacle of such conditions had affected its men.[64]

Particularly active in ensuring that the 221st's subordinate units imbibed the combination of guerrillaphobia, suspicion of the population, and anti-Slavic contempt was Captain Haupt's Operations Section. For one thing, Haupt repeatedly issued orders urging that all officers and NCOs down to the level of section commander be informed of the smallest attack and drum the necessary vigilance into their troops. "The possibility of arson and sabotage acts must be reckoned with everywhere," he declared. "The troops must be thoroughly informed of these events, be cautious to the utmost, and execute security measures consistently."[65]

If Haupt was moved by some measure of genuine concern for the troops, he was moved also by acute distrust of the population. Though Haupt was favorably impressed by the initial reception of bread, salt, and flowers euphorically showered on the German "liberators" by the ecstatic Polish population, his view changed within days.[66] By the beginning of July, he observed, the population's initial euphoria had vanished, to be replaced by passivity.[67] By 19 July his view had hardened completely. "The mood and manner of the population, the Poles included," he wrote, "is hostile through and through. There is no place for trust, chumminess, or letting one's guard down."[68]

Haupt's terse assessment is all the more striking for its contrast with reports by other military agencies. The Economic Inspectorate Center described the population's attitude as indifferent at worst, friendly at best.[69] Lieutenant Beck, meanwhile, did not allow his own contempt for eastern races to cloud his judgment about the need to cultivate their pro-German potential.

From Haupt, however, the talk from very early on was not of cultivation, but of coercion. The language of his instruction, issued on 13 August, that all village headmen be *ordered to compel* the peasants to employ all available labor in the coming harvest indicates a desire to subjugate the Slavic subhumans of his imaginings.[70] His attitude was even clearer over the *Leutnant Marx,* an armored locomotive the 221st obtained temporarily for pacification duty during July and August. Haupt told the train to employ "the harshest, most ruthless measures" in the areas assigned to it. He ordered it to roar into "suspect" villages to conduct lightning searches for weapons in the middle of the night. On 26 July he instructed the *Leutnant Marx* that local mayors were to be cajoled, on pain of death, into preventing sabotage upon railway stations, bridges, and technical installations. The fact that the *Leutnant Marx* was a highly mobile unit able to strike fast and hard must, Haupt believed, end any complacency the population might feel that otherwise thinly patrolled areas were somehow out of the division's reach.[71]

When it came to intensity of distrust, Haupt also outdid colleagues in other security divisions. The 403d Security Division, certainly, was also contemptuous of the population. Captain Wilhelm, its operations officer, described the population at the beginning of August as "natural slaves," inured to strict treatment and hard toil imposed by their masters.[72] Lieutenant Scharfenroth, the intelligence officer, wrote at the end of September that "the simple maxim 'whoever plunders is shot' is more effective than long-winded attempts at persuasion or public-spirited treatises."[73] Yet even these officers did not go as far as Haupt did when he effectively condemned the entire population as anti-German; Wilhelm, for one, drew the opposite conclusion.[74] The extremity of Haupt's distrust of the population indicates that it was not just calculated to impress superiors or harden the troops, and not just a reaction to difficult conditions. Instead, it appears instinctive, driven by genuine, venomous anti-Slavism.

For many officers at subdivisional level, meanwhile, the brutalizing potential of this interaction of frustration, fear, distrust, and racial contempt is likely to have been strengthened by feelings of personal resentment. The source of this resentment was the contrast between their current situation and the triumphant experience of Blitzkrieg campaigns—whether past campaigns in which they themselves had participated, or the present campaign, in which they were barred from participating.[75] Belonging to an institution that idolized maneuver warfare as much as the Wehrmacht did can only have intensified the feeling.

Notions of having been "dumped in a backwater" were expressed in a letter written in mid-July by Lieutenant Helmut Hahn of the 258th Infantry Division: "Yesterday, a minor mutiny flared up over the surprise news that we're to remain in this area as occupation troops. All want to push on into the Russian interior and share in the spoils . . . You get the impression that the men are literally burning to get to grips with the enemy."[76] For the 221st Security Division, memories of still more recent triumphs may have exacerbated resentment: its obscene aftermath notwithstanding, the capture of Bialystok was, militarily, an achievement that was to remain unmatched by any other Eastern Army security division. And no officer in the 221st felt such deprivation as keenly, perhaps, as General Pflugbeil himself.

Of all the generals who commanded Army Group Center security divisions from 1941 to 1943, Pflugbeil was the only one in charge of a front-line combat formation, the Kurland Division, at the end of the war.[77] His execution of the battle of Bialystok suggests, moreover, that his ambition was matched by his abilities. It was Pflugbeil himself, not his superiors at corps or army level, who decided it would be the 221st Security Division that would take the city.[78] Though Pflugbeil, at fifty-nine, was no longer a young man, such drive and independence suggest a veritable "man of action." The flip side of such potential, however, was that rear-area security—drab, frustrating, and far from the front—was hardly the ideal stage on which to realize it. And Pflugbeil would have known it.

The final point is that these frustrations were felt by officers and troops on whom the Wehrmacht's institutional attitude to guerrilla warfare, and the enshrinement of that attitude in the criminal orders, are already likely to have made an impression. Even then, this combination had yet to bear its full brutal fruit. Yet the fact that the combination was there, and was already hardening conduct, is another reason why the *potential* for *great* brutality, were circumstances to become more difficult, was there also.

The criminal orders the Eastern Army received before the invasion of the Soviet Union were a blueprint for unleashing the Wehrmacht's nazified antiguerrilla ruthlessness against Jews, Communists, and the wider population. But in the early summer of 1941, officers and units in the field did not mete out terror and oppression to all these groups equally. They victimized Jews and Communists not only out of ideological contempt, but out of particular "pragmatic," albeit callous, reasons also. Meanwhile, the absence as yet of any genuine partisan movement to speak of assured the Germans initially benign circumstances that reduced their proclivity for terrorizing the wider population. The ruthlessness Eastern Army security officers exercised at this early stage makes for a nauseating spectacle, then, but one that to a great degree was not only ideological but also selective, calculating, and determined by particular circumstances.

Precise motives varied. In addition to harboring ruthlessly pragmatic motives, the three central figures in the 221st Security Division's security campaign clearly were virulently disposed toward the Reich's "ideological enemies." The directives the division issued propagated such sentiments among its subordinate units. General Pflugbeil, meanwhile, probably was not the only officer whose frustrated front-line ambitions further hardened his attitude to rear-area security by breeding in him the resentment many rear-area officers felt at being relegated to a backwater. Major Haupt, the operations officer, displayed a contempt for the Slavic population which outdid that of many of his colleagues.

At the subdivisional level particularly, a further dynamic was at work. In addition to preexisting prejudices, the input of the criminal orders, the particular ruthlessness of some subordinate commanders such as Colonel Koch, and a general experience, be it secondhand or direct, of Soviet ruthlessness, the 221st's subordinate regiments and battalions were affected by the sometimes fearful, often frustrating, and usually uncomfortable experience of the war in the rear at closer quarters. Such were the division's still relatively favorable circumstances that this dynamic did not reach anything like its full brutalizing potential in the early summer of 1941. But the signs were there, and, in tandem with the other potential sources of brutalization that were present, they were already sufficient to nurture more indiscriminate harshness.

From the late summer of 1941, all these forces intensified and *combined.* Together, they launched a vicious radicalization of the campaign.

3

Bloodshed Mushrooms

In both the Eastern Army's conduct of antipartisan warfare and the emergence of Nazi Germany's wider campaign of ideological extermination, the late summer and early autumn of 1941 were a pivotal period. In the occupied Soviet Union, the body count of noncombatants labeled "partisans" exploded.

An extreme example of such bloodletting was the actions of the 707th Infantry Division in the newly created General Commissariat of White Ruthenia.[1] General von Bechtolsheim, the divisional commander, and the operations officer, Lieutenant-Colonel von der Osten, were possessed of a poisonous anti-Semitism, and were clear about what they expected from their troops: "The Jews, the spiritual leaders and carriers of Bolshevism and the Communist idea, are our *mortal enemy*. They are to be exterminated."[2] Their unit went on to shoot 10,431 of its 10,940 (mainly Jewish) "prisoners," while itself sustaining losses of two dead and five wounded, during October and early November.[3]

But the death tolls that other security divisions exacted, and the contrasts between those death tolls and their own losses, were stupendous also: "The 403d Security Division, in October alone, shot 1,093 'partisans' at no significant loss to itself."[4] The war diary of the 286th Security Division records the killing, at a cost to itself of 8 dead, of 715 partisans during the same period.[5] The fact that security divisions compiled their war diaries daily, on incomplete information, means that the true figure the 286th accumulated was probably much higher.[6] In the ten weeks from the middle of September, the 221st Security Division amassed a body count of 1,746 partisans—killed, it claimed, in combat, or shot after capture—for the loss of 18 dead.[7] So vast are these disparities that the "partisan" body counts clearly numbered far more defenseless noncombatants than actual partisans. Moreover, many of the large numbers of "partisan" prisoners each division took are likely to have been killed by the SS units to which they subsequently were handed over.[8]

Though the Wehrmacht's antipartisan campaign had already shown signs of considerable ruthlessness in the early summer of 1941, this volume of bloodshed constituted an enormous leap. The main circumstance that provided the overall push was the failure to achieve quick victory over the Soviet Union in 1941. The pressures these reverses created magnified the effects of brutalizing forces already at work.

From the late summer of 1941, the momentum of the German advance into the Soviet Union stalled. At the highest level, there had been strategic vacillation as Hitler and the generals in turn committed the bulk of the Panzer forces to the advance on Moscow, diverted them to the flanks to aid the advance on Leningrad and the agricultural and industrial heartlands of the Ukraine and the Don Basin, then diverted them back to the drive on the Soviet capital. In the field, the tremendous strain the advance placed on men and equipment, the ongoing ferocity of Red Army resistance, and, increasingly, the muddy chaos brought by the autumn rains all confronted the Germans with a fearful ordeal every step of the way. Even Army Group South's seizure of Kharkov in October, Army Group Center's renewed drive on Moscow, and the capture of more than 650,000 Red Army troops in the Vyazma Pocket west of the capital could not conceal the magnitude of the difficulties now accumulating. Nor could they conceal the fact that, even before the first snow fell, the German advance in general was slowing to a crawl.

Eventually—and, as it would turn out, fatally—the advance slowed beyond the point where victory in 1941 was still possible. By the beginning of December, German troops were at the gates of Moscow. Whether capturing Moscow would have dislocated the Soviet Union's government and infrastructure sufficiently to defeat her is debatable anyway. In any case, the onset of winter proper and mass counterattacks by a hundred fresh Soviet divisions rushed from Siberia nailed any lingering hopes of German victory that year. The German line in Russia did hold against the Soviet counteroffensive that fell upon it during the months that followed, but it buckled fearfully. The Eastern Army, then, was in it for the bitter duration.

Even before this, however, the arduousness of the German advance and the dwindling likelihood of a successful resolution of the campaign in 1941 was having a dramatically radicalizing effect on Eastern Army and SS conduct in the rear.

For one thing, the SS and other agencies now took a momentous step toward a "final solution of the problem of European Jewry"—a decision to exterminate the Jews of the occupied Soviet Union.

The progression from ghettoization and "selective killings" to innumerable mass shootings of Jewish men, women, and children across the German-occupied Soviet Union from August 1941 onward was a massive stride down the path that ended, ultimately, in the gas chambers of Auschwitz. Whether the SS had been planning it before Barbarossa, and how far the Einsatzgruppen and other agencies in the field took the initiative in the months following the invasion, are questions that, like many concerning the origins of the Final Solution, have vexed historians for decades. What is increasingly clear, however, is that the Reich's inhuman anti-Semitic policies—in particular, its practice of corralling the Jews of its eastern territories into heaving, disease-ridden ghettos—contained the seeds of radicalization of those policies.[9]

So insurmountable were the economic and logistical problems involved in ghettoizing hundreds of thousands of human beings, so limited the manpower to oversee them, that the amoral Reich agencies on the spot started considering more drastic solutions to the Jewish "problem." This development stoked those agents' ideological convictions, personal ambitions, and ruthless technocratic attitudes to fuel a truly genocidal dynamic. As the Wehrmacht's increasingly obvious inability to beat the Soviets in 1941 closed off the option of banishing the Jews en masse to the region east of the Urals, the dynamic accelerated. Though it would vary in form and timing across regions, the process that now unfolded would result in an extension of mass killing by the Einsatzgruppen, the greatly expanded number of Order Police battalions, newly arrived SS infantry and cavalry brigades, and numerous native auxiliary units, to encompass all Jewish men, women, and children in the Soviet Union.[10]

Merely to assist in this process constituted, by the very nature of the task, a radicalization of the Eastern Army's own conduct. It would be wrong to accuse the entire Eastern Army of collusion; indeed, its own files record at least a few instances of open opposition.[11] Yet the process would not have been feasible had not Eastern Army units already concentrated the Jews of their own jurisdictions en masse, thus making them easy for the SS and Police to get at, and provided those agencies with all manner of practical assistance. Nor would it have been feasible had the leadership of both the Wehrmacht in general and the Eastern Army particularly not assented collectively, silently or otherwise, to the entire murderous undertaking—and justified their own collusion as being in the "interests of security."[12]

Historians are at odds over what persuaded the Wehrmacht and the Eastern Army to go this far. Senior field commanders may have been swayed by any combination of the ideological—a genuine belief, fed by those cases in which it was true, that Jews and Bolsheviks were one and the same—and the ruthlessly pragmatic. The latter was formed not just by the ongoing belief that such actions could "impress" the population, but also by the Eastern Army's continuing, indeed rising, need for security assistance from SS and police manpower.[13] The reservations of some may well have been eroded by the fact that SS officialspeak depicted the spiraling butchery the Einsatzgruppen were now meting out as a "necessary security measure" against acts of treachery and sabotage committed by Jew-Bolshevik subversives. Einsatzkommando 8, which operated in the 221st Security Division's area, was typical. It justified the murder of 627 Jews north of Mogilev on the grounds that they had been participating in sabotage, for instance, and legitimized the massacre of 3,726 Jews in Mogilev itself as a necessary response to their involvement in sabotage, their refusal to work, and their support for the partisans.[14] Such rationalization could strengthen the conviction, which many officers already held, that Jew equaled Bolshevik equaled partisan. But in the increasingly pressured, frustrating situation in which the Eastern Army security forces found themselves, they also could ensure that other officers, who otherwise might not have been such convinced ideologues, came increasingly to harbor this perception also.[15]

But beyond this general level, quantifying and explaining the collusion of *particular* Eastern Army units in these killings can be next to impossible. Indeed, many Eastern Army officers felt a direct interest in keeping the record so vague. Such officers certainly had it in them to support all manner of anti-Semitic persecution. But the escalating Einsatzgruppen campaign, encompassing as it did the extermination of *all* Soviet Jews, irrespective of age or sex, was something else. Though such officers might still facilitate it readily, especially given the "security-related" rationale with which they could convince themselves that such actions were right, most were anxious to preserve a charade of decency or, more practically, avoid implicating themselves for fear of future answerability. Scattered hints and references aside, then, their silence on these matters is deafening.

But the question of how far, and through what mechanism, the increasingly murderous handling of the Jewish question fueled the mushrooming killing that Eastern Army troops began, from late summer, to mete out in their *own* security campaign, is something that can indeed be investigated.

To be sure, there are strong signs that Hitler and the Armed Forces High Command endeavored to embroil the Eastern Army in the extermination of the Soviet Jews. The decree that Field Marshal Keitel issued on 12 September, which among other things ordered "ruthless, energetic, and drastic measures above all against the Jews, the main carriers of Bolshevism," and forbade the employment of Jews as labor under most circumstances, exemplifies the orders that were issued.[16] Field commanders followed suit. A series of directives in the autumn of 1941, issued by numerous higher-level field commanders, combined ideological fervor with "pragmatic" military arguments. They stressed the "military necessity" of combating the Jew-Bolshevik menace in the German rear with the utmost severity, in the process identifying Jews as the source of all the unrest there even more explicitly than before. The "Reichenau Order" exemplifies these directives. Reichenau, commanding the Sixth Army in the Ukraine, stressed that "the soldier must have complete understanding for the necessity of the harsh but just atonement of Jewish subhumanity. This has the further goal of nipping in the bud rebellions in the rear of the Eastern Army which, as experience shows, are always plotted by the Jews."[17]

In the Army Group Center Rear Area, similarly pitiless directives emanated to the security divisions from General von Schenckendorff's command. In early October the general issued the booklet *The Partisan, His Organization, and How to Fight Him*, which declared that "the enemy is to be utterly annihilated. It is difficult, even for the toughest soldier, to decide swiftly between life and death for apprehended partisans and suspects, but the decision must be borne, and any personal feeling is to be banished ruthlessly and mercilessly."[18] Two weeks earlier, at a special antipartisan conference of Eastern Army and SS officers held by Schenckendorff, the maxim "Where there's a Jew there's a partisan, and where there's a partisan there's a Jew" had been drummed into all present.[19]

Historians disagree over the precise motives for this ideological injection. Along with the probability that some officers, perhaps a great many, clearly *believed* all this, is the argument that their ongoing need for SS assistance in the rear compelled them not only to acquiesce in genocide, but also to take steps to ensure that their own soldiers were given a military justification for such a scale of killing.[20] Other historians still find an explanation that lies primarily not in the unfolding of SS genocide, but in the increasing difficulties that both the Eastern Army's security effort and the entire eastern campaign encountered from late summer. Defeat, they argue, was not contemplated, but a lengthier campaign certainly was. It was more essential than ever, then, that the troops felt fortified for the task ahead. The Jew-equals-Bolshevik-equals-partisan equation fitted this purpose. Blaming "Jew-Bolsheviks," already a popular hate figure, for sabotage and resistance in the German rear could both stoke the troops' indignation *and* channel it into even harder, ideologically inspired fighting spirit.[21]

Whatever their motive for these exhortations, field commanders now could point out not only that some Communist functionaries were Jews, but also that Jews were responsible for rear-area resistance. Nor is this surprising: facing annihilation at the hands of the Einsatzgruppen as they did, they had every reason to resist. The 286th Security Division, for one, remarked in early November that a stream of Jewish recruits to the partisans, compelled to flee their homes in the face of the Sicherheitsdienst (Security Police) killings, were "fighting for their lives."[22]

The officer writing this report seems to have recognized Jewish resistance for what it was—a desperate attempt to survive—but instances such as these were meat and drink to field commanders intent on drilling the Jew-equals-Bolshevik-equals-partisan equation into their troops. Moreover, like the criminal orders before them, the field commanders' exhortations of autumn 1941 did not just invoke an ideologically infused spirit of harshness. Resembling incitements rather than orders, they also played on the careerist ambition that the leadership principle so often harnessed to such ruthless effect.

The key questions for us here are why, and to what extent, the 221st Security Division itself was receptive to these exhortations.

Both General Pflugbeil and various division-level departments were already endeavoring in the early summer, out of genuine conviction as well as any pragmatic assessment, to persuade their subordinate units that the Jews were carriers of Bolshevik contamination and, therefore, the ultimate source of any sabotage or other difficulty the division faced. Below divisional level, meanwhile, one regiment had among other things gleefully subjected the Jews to the most humiliating public degradation, and the commander of the other had identified the Jews as so great a threat that he had sought their mass internment and elimination even earlier than the division itself had wished. It is a damning record. Overall, it is suggestive of men who, on grounds of both ideology *and* twisted, brutal pragmatism, would have seen calls to kill Jews as partisans as a call to pleasure as well as duty. The course that events took, however, was less straightforward than this.

The proliferation of anti-Semitism in higher-level security directives from late summer certainly fed the 221st's mushrooming killing rate to some extent. Its subordinate units enacted the "Jew equals Bolshevik equals partisan" maxim many times. On 21 October the Eighth Company of the 350th Infantry Regiment shot four Jewish Communist Youth members whom it had seized attending a secret meeting. Eight days later the regiment reported the shooting of a Jewish bank director caught with false papers. On 31 October the Eighth Company again shot seven Jews whom it labeled partisan accomplices. A yet greater "success" had already been achieved by the 350th's third battalion; on 12 September this unit reported that it had shot 22 Jews and one Communist for supporting the partisans.[23] The 45th Territorial Regiment read from the same script; at the end of October it reported that it had tried to locate an armed band of 60 to 70 Jews southeast of the town of Rechitsa. It had greater success in the following days, however; on 2 November it reported the shooting of six Jews and on 8 November that Territorial Battalion 302 had shot three fugitive Jewish Red Army prisoners "trying to escape."[24]

In each case, the units responsible troubled themselves to identify the victims as Jews. Thus did they exhibit a mentality that, in line with what was being urged from above, did indeed equate Jews with partisans. The fact that these reports emanated from the entire spectrum of the 221st's subordinate regiments and battalions shows, moreover, that the mentality was widespread.

Nor was it restricted to the 221st. Some units in other security divisions perpetrated instances of killing vastly more sickening even than these. Worst of all the formations in the Army Group Center Rear Area were certain units of two infantry regiments subordinate to the 286th Security Division, the 354th and 691st. On 4 September men of the 354th shot 51 Jews in reprisal for an incident in which a German journalist had been killed and two German soldiers wounded. In the first week of October, units of the 691st Infantry Regiment killed twenty-two Jews in Esmon "shown to be working with the partisans," and nineteen in Golovchin. These Jews were shot not because any German soldiers had been killed, but because one soldier had been wounded in the arm.[25] And glimpses of a private soldier's diary for October shows that the worst these units were capable of was not even officially registered. Corporal Richard Heidenreich of the 354th Infantry Regiment described a mass shooting of around a thousand Jews in the Minsk area that his battalion itself carried out.

> October 5th, in the evening our Second Lieutenant selected fifteen men with strong nerves . . . We waited for the morning in tense expectation. We were ready at 5 o'clock prompt, and the First Lieutenant explained what we were to do. There were approximately 1,000 Jews in the village of Krupka, and these all needed to be shot today . . . After our names were read out, the column marched to the nearest swamp . . . A second lieutenant and a company sergeant-major were with us. Ten shots sounded, ten Jews were blown away. This went on until all were taken care of. Only a few of them kept their composure. The children clung to their mothers, women to their men . . . A couple of days later a similarly large number was shot in Kholoponichi. I was involved here too.[26]

As a depiction of the dreadful human cost the Eastern Army's security campaign exacted that autumn, from which no rigorous analysis of the causes, important though such analysis is, can detract, Heidenreich's diary needs to be cited.

But Eastern Army security units in the central sector of the Soviet Union, even during the escalation of late summer and autumn, did not target and kill Jews on this scale all that frequently. The actions Heidenreich describes prompted one of the few significant criminal investigations of Eastern Army members that the postwar Federal German government carried out. Most other actions did not.[27] There may have been many reasons for the fact that investigations were not pursued, but the scale of the killing was probably one of them. Of course, for any Jew who perished in the Eastern Army's "security" campaign, scale was meaningless. But for a historian seeking to explain why so many more people perished in that campaign during late summer and autumn 1941, scale is not meaningless.

Many Eastern Army security units in the Army Group Center Rear Area seem to have killed Jews to a degree that, widespread and merciless though it was, rarely assumed as ghastly a scale as that perpetrated by Heidenreich's unit. The figure of 700 or so "partisans" whom, according to the divisional war diary, the 286th Security Division's subordinate units killed between mid-September and the end of November clearly excludes the 1,000 Jews who were butchered in the action recounted by Heidenreich. Of these remaining 700, fewer than 100 Jews were reported killed.[28] The 43 victims who perished when the 221st Security Division's subordinate units put the "Jew equals Bolshevik equals partisan" equation into action, meanwhile, must be weighed against the 1,650-plus other deaths they inflicted between mid-September and the end of November.

Of course, one reason why the security divisions' war diaries do not record the killing of more Jews was that the Einsatzgruppen, aided and abetted by those same divisions, were making an excellent job of it already. And indeed, other central sector Eastern Army units—particularly those that belonged to those infantry divisions which, like the 707th, had commenced security duty more recently —massacred Jews to a sometimes infinitely greater extent.[29] But overall, the picture of the Eastern Army security campaign in the Army Group Center Rear Area that emerges shows that, while the actions of some units and their officers were more ruthlessly anti-Semitic than others, much of the killing was not directed against Jews.

Cold pragmatism and *general* antipartisan ruthlessness, qualities encouraged by the criminal orders, but intensified by the mounting pressure the divisions faced, proved more powerful components of the mounting brutality than did anti-Semitism. And though it may indeed have been the pressures of a lengthening campaign that inspired some senior commanders to urge their troops to go after Jews with a vengeance, the concrete effects of these pressures on units in the field actually steered much of the mushrooming brutality in other directions. The major impetus for *this* ruthless dynamic was emerging in late summer 1941 also.

In mid-August 1941 the eastward expansion of the new, civilian-administered Reich Commissariat Ostland relieved the Army Group Center security divisions of the westernmost portions of their jurisdictions. But in the new territory to the east with which they were saddled instead, conditions were far less benign.

Upon the populations of both eastern Belorussia and the strip of greater Russia immediately beyond it, the war was inflicting hardships far worse than anything the populations of Poland or western Belorussia had hitherto endured. Here the Soviet authorities had had time to enact a Stalin order to uproot and evacuate the fabric of industry and commerce before the German advance reached this far east. Thousands of specialist workers, civil servants, doctors, and managers had gone with it. The mass unemployment, hunger, and complete dislocation of the social fabric that resulted blighted the mass of the population that remained.

The reports of Einsatzgruppe B depict the deprivation vividly: "the flight of the functionaries has brought life in general to a standstill. The population pours back to the cities in its thousands, where instead of any basis of life they find only ruins . . . [B]ecause the collective farms aren't functioning and the depots stand empty and unoccupied, the small shops and distribution points can't function either. Despite the harsh measures that have been put in place, plunder is universal."[30] Three weeks later, on 5 August, it reported that "east of Minsk . . . the provisioning situation is catastrophic. For all supplies were destroyed by the Soviets."[31] Desperate mass foraging sprees by thousands of townsfolk into the surrounding countryside stoked enormous tension between urban and rural populations, and transformed order into chaos there also.[32]

For the Eastern Army, all this rendered the task of administration far more difficult. Hunger generated a wretched flood of refugees and Red Army fugitives whose desperation often drove them to join embryonic partisan groups. Misery and upheaval combined with a greater residue of Communist sympathy in the population—lengthier as the exposure of this region's population to Soviet propaganda had been—to create even more fertile ground for fledgling partisan groups.[33]

These ingredients marinated with the first stirrings of popular disappointment that the German occupation was not going to herald the bountiful existence it had portended. Although a pragmatic need to secure the population's cooperation diluted the murderously utilitarian "hunger policy" the Reich's planners had formulated originally,[34] the level of requisitioning that took place still provoked intense bitterness. "Among the population of the erstwhile Soviet Republic of Belorussia," Einsatzgruppe B reported on 5 August, "a worsening in the mood has recently become apparent. This is due, above all, to constant plunder and requisitioning, in both town and country, by the German troops."[35] More practically, the Soviet authorities in eastern Belorussia had also had time to lay more concrete foundations for underground resistance.[36]

In such an arduous context, the potentially brutalizing frustration the security divisions had already been feeling in early summer could only intensify. By the end of August, in the Army Group Center Rear Area at any rate, pressure for a wider radicalization of Eastern Army security measures, directed not just against Jews and Communists, was mounting.

In September, the storm broke. The sixteenth of that month saw the expiration of a jurisdictionwide deadline after which, General von Schenckendorff had ordered, every "escaped Red Army soldier still roaming around" in the territory between the Rivers Beresina and Dnepr was to be viewed as an irregular and shot on sight.[37] What happened next is clear in the divisional war diaries: the 286th Security Division reported killing 26 Red Army fugitives and partisans in the fortnight up to the 16th, 119 the fortnight after. The equivalent figures for the 403d were 9 and 62, for the 221st itself 73 and 221.[38] So imperfect were the Germans' techniques for recording their security operations' death tolls during 1941 that the real figures were probably a lot higher. The "before–after" contrast, however, is clear across the board.

The Army Group Center security divisions did not simply jump at Schenckendorff's call. The 221st Security Division's hands, as the figures indicate, were particularly bloodied even before the sixteenth. Its especially trying conditions had already provoked its officers to ruthless, independent action.

At the end of August the 221st, more so than the 286th and 403d Security Divisions at this time, experienced a rise in genuine partisan activity. On their own, the attack on a rail building on 29 August, the killing of four members of Guard Battalion 701, and the death of an officer in an attack on a roadblock on the thirtieth may look trifling.[39] But the already-pressured units that experienced them would have found them anything but. The inability to locate, kill, or capture partisans could only swell the fear and frustration that by now were stoking brutality.

So it was here. Typical were the actions of a company of Territorial Battalion 352 at the end of August. Fired upon with the loss of one dead, unable to catch the culprits, it torched the nearest farmstead in reprisal and shot six of the male inhabitants despite having not a scrap of evidence that the men had been involved. Guard Battalion 701 encountered a thirty-strong group of Russian soldiers during an extensive operation around the areas of Bazevichi and

Klichev. Two of the group were killed in combat and eleven prisoners taken, nine of whom were reported "shot trying to escape." This, of course, was a commonplace euphemism for shooting prisoners out of hand. The frustration the battalion probably felt at the fact that seventeen of the enemy *had* escaped may have tipped it to such action.[40] Neither action was a wholesale massacre, but they were actions of a kind unrecorded by the 221st's subordinate units before the end of August. That both battalions were weaker unit types, likely to feel the pressures of the situation particularly keenly, is probably no coincidence.

A propensity for brutality increased as the division's problems multiplied during early September. The next blow fell when, amid the widespread transfer of Order Police battalions from rear to front, the 221st had to relinquish its principal motorized contingent, Police Battalion 309, to the Second Army. True, Guard Battalion 701 and the 350th Infantry Regiment retained motorized elements. But the growing acuteness of the 221st's motorization problem could not be ignored. None of its remaining trucks was able to travel across land, and it felt the need for dispatch riders and a divisional spotter plane sorely. The extension of the 221st's area as far east as the River Dnepr on 6 September could only exacerbate the strain.[41]

Whether through frustration or a desire to conceal their shortcomings, units in the field were even more likely to lash out in such circumstances. They might also be prompted to consider how they might destroy possible future sources of partisan activity. This motivation amounted to a death sentence for many of the refugees and Red Army fugitives in the 221st's jurisdiction. Even so, the contrast between the death tolls the division inflicted before the expansion of its territory and the far higher ones directly after is striking. Forty-three people had been reported killed in the fortnight leading up to the territorial expansion of 6 September. Another 43 were killed on the day after the expansion alone.[42] Though the jurisdictions of both the 286th and 403d Security Divisions expanded at almost the same time as the 221st's, in neither case did killing escalate immediately.

Very probably the *combination* of extended territory with the sudden loss of mobility and rise in partisan activity was decisive in prompting the 221st's ruthless response.[43]

Circumstances, catalytic though they were, did not fuel the escalation alone. The ruthless independence of mind of the officers who commanded the 221st Security Division was crucial also.

At the division's head was an officer whose personal sense of frustrated ambition was probably especially pronounced. In view of this, General Pflugbeil's alarmed reaction to the attacks in a communiqué of 31 August is telling: "These incidents show that these parts of the division's jurisdiction cannot in any way be considered pacified, and must be approached by the troops with the greatest possible watchfulness . . . Enemy actions against the troops must be countered immediately with the harshest measures . . . I make every unit commander responsible for ensuring that the troops be reminded of this repeatedly."[44]

Perhaps the clearest contribution the 221st's divisional level made to the radicalization of its security campaign, even though General von Schenckendorff's 16 September deadline was the more decisive cutoff point in the process overall, was the directives it issued on 6 September.

Six September was the day the 221st's jurisdiction was extended, and ten days before General von Schenckendorff's deadline expired. On it, Lieutenant Beck issued a directive urging the troops to show the utmost vigilance in ensuring that captured commissars be identified as such and receive what was coming to them.[45] Even more significant for the brutalization of "antipartisan" conduct—and, because it went out on the same day, a likely sign of ruthless interdepartmental coordination—was the directive issued by Captain Haupt. This stated that "the underhandedness of the partisans, and the proven collusion of the Jewish population, mean that commanders must exercise their power even more intensively and severely than before if setbacks for the troops are to be avoided."[46]

This simultaneous appeal to ideological and military sentiment did not spur the troops to kill Jews en masse. But given the timing of both directives, it seems that they were driven in the first instance not by anti-Semitism or anti-Bolshevism—sentiments that both officers almost certainly harbored—but by another motive. Their likeliest purpose—and the troops' subsequent behavior suggests that they were successful in this—was to strengthen the troops' obduracy of spirit, driving them, in the harsher situation in which they were about to find themselves, to a more ruthless execution of security measures *generally*. Such a process follows the pattern, suggested by some historians, of directives that used ideological language to harden the troops' conduct of their military duties overall.

The composition of the death toll that mounted over the following weeks and months reveals still more about the makeup of the motives that drove the killing that autumn.

Career-minded officers at all divisional levels certainly would have seen by now, if not before, that a pitiless attitude to security was a treasured commodity. There is every reason to suppose that a careerist desire to impress superiors fed the tally of "partisan" dead even further. Ruthlessness certainly seems to have brought career rewards for Captain Brandt. This 221st Security Division officer bemoaned the failure of his men to display the "harshness" that antipartisan warfare demanded, and wrote in October that "it is unacceptable that officers have to do the shooting while the men watch. Most of the men are too weak. This is a sign that the true meaning of 'partisan warfare' is something they have never learned, or at least have been badly taught."[47]

Brandt, it seems here, was ministering tender mercies to his prisoners personally, and it was this ruthlessness that may well have led directly to his appointment as commander of the 221st's specialized, mobile partisan combat battalion, at that time the division's most dynamic unit, on 7 September.[48]

The career trajectory of Colonel Koch, the commander of the 350th Infantry Regiment, was similar. This officer, whose desire for a harsher line against Jews in August 1941 had been too fierce even for division-level tastes, was in December promoted and appointed commander of the 454th Security Division in the Ukraine.[49] Career-minded officers at all levels of the 221st may also have been mindful that their superiors were comparing them for ruthless effectiveness with the SS Cavalry Brigade. For this unit, assigned in September to cleansing operations in part of the 221st's jurisdiction, "effectiveness" meant butchery on the greatest possible scale. Its operations against "Jewish bandits" in the Polesje marshland in August had showcased to dreadful effect the Brigade's way of doing things.[50]

But while careerism, doubtless to a large extent channeled and brutalized by the National Socialist leadership principle and incited by the criminal orders, may well have contributed to the general ruthlessness, it did not determine whom that ruthlessness was directed against. For units in the field, the now-burgeoning presence of *genuine* partisan groups, however small-scale and ineffective, might intensify brutality toward the wider population. For practical experience now was teaching the Germans that it was general civilians, not Jews, who were succoring fledgling partisan groups the most extensively.

True, the bulk of the population, having generally adopted a "wait and see" attitude toward the Germans, were still wont primarily to reject the partisans now emerging in their midst. But this was not necessarily how lower-level Eastern Army field units saw things. After all, the undetected presence of a small number of Communists or other partisan sympathizers in a particular village might lead, in next to no time, to the forging of stronger links between villagers and partisans.

Signs of such accommodation were frequent. Thus the 350th Infantry Regiment's Reconnaissance Section reported, on 14 October, that the antipartisan inhabitants northwest of the highway near Klichev were actively assisting the German cause, but that those in nearby Choduny were firmly propartisan. It urged special care over villages situated near forests and rivers, for here partisans on spying missions were posing as harmless civilians.[51] Similarly fearful were reports from the 286th Security Division. One of its battalions reported on 23 September that Bolshevik functionaries, not pro-German sympathizers, still occupied many posts in the native administration.[52]

Nor need villagers who assisted partisans or Red Army fugitives feel any actual enthusiasm for the Soviet cause. A natural desire for a peaceful existence, and a fear of the violent marauding of which both partisans and Red Army fugitives were only too capable, could be incentive enough. According to Truman Anderson, for Soviet villagers "a pragmatic day-to-day calculus of personal survival played a much more important role than did either pro-German sentiment . . . or Soviet patriotism."[53] This view is borne out by excerpts from a partisan diary for September and October 1941. The diary, found by one of Army Group North's security divisions, the 281st, describes villages in which "the population goes out of its way to support us." More commonly, requests (demands?) for food by the partisans were refused, but the villagers employed heart-rending stories to convince the partisans of where their "true" sympathies lay: "The farmers' attitude is that they'd gladly help us and have no reason to be pleased at the arrival of the Germans. But 'nothing doing.' The Germans frighten them that much. Peasants are even threatened with the burning down of their villages if they supply the partisans." And the villagers' report of sex-starved German soldiers who, unable to find any personable-looking girls or women in the village, had raped some farm animals instead, may have been a tale concocted to convince the partisans further of the disgust with which the villagers regarded the Germans.[54]

Of course, the villagers may well have told an identical story about the partisans to the next German unit that came their way. But the Germans' growing realization of how conditional native loyalty was, was unlikely to cement their own trust in the population.

Certainly, growing distrust of civilians, combined with anti-Slavic prejudice and the harshness urged by the criminal orders, was likely to fuel increasing severity. The actions of another of the 221st's subordinate units, Feldkommandantur 551, exemplify this phenomenon. A directive it issued on 8 September held entire villages responsible for any failure to capture saboteurs. "If no culprit is caught," it declared, "the German Wehrmacht will enforce order and security with countermeasures against the general population." It also decreed that anyone failing to participate in gathering the harvest or relinquishing livestock in line with German-imposed regulations faced a charge of sabotage.[55]

No Army Group Center security division seems to have distrusted the general population more during the autumn of 1941, nor behaved more ferociously toward it, than the 403d Security Division.

By October 1941 the 403d, like the 221st and 286th, had already escalated the killing of "partisans" across its jurisdiction to terrible effect. Developments that month caused the division's fury to intensify, and the villages of its jurisdiction felt the effect.

Such distrust certainly emanated partly from a wellspring of racial contempt. Both the operations officer, Captain Wilhelm, and the intelligence officer, Lieutenant Scharfenroth, had already displayed this contempt during the summer of 1941.[56] Their scorn had not subsided by autumn. In his report for October Scharfenroth could not resist sneering at the population's "lethargic peculiarities," and Wilhelm harbored similar views. By now, however, derision mingled with increasing distrust. Though the 403d had originally judged the population, however wretched, slavish, and idle it may be, as essentially pro-German, Scharfenroth's report for October listed several reasons why this initially pro-German mood was now souring: "hunger, the long duration of the war, treatment of the Jews (!), punishment beatings and the scale of German administration . . . which they feel points toward permanent subjugation and annexation of their land."[57]

It was a sharp deterioration in circumstances that, in the autumn of 1941, seems to have converted a ruthless attitude into the mass burning of villages. In October, at the very time more than 1,700 of the 403d's troops were lost at the stroke of a pen as its artillery and some of its security units were transferred to duty elsewhere, the division's Operations Section reported an increase in partisan activity.[58] The directive issued by Captain Wilhelm in response on 11 October ordered "collective reprisal measures against any village where either cooperation with the partisans is uncovered or ammunition or weapons are found."[59] The division's subordinate units were swift to respond. Several "propartisan" farms were burned down immediately. More reprisals, in retaliation for further, unspecified sabotage acts, were carried out a week later. On 23 October another village was burned down, and on the twenty-seventh yet another three.[60]

The 221st Security Division did not execute measures against the rural population with such systematic ruthlessness. But for some of its units, mounting fear, frustration, and distrust may well have helped to fuel a jumpy, "shoot first, ask questions later" mentality that could only increase the likelihood of civilian deaths at their hands. In the divisional war diary, where all the talk is of killing actual partisans, there is no mention either of this fear-induced motive or the fact that it was civilians who were most likely to die in consequence. This omission, however, probably stemmed from the fact that the wild, knee-jerk nature of such killings, unlike the systematic pyromania practiced by the 403d Security Division, reflected badly on the all-important "discipline and self-control" of the units that committed them.

In late October and November, however, the 221st Security Division received a fresh brutalizing impetus. The victims this time were forest-dwelling refugees and Red Army fugitives.

From late October the 221st Security Division's killing campaign, unlike those of the 286th and 403d Security Divisions, accelerated sharply again. Of the 1,700 "partisans" it reportedly killed between mid-September and the end of November, more than 1,110 perished in the weeks after 26 October.[61]

As autumn drew on and a longer campaign grew increasingly likely, the need to destroy the basis of any *future* partisan movement grew urgent.[62] The implications of a communiqué from the 286th Security Division are obvious: "In part, these people are prisoners who have escaped from or been left behind by the prisoner-of-war columns marching through the locality. In part, they've been sent to the rear by front-line troops accompanied not by German personnel but only by the general instruction 'go west.' Most were wandering around weaponless. However, this doesn't rule out the possibility that wandering individuals, particularly officers, join partisan groups that they stumble across."[63] General von Schenckendorff, too, was extremely anxious to "prevent the movement of refugees by whatever means," and individual units, such as Army Rear Area 580, ordered that refugees, "as a matter of principle, be arrested or liquidated."[64]

Armed or not, then, people such as these would be considered legitimate targets in any Eastern Army drive to annihilate potential future partisans. If the security divisions were indeed thinking in this way, they almost certainly would have meted out such treatment to any Red Army soldiers found to have escaped from German prisoner-of-war columns. Divisions certainly would have been disinclined, with the strain on manpower that afflicted all of them, to commit personnel to escorting recaptured Red Army soldiers to the nearest prison camp. In the 221st Security Division's jurisdiction at least, the problem of escaping prisoners of war was now acute.[65]

And if anything, the specter of a burgeoning partisan movement tormented the 221st Security Division even more than it did its fellows. Such was the demoralization besetting the 221st that it regarded the prospect of success against such a movement with particular pessimism.

No security division escaped this demoralization. Its endemic nature prompted General von Schenckendorff to issue guidelines on 19 September for the "training of troops in difficult conditions" across the entire Army Group Center Rear Area. "The ongoing need to train the troops must not, even under present circumstances, be neglected," Schenckendorff declared. The guidelines stressed the importance of keeping the troops sharp, and ensuring that training, whether of newly arrived units or of units already in the field and growing "stale," be maintained even in the midst of the myriad occupation duties the troops were straining to fulfill. On no account were the troops to go for weeks without firing a shot, and officers and NCOs must be trained thoroughly to ensure that they provided the necessary leadership.[66] None of the guidelines, of course, came anywhere close to addressing the divisions' fundamental failing: troops too few in number, too low in quality, and with too little mobility.[67] Mobility, for one, was further hamstrung when Army Group Center ordered its security divisions to use fuel as sparingly as possible to ensure that enough remained for its final drive on Moscow.[68]

But the 221st seems to have been affected particularly badly. In October it was saddled with responsibility for new, particularly partisan-infested areas to its east. Moreover, at a time when partisans were increasingly targeting rail supply, it was made to guard a greater number of railways.[69] Worst afflicted by all this were the territorial units. These were by now encountering ever-greater difficulties even in guarding supply routes. On 17 September the 45th Territorial Regiment informed the division that it urgently needed better-equipped railway guards. Of the eight men on duty in Teluscha, for instance, only one man had a pistol and two men rifles.[70] A divisional report of 12 October to Army Group Center Rear Area command pointed out that, apart from its partisan combat battalion and the 350th Infantry Regiment's reconnaissance unit, the 221st no longer possessed any forces to combat actual partisans.[71] That the 350th Infantry Regiment and the 45th Territorial Regiment were by 4 November missing 10 percent of their full strength, then, was alarming indeed. When the 221st's Operations Section now described the division as possessing all the fighting power of a "badly equipped brigade" and that it was, "in its current state, a failing body," it probably was not exaggerating too wildly.[72] Major Heinz Brenner, who had replaced Captain Haupt as operations officer in early November, asserted that the genuine, active partisans in the division's area were adequately supplied, were being increased in number by an influx of Soviet parachutists, and would survive into the winter simply because the division was incapable of preventing them.[73] The 221st's sense of helplessness in the face of the burgeoning partisan movement confronting it was more palpable than that of its fellow security divisions. Neither the 286th nor the 403d Security Division expected the partisan movement to grow in the foreseeable future. They also found solace in the fact that the partisans' precarious supply situation was restricting them to foraging for food rather than inflicting damage upon German supply, personnel, and administration.[74]

Such by now was the 221st's officers' view of their situation that they probably saw their best course as being less one of taking *effective* preventative action (now no longer possible in such dire conditions) than one of killing as many potential partisans as possible, as quickly as possible. Its sources never explicitly acknowledge it, but most potential partisans would have been unarmed Red Army fugitives and refugees. Many such refugees may have been Jews fleeing from the SS; but the Eastern Army soldiers who killed them may not even have known what their ethnic identity was. If they did, they didn't bother to record it. By this point an obdurate frame of mind, nurtured both by the institutional harshness embodied in the criminal orders and, most immediately, by pressure of circumstances, would have rendered notions of "prevention," however spurious, motive enough for such a swathe of slaughter.

From the late summer of 1941, the Eastern Army security units of the Army Group Center Rear Area enmeshed themselves in the SS genocide of the Jews and in the process of anti-Semitic killing in their own security campaign. In doing so they were responding to promptings from increasingly radical higher-level directives. In this capacity, the seedbed of anti-Semitic ruthlessness that the campaign of early summer had displayed certainly proved fertile.

Even so, it was the increasingly testing circumstances the security divisions faced, as the duration of their rear-area tenure lengthened and the strains that beset them intensified, that brutalized the security effort of late summer and autumn most decisively. Subdivisional units experienced this reality most directly and uncomfortably, but their division-level superiors were well aware of it also. Not only did it provide the greatest immediate push to mushrooming brutality; it also determined whom that brutality was directed against. And the 221st was far from the only security division whose circumstances fueled a brutality that, though it might be expressed in anti-Semitic directives, was not in fact inflicted primarily upon "Jew-Bolsheviks." The victims of this wider, higher death toll hailed to a great extent from the ranks of Red Army fugitives, but also of civilian refugees—both groups constituting a potential nucleus of future partisan groups. They also hailed from a wider population viewed not only with mounting anti-Slavic contempt and a distrust born of institutional guerrillaphobia but also, most immediately, with the mounting sense of frustration units felt at their increasingly intractable circumstances.

In all this, those officers who—for whatever ideological, careerist, or brutally utilitarian reasons—embraced the ruthless conception of antipartisan warfare particularly readily, would have made for the most willing perpetrators. The butchers of the 707th Infantry Division were by far the most extreme example.[75] But the intense, all-consuming difficulties now experienced across the board ensured that many more officers were likely, even if not with results quite as bloody, to embrace that conception more readily.

Ultimately, shortages in time, manpower, and equipment prevented any Army Group Center security division from destroying the partisans before winter. In mid-December, Einsatzgruppe B reported that the partisans in eastern Belorussia, after inauspicious beginnings, were now wreaking severe disruption. With the onset of winter they had stepped up plundering of villages in order to supply themselves and, in order to keep their location secret, were operating far from their bases.[76]

It was a portent of the vastly different and more difficult situation the security divisions would face the following year.

4

The Rules Change

During 1942 the Eastern Army security forces in the Army Group Center area faced a situation that scarcely resembled that of 1941. The principal overall cause, in that it intensified brutalizing traits that were already there, was the course of the war itself.

Accompanying the failure to defeat the Soviet Union in 1941 was the recent entry of the United States into the war on the Allied side. As 1942 wore on, the significance of both for Germany's ability to conclude the war on anything like acceptable terms grew increasingly plain. For many in the hierarchies of the occupation authorities and of the National Socialist regime itself, the new reality meant that the war against the Soviet Union must be waged with greater ruthlessness, commitment, and ferocity than before. Only thus could the Red Army be stemmed, the subjugation of the occupied rear completed, and the wholesale plunder of its working population and economic materials for the good of the German war effort achieved. The exploitative element of occupation came increasingly to the fore, and more generally, pressure, indeed desperation, lent already brutal German maxims a new urgency.

This new injection of viciousness also made both occupation and antipartisan warfare still more difficult. Increasingly brutal, rapacious policy could only alienate a population whose cooperation the Germans now needed more than ever. At the same time, the perceived importance of front-line troops at rear-area troops' expense, now heightened as a result of the Red Army's resurgence, further deprived the Eastern Army's security forces of the volume and quality of men and equipment that the effective prosecution of occupation and antipartisan warfare demanded. Moreover, the Eastern Army had to strip its security forces even further to the bone to help counter the Soviet offensives of the winter of 1941–42. The combination of growing popular support and waning German effectiveness enabled partisan groups, finally, to establish themselves properly. They were now able to found a base from which they would later strike out and inflict mounting disruption upon German supply, administration, and economic exploitation.

It is unsurprising, given the combination of ruthless preexisting attitudes and the mounting pressures of the war, that intensified German terror stymied the efforts of those officers who believed that increased *cultivation* of the population was the only sensible response to the new reality.

Upon the German security effort in the Army Group Center area, as upon the course of the whole eastern war, the Soviet counteroffensives that fell upon the German front line from December 1941 had far-reaching consequences. In places the Germans, facing powerful assaults from fresh Red Army divisions from Siberia and the worst winter in Russia that century, were driven back more than 300 kilometers. The uncompromising "stand and fight" order that Hitler issued—a rare occasion on which this kind of order, frequently issued to disastrous effect by Hitler, actually had some sense behind it—did prevent the retreat from degenerating into a rout. By February 1942 the front was beginning to stabilize, and the Red Army, after its winter exertions, was in a state of increasing exhaustion. Indeed, it would face a long and arduous road before attaining the level of fighting power it would need for ultimate victory. And yet, though its own offensive had petered out by early spring and it now had to contend with German counterattacks encircling still more of its own troops, the Red Army had shattered the Germans' last hope of quick victory.

Though the Germans were able, during the next spring and summer, to take the offensive again, so massive had been their losses of men and material that they now lacked resources for a general attack all along the front. From May through November they were forced to concentrate their main effort on the southern sector, in a powerful and ultimately fateful armored drive on the Caucasus oil fields and the city of Stalingrad.

In the Army Group Center area as elsewhere, the commitment of as many troops as possible to stemming the Red Army's winter offensive compelled both the army group rear area and the individual army rear areas to dispatch their mobile troops to the front. The territorial and guard battalions that were left were now saddled with responsibility not only for guarding supply lines and other installations but also for prosecuting active operations against the partisans. For the partisans themselves, this drastic diminution of German fighting power provided just the respite General von Schenckendorff and his subordinates had dreaded. For here was the window of opportunity the fledgling partisan movement needed to build and consolidate the organization and fighting power that had previously eluded it. With the partisans much closer to a front line now much farther west, the Red Army and Red Air Force seized all opportunities for supporting them. Ground-based and airborne Red Army detachments, officers, and specialists were sent into German-occupied territory to establish contact with the partisan groups, train them in guerrilla warfare, sabotage, and subterfuge, coordinate them, and enlarge them with local recruits either willing or press-ganged.[1]

Such efforts were aided in no small measure by a popular mood that now was shifting against the Germans. For one thing, the Soviet counterattacks made German victory appear no longer inevitable. A population now having to reckon with the possibility of eventual Soviet reprisal against anyone who had assisted the Germans no longer felt so eager to cooperate with them.[2] Moreover, German occupation policy was taking such brutish, rapacious, and devastating forms that there were fewer reasons for the population to support it.

For one thing, with an end to the war no longer in sight, German occupation meant an indefinite perpetuation of chronic food shortages and economic disruption.[3] The population's mood was further blackened by the behavior of the Germans themselves. By the spring of 1942, the cooperative, cautiously optimistic "wait and see" philosophy of 1941 was rapidly being replaced by disgruntlement and disgust at the often-intolerable requisitioning levels, the mass death, through hunger and neglect, of Soviet prisoners of war, the plight of refugees, and the mass murder of Jews (this despite the considerable anti-Semitism harbored by the population itself). On a personal, day-to-day level, the arrogant, heavy-handed behavior of the German soldiers in the population's midst intensified such odium.[4]

The importance of an effective partisan movement, and the changing circumstances that increasingly favored its effective consolidation, were lost neither on the top levels of the Soviet command nor, indeed, on Stalin himself. Thirty May 1942 saw the founding, in Moscow, of the Central Staff of the Partisan Movement. This body assumed responsibility for harnessing every aspect of partisan warfare for the maximum benefit of the Soviet war effort.[5]

The partisans themselves spent much of 1942 attacking supply routes and economic installations in the German rear. But their main priority was to make contact with and establish themselves among the occupied population. This strategy would give them the firm basis of territory and recruitment with which to establish and strengthen themselves in preparation for the greater blows they would later inflict. It also would hinder the Germans' own efforts to harness essential popular cooperation in their own administration and exploitation of the territory they occupied. The Eastern Army forces, depleted as they now were, were powerless to prevent the partisans from thus establishing themselves in many areas.[6]

In their efforts to secure the population for their cause, the partisans employed both propaganda and terror extensively. Initially they relied on the spreading of rumors to unsettle the population, and on the copious quantities of leaflets the Red Air Force dropped in their service. As time went on, they employed their own printing presses to produce propaganda material, and they made extensive use of public speakers in the growing number of villages they controlled. In playing up the misery and hardships that German occupation policy was inflicting, partisan propaganda mined a particularly rich seam. It also highlighted promises the Germans had made, such as their pledges to privatize the hated Soviet collective farming system, and subsequently broken. "Now the Germans have taken the land from the peasants," read one partisan leaflet. "Like hungry insects they raid our dear fields . . . In order to cover up their pillage, the Hitlerite clique has worked out a so-called new agrarian order. What noise they have made over it! The Fascist propagandists say at every corner, 'The land to the peasants!' This is a brazen lie."[7]

Stress was also placed on alleged devastating German defeats and major Soviet victories, and on appeals to patriotic sentiments, to love of "Mother Russia" and evocation of past national glories, rather than on less effective political-ideological language. Such were the sentiments of one partisan leaflet: "Seven hundred years ago Alexander Nevsky crushed the ancestors of the Hitlerite bands; a hundred and eighty-two years ago Russian troops entered Berlin, crushing the equally 'invincible' armies of Frederick II. The Russian people destroyed the army of Napoleon, who dreamt of putting down Russia. In 1918 the young Red Army crushed the Germans at Narva and Pskov. The defeat of the Hitlerites is inescapable now that the Soviet people in their righteous wrath have risen."[8]

The prospect of a golden era of reform, encompassing measures such as the dissolution of the collective farms that Stalin would enact once the war was over, was also trumpeted. Indeed, in the hope of showcasing "Soviet reforming zeal," the partisans were often quick to enact such measures in the areas they controlled.[9] Stalin's hitherto-intense suspicion of the notion of a mass movement drawn primarily from what he saw as a potentially treacherous rural population gave way, in a September 1942 directive titled "On the Tasks of the Partisan Movement," to his and the Soviet leadership's full endorsement of the concept.[10]

Partisan ruthlessness also piled the pressure on the Germans. While the partisans promised much to those who participated in the "Great Patriotic War," they also went after pro-German collaborators with a vengeance. Collaborators were targeted and killed, sometimes along with their entire families, without a qualm. "Shot a traitor. Morale good!" was the comment in one partisan's diary. "In the evening, I went to do the same to his wife. We are sorry that she leaves three children behind. But war is war! Any humane consideration shown towards traitors is misplaced." "There's nowhere to go to get away from us," boasted one partisan leader to a village headman. "There is no salvation anywhere on Soviet soil for a traitor, and never will be."[11]

Terror, however, was employed selectively: by the autumn of 1942, though they were still showing no quarter to collaborating civilian administrators, the partisans were enticing members of armed native units in German service to defect.[12] A frequent tactic was to use ex-collaborators who had already "come over" as bait, as exemplified in the following extract from a leaflet: "Comrades! Follow our example . . . On 23rd September 1942, we . . . went over to the Red partisans. The partisans were very friendly in receiving us. After a friendly conversation we were told that from now on we were partisans and citizens of the USSR with full rights . . . We felt suddenly as if a different blood ran through our arteries, the clear and hot blood of a citizen of the USSR."[13] Meanwhile, though partisan requisitioning and recruitment certainly could degenerate into callous excess, both to a large extent were conducted in relatively orderly and systematic ways.[14]

A much darker side to the partisans' conduct was their strategy of driving a wedge between occupier and occupied by deliberately provoking vicious German reprisals against the population.[15] On balance, however, the rapacity, terror, and excess of the partisans were outdone by the increasingly onerous burdens and outrages inflicted by the German occupation. More and more, the population saw the partisans as the lesser of two evils.[16] In the words of Walter Laquer, "the partisan leaders . . . would have found it much more difficult to attract recruits had the Germans treated the population decently, but this would have been quite incompatible . . . with the character of the Nazi leaders, their doctrine, and their aims."[17]

The partisans' reception by the population assured increasing success for their efforts at subversion and sabotage. How successful the partisans were in establishing themselves in the Army Group Center region during the spring and early summer of 1942 is reflected clearly in the mounting disruption they wrought. There were 208 cases of rail sabotage recorded in August, for example, as against only 30 in April. Clashes between partisans and Germans rose sevenfold in the same period.[18]

Coming at a time when General von Schenckendorff's command had no prospect of being restored to its earlier strength, the development of partisan warfare was doubly alarming. Of the twenty-five territorial battalions active in the rear area in May 1942, Schenckendorff judged that eleven possessed zero fighting worth.[19] Other German agencies expressed similar alarm. In many areas, Einsatzgruppe B reported in June, "the lack of sufficient security forces means that it is not always possible to persecute the partisan war with the necessary severity. This shakes the confidence of the population and feeds the [partisans'] rumor mill."[20] A report by the 203d Security Division, dated 16 April, was even more despairing: "Listing all the individual attacks, all the disturbances inflicted by the partisans and 'bandits' upon rear-area security, would take up pages."[21]

Those reinforcements that were forthcoming over the summer of 1942—in the main, a limited number of Wehrmacht training formations, Luftwaffe ground troops, and men provided by the Reich's Hungarian, Slovak, and Rumanian allies—fell far short of what was needed. So ill-equipped and under-strength were these units that they made even the second-rate German training formations look impressive.[22]

The Luftwaffe field divisions offered a more formidable prospect. They had come into being through Göring's ambition to muscle in on the conduct of the land war. The divisions at his disposal, formed from retrained Luftwaffe ground personnel, were mechanized, well equipped, and of relatively good quality. But with these attributes came an approach to antipartisan warfare that often was so brutal that it drove the population further into the arms of the partisans and negated much of the divisions' combat value. Among Göring's directives to his antipartisan formations was an order to burn down the nearest village in the event of any railway explosion. General von Schenckendorff protested that the rail workers housed in such villages would be homeless and compelled to join the partisans, but this protest seems to have been ignored.[23]

Some further alleviation of the manpower problem came from the SS. From 1942 both the quantity and range of SS personnel expanded in the occupied areas, encompassing not just the Einsatzgruppe and Order Police units of old, but a growing number of combat formations of the Waffen-SS.

There were two ways in which the Eastern Army benefited from SS assistance over security during these years. In the army group rear areas and, less commonly, the army rear areas to their east, the Order Police and Einsatzgruppen provided extra manpower for Eastern Army antipartisan operations. Order Police battalions, soon to be redesignated officially as SS Police battalions, provided full combat units.[24] The Einsatzkommando and Sonderkommando detachments of the Einsatzgruppen, their mass shootings of Jews completed, acted in an intelligence capacity by employing local informers to identify hostile villages. They also often acted as judge, jury, and—at a nod from the Eastern Army commander in charge of the operation—executioner, charged with screening partisan prisoners, accomplices, and "suspects," and disposing of those they saw as warranting elimination.[25]

Less directly, but of greater overall value to the Eastern Army's antipartisan effort, was the ongoing expansion of police and Waffen-SS forces for SS antipartisan actions. As a result the Eastern Army could relinquish responsibility for entire operations and, in some cases, regions. Arrangements were formalized in August 1942 when Hitler's Directive No. 46 made the Army High Command responsible for antipartisan warfare in the Eastern Army–administered army group rear areas and army rear areas, and the SS in the Reich commissariats farther west.[26]

Herein, however, lay one of the limitations in the help the SS provided for the Eastern Army's beleaguered forces: the bulk of its manpower was not committed to the army group rear areas and army rear areas in which the Eastern Army's security divisions operated. Moreover, with their increasing reliance on the SS, both Wehrmacht leadership and many Eastern Army field commanders fueled even further a degree of popular resentment that could only stymie further the effective prosecution of occupation. For when they allowed the SS an ever-greater slice of the security pie, they gave further free rein to terrible forces.

In the rear areas administered by the Eastern Army there operated a number of Order Police battalions—the "300-number" battalions, so called after the number of their unit designation—whose relatively youthful personnel were particularly fired by Nazi ideology. They often terrorized the local populations as brutally as they had the Soviet Jews during 1941.[27] But for the populations of the Reich commissariats, at the mercy of overall SS jurisdiction for antipartisan warfare, matters were even deadlier. Here the antipartisan campaign provided the SS with excellent cover to further its aim of wiping out what remained of Soviet Jewry—essentially the ghettoized populations still surviving in the Reich commissariats—and decimating the Slavic population so as to cull surplus mouths and clear space for future German colonists.[28]

Reports on the main SS-led antipartisan operations have been described as "thinly disguised records of genocide." Wilhelm Kube, general commissioner for White Ruthenia, wrote approvingly of a ten-week SS operation in his jurisdiction in which 55,000 Jews, "the main bearer[s] of the partisan movement in the East," had been "liquidated." The tally of "enemy" losses for Operation February, which the SS carried out during the month of the same name in 1943, recorded "2,219 dead; 7,378 persons who received 'special treatment' [in other words, they were killed after capture]; 65 prisoners; 3,300

Jews. Our own losses: dead, 2 Germans, 27 non-Germans; wounded: 12 Germans, 26 non-Germans."[29]

The quality of SS brutality was often as ghastly as the quantity. One Russian auxiliary in German service, nauseated by what he had witnessed during one reprisal against a Belorussian village in May 1943, recounted a spectacle of "women . . . hysterical . . . beaten into submission . . . huts set on fire . . . [a] girl, stripped naked, [with] one of her breasts cut off . . . the execution of the mayor by slow hanging and the death by shooting of the rest of the inhabitants."[30]

Of course, given the failure of such operations to target actual partisans, the utter popular alienation they caused, and the consequent surge in partisan support this was bound to engender, it is clear that such carnage was as self-defeating to the security cause as it is sickening to recount.[31] Even SS officers began to realize this; Herf, a police general in the east, assessed one operation of early 1943 in a letter to a colleague thus: "Yesterday, a *Gauleiter* [Nazi regional leader] . . . broadcast certain secret reports . . . showing that some 480 rifles were found on 6,000 dead 'partisans.' Put bluntly, *all these men had been shot* to swell the figure of enemy losses and highlight our own 'heroic deeds.' I am under no illusions that, this being the system, the winter 1943–44 will see the beginning of the end in the rear areas . . . The increase in guerrilla warfare is simply and solely due to the way the Russians have been treated."[32]

Though the Eastern Army had by the end of 1942 achieved some success in reducing the number of successful partisan attacks on the railways—static security being the only task many of their units were fit for—that success was strictly limited.[33] The rules of engagement, in the central sector particularly, were turning unambiguously against the Germans. No longer did they face a "potential" partisan threat of Red Army stragglers, refugees, and the "Jew-Bolsheviks" of diseased National Socialist imaginings. The threat confronting them now was one that increasingly menaced their ability to harness their jurisdictions in the service of the Reich's war effort.

Pressures generated by the essential ruthlessness of German occupation policy in the Soviet Union and a bewildering confusion of ruthless and restrained notions of antipartisan conduct were two more of the forces that combined to frustrate the realization of a genuinely constructive, long-term Eastern Army response to this challenge.

During 1941, as prospects of rapid German victory over the Soviet Union progressively dimmed, numerous Eastern Army figures already saw the potential for support in a tentatively pro-German population. They also saw the need for a more sensible, measured prosecution of occupation and security policy in order to exploit it. Alfred Rosenberg, Reich minister for the Eastern Territories, invoked the memory of the initially warm reception afforded the German troops in 1941, speaking of "a people who went through all the terrors of Bolshevism, and who now, happy about their liberation, put themselves willingly at the disposal of Germany."[34]

During 1942, schemes emerged in the Eastern Army–occupied zone for raising a "liberation army" of former Soviet prisoners of war, under the renegade general Andrei Vlasov, to fight alongside the Germans, and for granting a limited measure of political autonomy to the subjugated regions.[35] At the most basic level, cultivating the population was crucial to smooth administration and economic exploitation, and to the increasingly pressing business of recruiting locals into the German-led native auxiliary force, the Ordnungsdienst (OD). The OD, which the Germans had initially envisaged as a further source of static security personnel and local knowledge in active antipartisan operations, would assume a far more extensive, active role during 1942. Recruitment of civilians into the Ordnungsdienst (Order Service, or OD) and of former prisoners of war into new "eastern" security battalions gathered pace.[36] All this constituted an attempt to reconcile the need for military pacification with the need for engagement in a more viable and conciliatory way.

But successfully engaging the population, and thereby also, crucially, denying the partisans its support, needed more than this. It also needed an effective challenge to the brutish National Socialist view that the occupied Soviet Union was nothing more than an immense source of economic wealth and expendable, stupefied labor.

Several initiatives did seek to challenge this outlook. Some military and civilian administrators saw the announcement, in February 1942, of reforms to break up the widely despised Soviet collective farming system as heralding a flagship occupation policy that would assure popular support for the German cause.[37] Colonel Reinhard Gehlen of Foreign Armies East, the army intelligence center for the Eastern Front, was at the head of higher command efforts to rally the population against the partisans. "If the population rejects the partisans and lends its full support to the struggle against them, no partisan problem will exist," Gehlen asserted.[38] The Army Group Center Rear Area, like other jurisdictions, enacted a raft of propaganda measures. They included theater shows, cultural exhibitions, and a massive leafleting effort designed to convince the population of the benevolence of German occupation policy and the criminality of the Soviet regime and the partisans themselves.[39]

But the effectiveness of all these efforts was blunted by the fact that they never posed a fundamental challenge to ruthless economic interests, or to racist preconceptions of the population. Even Gehlen himself felt it necessary to stress that, though he saw a need to woo the population more effectively, he fully recognized the Russians' "objective inferiority" and natural status as "objects of exploitation."[40] The ruthless, ideological, and exploitative dynamic of Nazi occupation policy in the east, then, proved an implacable obstacle to any successful cultivation effort. And increasingly, as part of the endeavor to put Germany's war economy on an increasingly "total" footing, it was the exploitative element that proved most devastating.

Two cases demonstrate this clearly: the failure of agricultural reform, and the mass procurement of eastern labor for the German war effort.

Actual implementation of the breakup of collective farms, enticing though the prospect had sounded, was patchy and halfhearted. Much of this failure was due to the dislocation of agriculture caused by the partisans themselves. Much was due also to the cynicism and contempt with which German agricultural officials regarded the ability of docile, half-witted Russian peasants to show the competitive spirit necessary for a private enterprise system to work. But the most fundamental reason for the reform's failure was that the Germans believed that the needs of their own war effort demanded intensive control of farming in the east.[41] Consequently, alongside the ever more acute food shortages caused by economic dislocation and the Germans' own increasingly voracious requisitioning, rural resentment at the Germans' failure to honor their promises was bitter indeed.[42]

The issue of "eastern workers" on labor service in the Reich was to prove an even bigger time bomb. Mobilizing the Reich's war economy meant, among other things, mobilizing the able-bodied population of occupied Europe. The Reich Ministry of Labor, headed by Fritz Sauckel, instructed German administrators in the occupied Soviet Union to order, "with all the requisite vigour, those measures necessary to bolster voluntary recruitment of workers for deployment in Germany."[43]

To try to ensure that they met their quotas of workers for labor service, the authorities went on to employ a combination of material promises and coercion, financial and physical, that had first been employed in Poland.[44] Recruitment efforts vigorously trumpeted the comforts and financial benefits of employment in the Reich. But the authorities, as a means of "encouraging" work in Germany, also set the support allowances they paid out to every Russian family at such pitifully low levels that Russians would have no practical choice but to enroll for labor service. Further "incentive" was to be provided by the nightmare prospect of eventual forced recruitment. By early October 1942, eastern workers accounted for 697,000 of the 3,159,000 foreign workers employed in the Reich—an increase of 17 percent over their number just two months previously. But rumors about the often-appalling conditions in which eastern workers in the Reich lived and worked were already rife.[45] Labor service, then, like the failed agricultural reform, could only exacerbate the festering popular resentment that the partisans were increasingly well placed to exploit. "Whoever Goes to Germany Will Perish" was the title of one partisan leaflet.[46]

Another immense barrier to cultivating the population was the ruthless brutality that many German officers, Eastern Army as well as SS, advocated in the conduct of antipartisan warfare itself.

Many officers, possessed of ruthless attitudes already and further frustrated by the intractabilities of their situation, preached nothing but the harshest severity against the partisans. Typical was an order of the 207th Security Division, stationed in northern Russia. "The fight is to be executed ruthlessly," it declared. "It is a question of exterminating partisans, not taking them prisoner—unless this is necessary for gleaning information."[47] Other officers urged a crackdown not just on the partisans but on the whole population. In their eyes, the only language the "eastern character" understood was that of harshness, the only means of overcoming the partisan menace the pitiless infliction of that harshness upon the population.

Those officers who were particularly "far gone" ideologically could draw no distinction between partisans and population. General von Bechtolsheim, commander of the 707th Infantry Division, left no doubt as to where he stood when he wrote, in March 1942, of the "criminality" inherent in the population, "consciously grown and nurtured here for a quarter of a century. All are guilty, young and old, men and women, and not just any individual sector of society. So the battle must be carried out with the utmost ruthlessness!"[48] But Bechtolsheim's views were only an extreme example of a wider mental malaise. Thus could Russian villages be put to the torch, their populations butchered or evacuated, on the flimsiest of pretexts. The discovery of a single cache of arms or ammunition might be all it took.[49]

The main mechanism that converted such attitudes into murderous reality was the large-scale operations. The Eastern Army security forces, so often lacking the manpower for sufficiently extensive longer-term occupation of areas susceptible to the partisans, came increasingly to favor these lightning "butcher and bolt" operations.[50]

The typical pattern of a large-scale operation was shaped by a dynamic that converted it, more often than not, into the embodiment of carnage.[51] A designated area would be cordoned off; then, with some troops assigned to hold the perimeter to prevent the enemy from breaking out, the rest would advance to a central point, combing the area for partisans as they went—at least, so went the theory—vetting the villages for "suspect elements," stripping them of much of their food supply so as to deprive the partisans of it, and "resettling" much or all of their populations.

But because the daily "target areas" were often so wholly unrealistic, the distances and terrain they encompassed often immense and nigh-on impenetrable, pressure for results was enormous. A German report of February 1942 gives a quite surreal flavor of how such exhausting efforts could bring so little reward:

Scattered bloodstains on the snow indicated that we were on the right trail. After one hour we reached the end of the sled tracks.

From there on faint footprints were observed which followed winding forest paths. Here and there more bloodstains appeared. Frequently, secondary tracks led off into the forest, obviously made to confuse pursuers. Zigzagging back and forth in the forest I lost my sense of direction. At 1400 . . . we came to a clearing . . . According to [our] prisoner we were still about two miles from camp. Knee-high snow made movement difficult . . .

After another twenty minutes' march we came to another small clearing where one track branched off to the left. We had all gone past, when an OD man who had followed that track called our attention to a man standing in a fir thicket . . . He had already opened fire on us . . . We returned the fire as the man turned and ran . . .

With the OD men and three or four of our men, I formed a skirmish line and moved forward through the forest. The fleeing man, of whom we caught occasional glimpses through the trees, fired on us several more times. After we had moved on another 500 yards or so, I suddenly found myself in a clump of scattered fir trees. Catching sight of horses' hooves hanging out of the trees [carcasses hung there for storage], I thought I had come upon the dugout we were looking for. As I circled the spot, I was fired upon from nearby. I took cover and noticed for the first time an excellently camouflaged bunker-like structure about thirty yards away. I ordered hand grenades thrown into the bunker . . . It was empty . . .[52]

What precise brutalizing dynamic seized hold of individual large-scale operations is something the gaps in sources usually render difficult to construct. It often seems, however, that the Germans, frustrated by the fact that their quarry so frequently slipped through the net, turned on the population instead. Any combination of frustration, pressure for visible success, a belief that decimating the potentially partisan-friendly population was a legitimate means of combating the partisans, and the preexisting guerrillaphobia and racial contempt nurtured further by the criminal orders, may have played a role.[53] Jacob Grigoriev, whose own village was sacked in such a killing spree, provided a nightmarish glimpse of such actions when he testified at the Nuremberg trials:

On the memorable day of 28th October 1943, German soldiers suddenly raided our village and started murdering the peaceful citizens, shooting them, chasing them into the houses . . . three German machine gunners came in, accompanied by a fourth carrying a heavy revolver. We were ordered into another room. We went, all nineteen of us, and were lined up against a wall, including my two sons, and they began shooting us with their machine guns. I stood right up to the wall, bending slightly. After the first volley I fell to the floor, where I lay, too frightened to move. When I came to, I looked round and saw my son Nikolai who had been shot and had fallen, face downward . . .

[I]n the second hut where my wife and son had been taken . . . the German soldiers, having driven the people into the hut, opened the door and began shooting with their machine guns

... people who were still half alive were burning, including my little boy, Petya, who was only nine years old.[54]

For the Germans, any perceived benefits from such butchery were usually fleeting anyway. Paltry manpower levels usually prevented them from *occupying* recently cleansed areas, and thus ensuring that the partisans would not reestablish themselves there.[55] The death tolls these operations spawned could be staggering. An early, particularly vile example of a large-scale operation, described by one historian as "first in a chain of campaigns of plunder, murder, and population clearance against the farming population of Belorussia," was carried out by the 707th Infantry Division. Operation Bamberg, first in a series of such operations carried out in the Bobruisk region during the spring and early summer of 1942, exacted a death toll of over 4,000 "partisans" at a cost to the 707th of seven dead and eight wounded. The operations the 201st and 286th Security Divisions executed in the Polotsk-Vitebsk region of northern Belorussia between August 1942 and February 1943 were only marginally less bloody. The 286th, for instance, notched up nearly 3,000 victims, during Operations Griffin, Lightning, and Winter Forest as against 54 dead on its own side.[56]

Between extreme ruthlessness and the increasingly merciless, rapacious dictates of Nazi occupation policy on the one hand, and the need for a saner approach to antipartisan warfare on the other, there were some higher-level attempts to "square the circle" with more measured antipartisan directives. Ultimately, they failed. In the meantime, however, a series of higher-level directives was issued that amply illustrate the destructive contradictions that lay at the heart of Eastern Army antipartisan efforts and allowed brutality free rein.

One embodiment of these contradictions was General von Schenckendorff himself. He certainly *sounded* critical over the unjustified burning of villages, the shooting of innocent civilians, and what he described as the "soldiers' urge to see something burning." But he also worded his directives in a way that allowed brutality "should circumstances dictate." Such, for instance, was an August 1942 decree stipulating that "collective punishment measures, so far as they involve the shooting of inhabitants and the burning of villages, are without exception to be carried out only by order of an officer at the level of battalion commander or higher." Thus the decision was left to the discretion of officers who, if not actually on the spot themselves, were not far removed from it—a recipe with as much potential for extreme ruthlessness as for restraint. That Schenckendorff himself realized this is suggested by the discrepancy between the wording of this directive and the language that was used in the Army Group Center Rear Area's war diary, which claimed that Schenckendorff had on this occasion imposed a total ban on the burning of villages.[57]

Other directives cloaked their acceptance of all manner of ruthlessness in the language of "moderation." "Anybody, including women," Schenckendorff wrote in September 1942, "of whom it is proven that they either belong to a bandit group, have actively aided the bandits, or carried out reconnaissance for them, is to be dealt with as ordered [in other words, shot]." Then came what Schenckendorff evidently saw as a show of humanity. "Children fall into this category only when they are old enough to understand the implications of their actions. Such understanding is beyond children of ten; these are to be punished but not shot."[58] This directive, then, allowed a child aged ten or under to be "punished" (the details of which were to be left to the troops on the spot) and a child of eleven to be shot.

Whatever Schenckendorff's precise motives in issuing such directives, the impression they created further down the command chain must have been that restraint, while desirable, could be cast aside at any time. A corpus of directives emanating from the very highest command levels would have reinforced this impression.[59]

Hitler himself issued the first of these, Directive No. 46, on 18 August 1942. This asserted that just treatment for the population and en masse recruitment of civilians to fight the partisans were necessary. But it also urged unprecedentedly harsh punishment of civilian support for partisans, and stressed that officers and men must guard against "misplaced confidence" in the population. In other words it argued, virtually in the same breath, that though the population must be cultivated it could not be trusted. The Commando Order of 18 October renewed the plea for severity: "Only where the struggle against the partisan nuisance was begun and carried out with ruthless brutality have successes been achieved . . . Throughout the Eastern Territories, the war against the partisans is therefore a struggle of total annihilation of one side or the other."[60]

Attempts by the Armed Forces High Command to come up with a more sensible strategy were stymied by that organization's closeness to Hitler. Its "Combat Directive for Anti-Partisan Warfare in the East" of November 1942 was vague on the issue of partisan deserters. It merely stipulated that they be treated as prisoners of war "according to circumstances"—whatever that meant—and that captured partisans and their supporters be shot or, better still, hanged. Officers on the spot, meanwhile, retained discretionary powers over whether to destroy villages. This directive, too, completely contradicted itself. It stated on the one hand that "unjust punishment shakes the confidence of the population and creates new partisans," but on the other that "the severity of our measures and the fear of expected punishment must restrain the population from aid or support of the partisans."[61]

Severest of all the higher-level directives of 1942 was the decree that Hitler issued through the Armed Forces High Command on 16 December. This ordered "the most brutal means . . . against women and children also" and declared that any scruples in this matter were treasonous to the German people. This order took the severity first exhibited in 1941's Barbarossa Decree to new extremes. While the earlier directive had granted officers discretion not to punish excesses against the population by the troops, Hitler's new directive *forbade* such punishment.[62]

In late 1942 yet another brutalizing element was added. With no end to the war in sight, the Reich's need for foodstuffs and labor from the occupied east was increasingly desperate. But it was growing progressively harder to provide them without estranging the Soviet population even further.[63] The partisans themselves, meanwhile, controlled ever-larger amounts of arable land. The Agricultural Section of the Economic Inspectorate Center reported that the partisan situation was preventing the requisitioning of "160 herds of cattle at approximately 600 heads of cattle each, 44 batches of potatoes of 500 potatoes each, and 150 batches of grain at 150 tons each. This is calculated as equivalent to the supply of an army of 300,000 men with bread for one year, meat for three months, potatoes for four months."[64] Brutal economic calculation dictated that the burden fall as far as possible on the "bandit areas."

Göring's directive of 26 October 1942 was significant in setting the pace:

1. When combating partisans and clearing partisan-infested areas, all livestock to hand is to be removed to a safe area, and the food reserves likewise cleared away to deprive the partisans of them.

2. The entire male and female workforce that may be liable for labor service is to be forcibly recruited and taken to the plenipotentiary for labor, to be used either in the rear areas or in the homeland. Children are to be specially accommodated in camps to the rear.[65]

Such measures would further meet the "military" aim, toward which the large-scale operations had worked to some extent already, of depriving the partisans of food and shelter.[66] Thus, increasingly, antipartisan operations were accompanied by officials from Reich economic agencies, the economic detachments.

The economic detachments and, above them, regional economic inspectorates had the task of overseeing the systematic seizure of livestock and crops. Wholesale evacuations were commonplace, the able-bodied members of the population being pressed into forced labor as the Reich's need for it grew ever more severe.[67] Economic officials could also hold the power of life and death over villages.

Those meeting their agricultural quotas—this being seen to prove not only the economic worth of their continued existence but also their pro-German loyalty—were likely to be spared annihilation and evacuation. But a shortfall of just one cow might spell obliteration. The culmination of this process, during 1943, would be the widespread creation of "dead zones." These were areas that the Germans, having given up trying to hold on to them in the face of partisan pressure, pillaged, evacuated, and devastated so that the partisans at least were denied their economic benefit.[68]

But already by the end of 1942, economic calculation had added to the increasingly lethal cocktail that characterized so much of the Eastern Army's antipartisan effort, and proved a massive impediment to more-constructive initiatives.

Thus it was not only the magnitude of the task facing the Eastern Army security divisions that changed during 1942, but its very nature. It is worth briefly revisiting the trio of tasks that occupation regimes often need to juggle: pacification, which involves combating the guerrillas directly; engagement of popular cooperation; and economic exploitation. In 1941, at the outset of the campaign, the Eastern Army had felt assured that its security effort needed to bother with only the first of these. And this, it believed, could be achieved primarily by employing terror, selective or otherwise, to stifle any popular will to resist. Well before the end of 1941, it was clear that the security divisions were incapable of achieving even this one task. From 1942, the prospect of a much lengthier campaign made it increasingly important for the security divisions to expend manpower, resources, and effort on the second and, increasingly, on the third also.

Negotiating all three is a difficult task for any occupation regime: it would be difficult not least for a security force weak in material, manpower, and administrative acumen, blinkered by doctrinal ruthlessness, and charged with upholding a general occupation regime of mounting rapacity. All of this augured badly for the effective prosecution of antipartisan warfare.

Region of the Army Group Center Rear Area, 1941–1943.

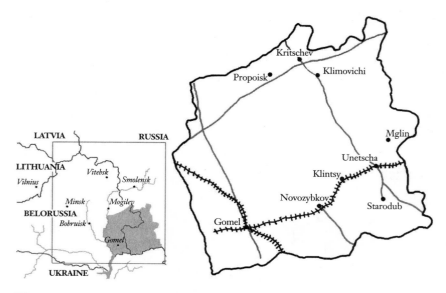

The 221st Security Division's jurisdiction, June 1942–August 1943. (Source: "Divisionsbereich," Sich.-Div. 221 Ia, file 35408/2, T-315/1681, NA)

German officers searching for partisans who have been cutting telephone wires try to glean information from villagers, 1941. The rarity of partisan attacks that summer often enabled German units, for a time at least, to cultivate relatively cordial relations with the population. (SV-Bilderdienst, Munich)

German security troops patrol the countryside in an improvised armored train. The 221st Security Division used such a train, the *Leutnant Marx*, to carry out spot-checks on the villages in its jurisdiction during the 1941 campaign. (Bundesarchiv, Koblenz)

A German soldier captures a Soviet soldier disguised as a civilian,
1941. Fugitive Red Army soldiers, stranded by the German advance,
increasingly were caught up in the rear-area "sweeps" to ferret out
dangerous elements, potential or otherwise, which the Germans conducted during the late summer and autumn of that year. It is almost
certain that this man, having fired upon Germans while disguised as a
civilian, was subsequently shot. (SV-Bilderdienst, Munich)

German soldiers burn down a farmhouse in response to shots fired from inside, 1941. Despite German attempts to foster local cooperation, retaliation for direct attacks could be swift and harsh. By autumn, facing mounting partisan activity, the prospect of a long campaign in the east, and intensifying strains upon their own personnel, the Germans were meting out such retaliation more frequently. (SV-Bilderdienst, Munich)

An increasingly common sight during 1941: partisans executed in Orel are displayed as an example to the townspeople. The National Socialist conception of military occupation held that terror was the means of ensuring a compliant population. As the year wore on, the Eastern Army's security forces increasingly acted in this spirit. (SV-Bilderdienst, Munich)

A German interpreter questions the women and children of a village whose
men have fled into the forests to join the partisans, 1941. The villagers' at-
tire suggests that the picture was taken in the autumn, the precise period in
which the German security campaign in the Army Group Center Rear Area
was undergoing a marked intensification in harshness and brutality. Though
the German soldier here seems to be trying to communicate reasonably, the
mixed emotions on the villagers' faces indicate severe unease at their situation. (SV-Bilderdienst, Munich)

General Johann Pflugbeil, commander of the 221st Infantry (later Security) Division, September 1939–June 1942. Under Pflugbeil, the 221st prosecuted antipartisan warfare with mounting ruthlessness, particularly during the explosion of killing in the security campaign of autumn 1941. During the first half of 1942 the 221st, facing a growing partisan movement, adopted more imaginative measures to win the population's hearts and minds, but much of its conduct remained very harsh. (BA-MA, Freiburg im Breisgau)

Partisans captured east of Kharkov in the winter of 1941 await their fate. (Bundesarchiv, Koblenz)

A Red Army soldier and partisan suspect who tried to pass himself off as a civilian to avoid capture is held and searched by German security troops. Note the expression of the soldier on the left. (SV-Bilderdienst, Munich)

Security troops search two partisans, aged fifteen and sixteen, in 1942. By now the partisan movement was growing increasingly active, dangerous, and widespread. Virtually no civilian, irrespective of age or sex, was beyond suspicion. (SV-Bilderdienst, Munich)

Native auxiliaries in German service, employed to hold their village and protect the harvest against partisans, are instructed in the use of a Soviet machine gun. Security divisions of the German Eastern Army increasingly depended on these often-unreliable troops, who themselves tended to be kitted out with a ragbag of uniform and equipment pieces from all manner of sources. (SV-Bilderdienst, Munich)

German soldiers root out partisans, 1942. The soldiers' relaxed swagger and immaculate uniforms strongly suggest that this was a staged photograph. The actual appearance of the Eastern Army's increasingly pressured security troops was by now very different. (SV-Bilderdienst, Munich)

A much more authentic-looking record of the capture of partisans by German security troops, 1942. (Bundesarchiv, Koblenz)

These civilians, found hiding in the reeds of a brook near a village in the Bryansk region in 1942, were suspected of being partisans. (SV-Bilderdienst, Munich)

General Hubert Lendle, commanding officer, 221st Security Division, June 1942–November 1944. Under Lendle, in the face of a burgeoning partisan movement, the 221st Security Division's conduct of antipartisan warfare displayed a growing awareness of the need to cultivate the support of the population rather than terrorize it. (BA-MA, Freiburg im Breisgau)

Men of a German Order Police battalion interrogate villagers in the Pripet marshes area, 1943. Many Order Police units, including several directly attached to Eastern Army units, were notorious for their brutality. Thus did they play a role in undermining the efforts of some Eastern Army officers, their antipartisan forces by now increasingly beleaguered, to prosecute a more conciliatory antipartisan campaign. (SV-Bilderdienst, Munich)

5

More of the Sugar, Less of the Whip

THE BATTLE FOR POPULAR SUPPORT, 1942

The 221st Security Division became grimly acquainted with the bitter, defensive fighting that engulfed the German front during the winter of 1941–42. During the winter months its staff and combat troops were committed to stemming the Soviet offensives in the sector of the Second Army. Between mid-December and mid-March, the 221st sustained losses of 395 dead and wounded. Its ordeal was worsened by the lack of quality of many of its troops.[1] Nor would the division gain respite once it returned to the rear area the following spring. In its sector, as across the entire Army Group Center Rear Area, the partisan problem had assumed a new, complex, fearful shape.

Any security division that followed the precepts of sense in such a situation would have seen the need to rein in the brutality of its troops, and to combine military force targeted at the partisans specifically with a sustained effort to cultivate both population and potential partisan deserters. Indeed, the officers who had coordinated the 221st's Security Division's profoundly ruthless conduct of 1941 now did try to follow saner dictates. Their efforts would be stymied by the dynamics of the wider occupation regime they were charged with upholding, and by shortages in their own resources. Yet, given the resources they had, they made a considerable effort.

Through both the mobile operations the division prosecuted

against the partisans in the Yelnya-Dorogobuzh region near Smolensk in the spring of 1942, and its static security tenure in the Gomel region of southeastern Belorussia from June of that year, the pattern becomes increasingly clear. It was one to which all division-level departments contributed. The replacement, in April, of the operations officer Major Brenner with Major Friedrich, and the arrival of General Hubert Lendle as General Pflugbeil's successor as divisional commander in June, if anything spurred the process. But their predecessors—men who had sanctioned policies of extreme harshness in 1941—played their part also.

General Pflugbeil and the rest of the 221st Security Division's staff returned to the rear on 21 March 1942. With their best formation, the 350th Infantry Regiment, left at the front, they were immediately sent into action east of Smolensk against the partisans of the Yelnya-Dorogobuzh region.

The Yelnya-Dorogobuzh partisans were as far removed from the scrappy amateurs of 1941 as could be imagined. They were numerous enough, and dangerous enough, to draw a body of German units into what would become the largest Eastern Army antipartisan effort of the war.

Operations Munich and Hanover, which committed the 221st against the Yelnya-Dorogobuzh partisans, encompassed mobile encirclements and attacks over a wide area. Acute fuel shortages, an execrable road system, appalling winter weather, and, as ever, poor fighting power tormented the 221st throughout. The spirited partisan counterattacks that fell upon it—of which the worst, after a disastrous attempt by the division to prevent the breakout of a large partisan group under General Belov, inflicted shocking casualties—exposed the wretchedness of its condition.

The antiguerrilla, anti-Slavic, and career-driven ruthlessness that had characterized the 221st's divisional command in 1941 continued to color many of the directives and exhortations issued during the Yelnya-Dorogobuzh operations. Even directives ostensibly meant to encourage decent treatment of the population used language and arguments that could work only in the other direction. "It must be made clear to every soldier," the Intelligence Section asserted in early April, "that any civilian whom he mistreats might join the partisans and then face him with a gun in his hand the following day."[2] By stressing how shaky the population's allegiance actually was, this kind of reasoning could only make the troops' distrust of the population even more venomous. Worse still was the Operations Section's directive of 24 March. This ordered, as a matter of course, bombardment of any village the division's troops had not yet captured or had yet to reconnoiter properly. It was a recipe for potentially massive death tolls of innocent civilians.[3]

The most dramatic directive was one the Operations Section issued on 6 May. Written with the dire conditions the division faced clearly in mind, it oozed a spirit of comradeship and social-Darwinist struggle in its appeal to the spirit of soldierly endurance the German military had long eulogized:

Every soldier must be made to understand clearly that any unauthorized retreat means certain death. He must also understand that the proper, decisive use of weapons and the right use of terrain ensure that success will be his. Every man needs to be fully aware that it is the worst possible disgrace for a soldier to allow ammunition, equipment, or dead or wounded comrades to fall into enemy hands. A soldier may die in battle, but he will have died a hero's death like so many who have died for Germany before him. The coward, however, must die, as all traitors fully deserve. Let there be no doubt that cowards will be dealt with mercilessly in full accordance with military law.[4]

Yet it was also during the Yelnya-Dorogobuzh operations that the 221st Security Division began to display a marked capacity for moderation.

The Yelnya-Dorogobuzh operations were the first prominent instance of the "decent," more sensible type of antipartisan warfare that numerous leading Eastern Army figures now increasingly sub-scribed to. Indeed, such was the character of the partisans in this re-gion that the need for such an approach was particularly pressing.

Among the partisans were large numbers of Red Army soldiers. Many had been holding out in the region since the German advance of the previous summer had isolated them. Others had escaped from prisoner-of-war camps or, having penetrated into the area during the Red Army's winter offensives, had recently been cut off by German counterattacks.[5]

The partisans' particularly military character presented a deep threat to the Germans. The main fear that haunted General von Schenckendorff was that, with so many military personnel in the area, new partisan recruits from the population would themselves be instructed and trained to full military standard. Admittedly, Eastern Army security units always had an interest in talking up the partisans' strength, as a means of deflecting attention from their own failure to defeat them. But the undeniable presence of so many military per-sonnel in the Yelnya-Dorogobuzh region made the partisans there a genuinely dangerous prospect—one the Germans simply had to de-stroy conclusively. Substituting a terror campaign against the popu-lation for decisive victory over the partisans, then, was even less of an option for the Yelnya-Dorogobuzh operations than for others. The size of the force the Germans would eventually commit to them—nine divisions by May 1942—shows the urgency with which they viewed the task.[6]

The Germans, then, had a particular interest, simply in order to reduce casualties, in getting as many partisans as possible to desert. Hence German appeals to desert held out the promise—a complete turnaround from previous policy—that commissars' lives would be spared. Deserters also were to receive decent treatment, and a major propaganda effort was to be employed to tell them so.[7]

Parallel propaganda efforts were to be directed at the population. In the spring of 1942 this strategy was still relatively easy. Schenck-endorff himself was one of numerous military and civilian fig-ures who now wanted to loosen the population's oppressive Stalinist straitjacket, increase religious and political freedom (albeit within an overall sphere of German domination), and privatize agriculture. The failure of these initiatives lay in the future. This, along with the fact that, in the wake of the Germans' spring counterattacks, ultimate German victory still seemed a strong possibility, meant that it was still possible to persuade the population that those initiatives were feasible.[8] February's announcement of agricultural reforms, Einsatzgruppe B recorded, had made a genuinely positive impression upon the population.[9] Moreover, because so many of the Yelnya-Dorogobuzh partisans were so obviously soldiers, the Germans had a better-than-usual opportunity—albeit one they didn't always take—to distinguish between partisans and population and to ensure that the latter did not fall victim to German terror and excess.[10]

How the 221st Security Division actually prosecuted its hearts-and-minds campaign was left to its own discretion. All its superiors cared about was that the measures worked.[11] Some of the measures the 221st went on to enact, sensible though they certainly were, were not unique. Its Intelligence Section was not alone, for instance, in believing that correct, disciplined rank-and-file behavior toward the population could bring good results. A directive of 24 March declared that "the troops are to be reminded at frequent and regular intervals that firm but fair and correct treatment of the population is the best weapon for maintaining security and keeping the partisans down. They are also to be reminded that mindless and violent requisitioning, particularly against persons protected by a German pass card [local militiamen, informers], can effectively destroy all efforts at pacification. Any officer or man who transgresses this order can expect the harshest punishment."[12]

The Intelligence Section also ordered "awareness of local needs and sensibilities" and strict observance of the dignity of Russian women. The population's grinding poverty meant that things apparently of little worth to the Germans were of the utmost value to civilians. Though requisitioning by the troops was to be tolerated, it was to be kept to an absolute minimum. It was also either to be paid for in cash or have a receipt made out for it. Above all, it was to be conducted in coordination with village headmen. Where possible, finally, each family was to be allowed the minimum necessary for survival.[13]

Every endeavor seems to have been made, meanwhile, to involve civilians in the antipartisan effort. Armed pro-German civilians were charged with guarding the many villages the division itself lacked the troops to occupy, and assisting headmen by arresting all nonlocals and taking them to the nearest German unit. Civilians could participate in other ways also, "particularly by eliminating any partisans who enter the village, or arresting them and handing them over to the Wehrmacht, along with any inhabitant who takes partisans in, supplies them, or assists them in any other way."[14] They also were to be rewarded for every partisan whom they brought in, with a bounty to be paid immediately rather than later.[15] Lieutenant Beck was also anxious to ensure that any transgressions the troops did commit against the population were punished properly.[16]

Over partisan deserters, meanwhile, the 221st was actually ahead of its fellow divisions. It recognized that, while partisans captured in battle should be shot as irregulars, potential deserters could be enticed with promises of treatment "not only better than that which prisoners of war normally receive, but [which] also improves on their previous experiences in the Red Army." Most important of all, it saw that "if such propaganda is to work, then deserters must actually receive better treatment." The deserter was entitled to numerous privileges, "simple rations as quickly as possible," and to "be allowed to keep his uniform and personal belongings." He could then be put to one of a variety of uses: as a sentry or specialist worker, or as a member of one of the new "eastern legions" the Germans were now raising from the vast pool of potential manpower languishing (and, if it didn't seize such opportunities to get out, dying) in their prisoner-of-war camps. He should also be allowed, in the wake of abolition of the collective farm system, to share in the benefits of land redistribution.[17] It was not until 18 August 1943, in fact, that an Armed Forces High Command directive stipulated better treatment for partisan deserters.[18]

Manifold instances of ruthlessness aside, then, the commitment of the 221st, or of its Intelligence Section at any rate, to hearts-and-minds measures as wide-ranging as resources allowed was at this stage stronger than most. Sanity also was evident when the division was transferred to static security duty in the Gomel region, under its new commander, General Lendle, in June.[19]

From arrival in the region, which straddles what is now southeastern Belarus and the area of Russia to the east of it, some of the directives the 221st Security Division issued did again display the ambiguity the troops could so easily interpret as a blank check for brutality. Such, for example, were the Operations Section's 12 July orders for Operation Triangle, one of the division's initial operations to comb the forests of its new jurisdiction: "Ruthless measures are to be carried out vigorously; unnecessary harshness, particularly the unnecessary burning of houses, is to be avoided."[20] The implication is clear: troops being urged to conduct themselves ruthlessly might well interpret the word "unnecessary" rather loosely.

But overall, the division's ruthlessness was even less pronounced than before. No longer was there nearly as much sign either of the dramatic, merciless exhortations of the Yelnya-Dorogobuzh operations, or of the distrust of and contempt for the population that had marked Captain Haupt's tenure as operations officer in 1941.

As before, the 221st executed a many-faceted campaign of constructive engagement; though very little of the occupation Administrative Section's material from this period survives, that of the Intelligence Section is comprehensive. It was necessary, the Intelligence Section recognized, to employ an extensive range of media.[21] The importance of winning and retaining the population's trust also was stressed by the 203d Security Division. "The Russian is as trusting as a child," its Administrative Section pronounced, "and wants to be treated as such. He is devoted and obedient, and used to poverty and privation. But if he feels his trust is being betrayed, or sees that promises are not being fulfilled, he becomes treacherous and deceitful and rears up against his master."[22]

And such by now was the population's experience of German occupation that the potential for holding out hope of something better was immense. Across the entire Army Group Center Rear Area, the population was groaning under the burden of appalling food shortages, mass requisitioning, and, increasingly, procurement of vast amounts of labor for service in the Reich via a combination of (often false) promises, financial pressure, and, in time, outright coercion. In the 221st's own area, the Intelligence Section described seething resentment at tax levels, ongoing food shortages, and the heavy-handedness (sometimes outright thuggery) of the Ordnungsdienst (OD) and allied Hungarian troops in the jurisdiction.[23] It is also likely, even though the 221st's reports, probably for fear of its reflecting badly on the division's discipline, remain silent on the matter, that its own troops were behaving in a similarly atrocious manner. In any case, the result, increasingly, was a boiling rage far beyond the control of the often ham-fisted abilities of the German-appointed native civilian administration.

It was too early to push the panic button. By no means was the population flocking en masse to the partisans just yet. Clearly, though, the 221st Security Division had an incentive to strain every sinew to engage the population in order to try to prevent the partisans from thoroughly exploiting civilian resentment in the near future.

Lieutenant Beck's Intelligence Section was, as before, at the forefront of the hearts-and-minds effort. Though it concluded that the Russian, having been saturated with propaganda during the Soviet regime, was highly receptive to it, it recognized that it had to be the right kind of propaganda. The population, it saw, hankered after information on world events and politics, and on National Socialism and how it affected people's everyday lives.[24] Similarly, Einsatzgruppe B described the population as possessing a "hunger for news" and information, particularly on agricultural reform and National Socialism.[25]

There was a particular yearning for information about the lives of German workers and farmers. The Intelligence Section, seeing an opportunity to contrast conditions in the Reich with the misery and deprivation of life in the Soviet Union, was swift to oblige. It arranged lectures on agricultural issues and produced a popular "agricultural calendar."[26] A "House of the People" for theater and film performances was opened by the propaganda staff in Gomel.[27] Even prisoners of war were used as propaganda pawns; the Intelligence Section's monthly report for October 1942 recounted that the transit camp in Gomel had given a "live musical sendoff" for prisoners of war being sent for forced labor in the Reich. Bizarre though it may seem, this apparently macabre gesture was reportedly well received by the civilians who witnessed it.[28]

The division also employed eastern workers home on leave from the Reich to give upbeat public talks on their experience of Germany, of the bountiful existence enjoyed by German workers and farmers, and of the favorable treatment of eastern workers there. "The performances were received with enthusiasm," the Intelligence Section reported, "and were interrupted by calls of 'If only we could live like that!'"[29] Talks such as these, given for Russians by Russians, were seen as especially effective because the speakers, recounting their own experiences in their own language, could employ all its linguistic nuances. Native Russian speakers were also used to recruit for the eastern troops. "The division's deployment on 5 December of suitably articulate officers of the eastern troops . . . speaking of their own experiences in their own language, achieved far greater success than German officers ever would have been capable of."[30]

It was over labor service particularly, the conditions of which would eventually undermine the 221st's relationship with the population like no other aspect of the occupation, that the Intelligence Section needed all the inventiveness it could muster. As well as holding talks by native speakers, its propaganda troops also displayed films on German life and "open letters" cheerily describing the happiness of eastern workers in the Reich.[31] The division also tried to reduce some of the hardships of labor service itself: "transportation in severe cold by rail truck, without straw or heating . . . with no consideration of comfort or space," and the objectionable press-gang methods, such as thuggish coercion and plying with alcohol, which the native administrators directly responsible for assembling labor often employed.[32] The Intelligence Section urged that recruitment in future be put on a much more responsible basis that left less room for abuse by the native civilian authorities.[33]

As before, neither the 221st's view of affairs nor many of its subsequent measures were unique. By now, an extensive propaganda effort was being enacted across the whole of the Army Group Center Rear Area comprising exhibitions, film shows, written material, and native and German public speakers. It also encompassed attempts to impress the population with better conduct of the troops themselves. Yet, even if General von Schenckendorff was sincere in his advocacy of "fairer" antipartisan warfare, three prongs of the 221st's cultivation effort in the Gomel region outdid both normal Eastern Army standards and superiors' expectations.

First, there was the division's use of the initial combing operations conducted across its new jurisdiction in July and August. These did not inflict the grotesquely high body counts now increasingly common in mobile Eastern Army antipartisan operations. Instead, the 221st used them to cultivate the population assiduously. During an operation in the Novosybkov area, the able-bodied men of numerous villages were sent to detention camps for security checks.[34] General von Schenckendorff had already instructed the 221st that the detainees must not be handled brutally.[35] The division itself, however, went further. Its plan was for those detainees due eventually to be sent home, the overwhelming majority, to be transformed into a potent propaganda weapon during their internment. This transformation would be achieved by treating them to antipartisan talks and films and to entertainment programs described as "merry prison camp evenings." When these men were released, the division hoped, they would be inclined to discount "horror stories" about conditions in the prison camps, and encourage fellow villagers to cooperate with their occupiers. Apparently the initiative was successful; nine days later the 221st reported that the areas it had so targeted had seen no further encounters with partisans.[36]

Then there were the Ankara operations of the winter of 1942–43.

These two operations were part of a campaign of mobile antiparti-san warfare that the 221st prosecuted in its especially troublesome northeastern sector. The 221st, along with the unit it had charged with direct responsibility for the operations, the 36th Security Regiment, ordered the troops combing the villages to adhere strictly to the quota levels of livestock and produce set by the German economic inspectorates.[37] Even those villages that had not met the necessary quota level, the division directed, were not to be subjected to unbridled requisitioning.[38] During the second Ankara operation the division strictly forbade the burning of villages.[39]

These measures contrasted starkly with the organized marauding that was gathering pace elsewhere. In Peter, a winter operation carried out by the neighboring 203d Security Division, "bandit-friendly" villages—in other words, those that had failed to meet their agricultural quotas—were stripped of all useful labor, and livestock, and then simply evacuated and destroyed.[40] Here, requisitioning seems to have gone well beyond fulfillment of quotas. Two-thirds of all produce and livestock were seized, and the villagers were left to survive on what remained.[41] And compared to some of the devastation the Germans were wreaking elsewhere, even Peter was a paragon of restraint. Economic Detachment Vitebsk was just one economic unit that was severely critical of the economic destruction wrought by antipartisan operations and the rapacity of the troops. It pointed out the effects upon farmers not just in economic terms but also in terms of how they viewed the German occupation.[42]

Particularly audacious, finally, was the 221st's deserter policy. A communiqué of 3 December warned that current guidelines—stipulating that partisans be spared only if they deserted with their weapons *before* an antipartisan operation, and that those surrendering during or after an operation, even if they brought their weapons with them, be shot—were dangerously counterproductive. After all, "an enemy with only the prospect of death staring him in the face [would] fight, bitterly and tenaciously, to the end."[43] This was an implicit condemnation of the provisions on deserters—which instructed that captured partisans be shot or, better still, hanged—in the "Combat Directive for Anti-Partisan Warfare in the East," which the Armed Forces High Command had issued in November.[44] What the 221st essentially was arguing was that all captured partisans, deserters or otherwise, be taken prisoner—a policy the Armed Forces High Command would endorse only in August 1943.[45] It was also essential, the 221st argued, "that promises of preferential treatment for deserters be kept under all circumstances. As soon as there is a failure to back the propaganda up with reality, that propaganda loses effect immediately." This statement, of course, implies that such promises had been broken before.[46] It is clear that the officers who drafted this communiqué were more concerned about executing sensible policy than about being perceived as overly "soft" by their superiors.

This was indeed the same 221st Security Division that had terrorized, then culled the population of its territory during 1941. It had not undergone some Damascene conversion to the cause of cultivation. This was a change that circumstances and perceptions had interacted in complex ways to bring about.

All the Eastern Army divisions fighting in the Yelnya-Dorogobuzh region during the spring of 1942 were aware, even if their conduct frequently failed to show it, of how fundamental constructive engagement was to the operations' success. For the 221st Security Division, however, the awareness was especially painful.

The enemy the 221st Security Division faced in the region contained an extensive core of regular troops cut off from their own lines by the German counterattacks of late winter 1941–42, supplemented by Communists, former destruction battalion members, Red Army escapees, and freshly procured civilians. The recent arrival of airborne troops had boosted their number. By mid-April 5,000 partisans, recruiting extensively from the population and incorporating ski troops, Red Army parachutists, and tanks, were reported in the Yelnya area alone.[47]

As the only rear-area unit involved in the operations—the rest were front-line formations drafted in temporarily—all the 221st had to commit against the partisans were second- and third-rate territorial battalions. Worse still, it had just been "reinforced" by a number of territorial battalions from the Reich whose men had neither fired a shot in anger nor thrown a hand grenade. The particular details of these units were sufficient to induce the blackest depression. Territorial Battalion 555, for example, had had its entire training program stopped between mid-October and mid-March as a result of a typhus outbreak that had killed fifteen men and hospitalized another seventy-two. Territorial Battalion 573 contained a complement of officers whose average age was over fifty, and a majority of companies equipped so irregularly that they had no idea what was in their own knapsacks.[48]

Operations Munich and Hanover exposed these shortcomings mercilessly. The Army Group Center Rear Area's Operations Section reported on 7 May 1942 that "the deployment of the territorial battalions within the compass of the 221st Division for the operation against Glinka has already shown that with such troops successes will be difficult to achieve. As a consequence of their inadequate combat training, the casualties sustained by these units are higher than those of front-line troops. Fifty percent of casualties are dead."[49]

If destroying the partisans was crucial, then, a unit like the 221st was in particularly dire need of help from both population and partisan desertion in order to achieve it. Indeed, it would have been surprising if more rational officers at the 221st's divisional level *hadn't* viewed the diligent courting of population and potential deserters as the best means of compensating for their formation's failings.

Deserters and pliable civilians could supply both more OD and militiamen and more information on partisans. Indeed, the division enacted an intelligence-gathering effort, involving both deserters and civilians in cooperation with various German agencies, which produced a highly detailed picture of the partisans.[50] Even more pertinently, each new desertion meant that "our own troops are spared sacrifice in blood."[51]

And as the operations went on, the returns on cultivation increased. Ultimately, even with all the defects that plagued the 221st Security Division particularly, the Germans' massive effort across the Yelnya-Dorogobuzh region could not fail to destroy the bulk of the partisans there. Increasingly, the population must have seen that, with the Germans back in control, it paid to get on their right side. Moreover, though German reports certainly had an interest in embroidering stories of grisly partisan excess, there is every reason to suppose that the partisans' mounting desperation in the face of the German offensive did harden their own treatment of the population. In their seizure of essential supplies particularly, they are likely to have given a progressively worse account of themselves. All this could only increase civilian willingness to cooperate with the Germans. Thus a report that one of the 221st's subordinate units compiled at the start of June, which described the misery the partisans had wrought upon the inhabitants of the villages of Boroviva, Sekerino, Spaskava, and several others, is probably essentially accurate. The partisans reportedly had razed the villages to the ground, destroyed agricultural tools, and seized nearly all the livestock except a handful of horses and cows. Sure enough, though much of the refugee populace had scattered to other villages, the civilians who remained responded positively to German propaganda.[52]

The principal spur to such constructive engagement was the division's situation throughout the operations. It was a substandard unit up against a partisan enemy trained and equipped to military standards. Were it to have any chance at all of rising to this challenge, the judicious wooing of population and potential partisan deserters was crucial.

Circumstances were similarly pivotal in the Gomel region. For one thing, the 221st arrived in its new jurisdiction to find that its predecessor there, the 203d Security Division, had failed to install an essential prerequisite of any effective counterinsurgency campaign— a proper intelligence system.[53] Thus did the 221st have to reckon with a dearth of detailed, accurate information on the partisans in the area. Reports on partisan strength compiled by the 203d's Feldkommandanturen and Ortskommandanturen bore little resemblance to reality, and no informer network was in place. The particularly comprehensive intelligence effort the 221st now had to undertake in order to compensate, which included a command for every battalion and Ortskommandantur to set up its own informer network, almost certainly increased its reliance upon a pliant population.[54]

Such was the state of the Gomel region partisans themselves that moves to entice desertion from their ranks were especially likely to succeed. The 221st identified six main partisan areas, the northeastern sector being the most infested, in its new jurisdiction. Three to four thousand partisans, combining Red Army stragglers and destruction battalion personnel from 1941 with locally raised recruits, many of whom were well equipped, were reported across them. But these partisans were both uncoordinated and filled out with press-ganged local recruits. In mid-September the Feodorov group was described as having been poor in morale and in mood after having being relentlessly on the march and in combat.[55] The great potential to lure deserters, then, was not lost on the 221st. "Among the partisans," it noted, "are a large number of amoral fellow travelers. The best means of weakening and undermining partisan morale is to target this particular group with an unrestricted propaganda effort enticing it to desert."[56] Partisan discipline, equipment, supply, and leadership all improved over the autumn. In October the Intelligence Section reported the presence of up to 15,000 partisans, greatly improved in terms of discipline, equipment, supply, and leadership, in the Kletnya-Mamayevka Forest. But the division's preference for an antipartisan campaign employing more sugar, less whip did not diminish.[57]

Probably the biggest incentive to sustain and indeed intensify cultivation was the fact that, when it came to allocating reinforcements, the 221st found itself massively disadvantaged. The scale of the partisan problem in the Gomel region certainly alarmed General von Schenckendorff and his Army Group Center superiors. But the scale of it elsewhere was likely to alarm them far more. In regions such as the Bryansk Forest area to the northeast and the Vitebsk-Polotsk area to the northwest, greater proximity to the front enabled the partisans to maintain particularly close contact with the Red Army. In the Vitebsk-Polotsk region particularly, this conjured the frightening prospect of partisans who might start having a serious strategic impact.[58] Facing a partisan threat of markedly greater magnitude in these areas, it is little wonder that Army Group Center so neglected the 221st's need for reinforcement. One of the Eastern Army units fighting in the particularly troublesome Vitebsk-Polotsk region—between the start of July and the end of November, it faced 272 successful partisan sabotage attacks on the railways as against the 221st's 117—was the 201st Security Division.[59] The 201st was accorded significantly more manpower than the 221st; in mid-October 1942, for example, twelve battalions had been assigned to it as opposed to nine for the 221st.[60]

But the 221st still had to administer an enormous area, and the overstretch was crippling. The effects were severest when the division attempted mobile operations. Operations in the areas south Novosybkov in July were just one occasion when the partisans were able to melt into the undergrowth in the face of the far-from-overwhelming force the division had mustered, then slip back into the area once the Germans, compelled by the manpower shortage to report for duty elsewhere, had left.[61]

The stress intensified in September 1942. It was then, at a time when it also had to oversee the harvest, that the 221st Security Division had to surrender Security Battalion 573 and the staff and headquarters troops of the 44th Security Regiment to duties elsewhere. Consequently, simply guarding the railways became a nightmare task. However tempting it might be for Eastern Army security units to exaggerate their adversities, the concrete facts—a wafer-thin spread of manpower across an enormous area—show that little exaggeration was needed. The 221st, at well below 7,000 combat strength, was responsible for an area of 30,000 square kilometers, 2,560 villages, and more than 1.3 million inhabitants.[62]

It also could expect little relief from its still poorly trained and ill-equipped native units. If German security forces were low on the list of priorities, the position of the OD, across the Army Group Rear Area in general, was often even lower.[63] On 20 August the 221st reported that the divisionwide OD force was 3,000 rifles short.[64]

Worse, if anything, was the state of Eastern Battalion 604. This unit, raised from former prisoners of war, was crippled by "a lack of machine-guns . . . clothes, footwear and medical facilities" and "only half the prescribed number of horses and trucks."[65] In September, now facing 13,000 increasingly disciplined, motivated, and well-equipped partisans, the division drastically deemphasized active security and hurled far more of its effort into guarding the railways.[66]

Compensating for lack of manpower, then, remained a considerable inducement to cultivate the population. Compensating for the substandard, sometimes frightful quality of it was another.

Even passive security, involving as it did often ridiculously long hours of sentry duty, might be beyond the ability of troops in the miserable state to which many of the 221st's units, in the face of the rigors of long-term service in the east, were sinking. Training, a grave concern to the 221st as to other security divisions, was especially difficult for troops scattered over an immense area guarding railway lines. The need for training and the sometimes hair-raising consequences of a lack of it were especially glaring among replacement troops. At the end of July, three of the division's security battalions received replacements of 11 NCOs and 309 men. Many of these, however, were either insufficiently trained or simply untrained.[67] Major Kriebel, the new operations officer, doubted that the batch projected for the end of August would cope with the hardships of antipartisan duty—it did, after all, possess an average age of forty. "Many of these very old people," he predicted, "will fall by the wayside when it comes to active operations."[68] The 221st's Operations Section was soon castigating the troops for their lack of preparedness. It reported that "heavy losses have had to be sustained as a result of the troops' negligence and carelessness in their conduct of the full range of necessary security duties. It must be hammered into the troops that, even in those areas where attacks have not recently taken place, they must maintain the sharpest state of alertness."[69]

Morale, inevitably, was beginning to skim the depths. By the summer of 1942, most of the troops who had been with the division since the previous summer had had no leave for twelve to eighteen months, some even longer.[70] The problem of leave was general to the Eastern Army. By April 1942, for example, 123,000 of the Ninth Army's combat troops had not been home for a year or more.[71] The possible damage to morale is illustrated forcefully in a letter written by the 198th Infantry Division's Corporal Otto Hirschfeld in the spring of 1942. "There are soldiers who'll soon have had two years out here without a break—and here are the Nazis claiming such problems don't exist! As ever, there's a big gap between talk and action. The officers, of course, get home sooner. It's the same old thing. Best not to think about it, but just accept your fate."[72]

The often-atrocious state of the roads heightened a sense of isolation. These were roads that a spell of rain could transform into a quagmire, hindering both movement and delivery of field post. The scattering of the division's troops in small strongpoints along the railway lines probably exacerbated isolation and damage to morale. An Operations Section report of 4 October described railway strongpoints in a state of disarray, with rifles, helmets, coats, and gas masks left lying around in disorder.[73] Dangers of illness from eastern conditions, usually thoroughly unhygienic at best, were particularly heightened for new, inexperienced troops recently transferred from the Reich. Within Territorial Battalion 557, for instance, gout and rheumatism were rife.[74] The prolonged lack of obvious success and the sheer boredom of passive security probably assailed morale further.[75]

Under other circumstances, the frustration such pressures could generate might have pushed the 221st, like many other units, to even more ruthlessness and brutality. But with the division blind in intelligence terms, robbed of its mobility, and unable to impose itself upon the population, they may simply have added to the sense of urgency pushing it in a more enlightened—albeit ultimately fruitless—direction.

The pattern repeated itself that autumn and winter. Granted, the onset of winter and the temporary loan of reinforcements finally enabled the 221st to execute some measure of mobile antipartisan action. But in the 221st's situation, any attempt at a sane long-term strategy ruled out injecting greater ruthlessness into the directives for that action. Though traversing frozen swamps and tracing partisan tracks in the snow might enable mobile operations to land some blows against the partisan movement, such by now was its growth in the region that they were hardly likely to destroy it outright. Mobile large-scale operations might also drive the troops, as they so often did, to excessive brutality. Alongside the threat to soldierly discipline this could pose, the 221st may also have feared, rightly, that it might embitter the population into embracing the inevitably resurgent partisans even more fervently the following spring. That the division couldn't rely on the long-term presence of the unit that had just reinforced it, the First Paratroop Training Regiment—a unit composed in any case of inexperienced trainees—probably strengthened its resolve in favor of moderation.

Though there is no written evidence that such considerations did indeed shape the 221st's thinking, they would certainly help explain why such mobile operations as the division did execute were concentrated only where the partisan problem was worst—its northeastern sector. They also help explain why the divisional directives for those operations were, again, relatively measured.

Essentially, whereas past studies have argued that severe conditions could fuel brutality, the 221st's conduct in the Gomel region as in the Yelnya-Dorogobuzh region shows that, if they deteriorated beyond a certain point, certain aspects of an increasingly difficult situation increasingly compelled restraint. If a unit was *so* weak, blind, or overstretched that it was unable to execute mobile operations or impose its presence in native villages for a commensurate length of time, then its ability to cultivate the population was likely to be limited. But the 221st's ability to terrorize and coerce it was nonexistent. Constructive engagement, difficult to enact as it might be, was its only means of easing the task of security at all.

A unit whose very different circumstances helped drive it in a much bloodier direction was the 201st Security Division. First, in order to cope with the demands of a particularly troublesome and strategically important sector, this unit was granted significantly more manpower, at least for limited periods, than the 221st. It might not be enough to attain an effective long-term presence across its jurisdiction, but it was enough to execute large-scale operations and, consequently, to kill civilians en masse. The ideological inclination of the divisional commander is unlikely to have hindered such a course of action; General Alfred Jacobi was described glowingly by his superiors as "involving himself actively in the political issues of the moment, enjoying particularly good relations with the [Nazi] Party and its subdivisions."[76]

In the five months from the beginning of July and the end of November 1942, the 221st Security Division reported that it had killed 687 partisans, at a cost to itself of 182 dead and 207 wounded.[77] This is a massive disparity by any reckoning, one that indicates that the indiscriminate killing of civilians went an enormous way to fueling that disparity. Yet by the same token, the division's own losses show that the enemy it faced could indeed show its teeth. In no sense could the same be said of the 201st Security Division. The 201st killed 864 "partisans" in combat, and condemned a further 245 to a quick dispatch from the Secret Field Police, in the month of September alone. And just ninety-nine rifles, pistols, and machine guns were yielded from the 1,100-plus body count. The 201st itself, meanwhile, suffered 8 dead and 25 wounded.[78]

The difference over partisan deserters was even more marked. Between 18 June and 31 December 429 such deserters came over to the 221st. During almost the same period, 43 came over to the 201st.[79] Perhaps partisans endeavoring to come over to the 201st had been shot in the attempt. Then again, perhaps most partisans, having seen how the 201st did business, were not likely to try this in the first place. And worse was to come: Operations Snow Rabbit, Lightning Ball, and Thunderbolt, conducted by the 201st during the early months of 1943, killed more than 6,500 "partisans and accomplices" for the loss of 159 German dead.[80] These degrees of carnage, it seems, left the 201st's division-level officers unmoved.[81]

The 201st's particular relationship with the SS and Order Police, meanwhile, not only increased the body count in the division's operations, but may well also have increased the division's inclination to brutality. On the former score, the extensive assistance rendered by Einsatzkommando 9 of Einsatzgruppe B stoked the death toll further. In Operation Lightning Ball, for example, Einsatzkommando 9 and Secret Field Police units killed 1,204 people whom the 201st had handed over to them.[82] This sort of assistance relieved the 201st of an "awkward" choice between expending scant time and resources in committing its own troops to guarding "suspect, non-able-bodied elements," or endangering the troops' discipline by giving them orders to butcher such captives. The Einsatzkommando could dirty its hands with the task instead—indeed, would do so readily.

As in 1941, however, the SS was not just the Wehrmacht's facilitator; it was its rival also. Waffen-SS and Order Police units operated in the Vitebsk-Polotsk region in far greater numbers than they did in the 221st's area. There were seven major Eastern Army–led operations and three SS-led operations in the region between August 1942 and June 1943.[83] The presence of such units may well have generated a particularly direct institutional rivalry and career pressure, just as that of the SS Cavalry Brigade had done in 1941, for all antipartisan commanders in their vicinity. Thus may the 201st's officers have felt spurred to an even more zealous display of "necessary" ruthlessness.

The 221st Security Division neither enjoyed such levels of manpower or Einsatzgruppe assistance, nor felt the brutalizing pressure of such rivalry. Einsatzgruppe involvement in the 221st's antipartisan effort usually went no further than screening suspects. At most, it stretched to providing small, armed contingents for individual operations.[84] There was only one Order Police unit, Reserve Police Battalion 91, in the 221st's jurisdiction. And this unit, composed as it was of reservists not regulars, was perhaps less likely than many to act with fanatical ruthlessness. Neither the 221st's ability to employ brutality nor its inclination, then, was as great as the 201st's.

Committed, at least for now, to a sustained hearts-and-minds campaign, the 221st almost certainly would have felt compelled to intensify it by the fact that the partisans' own hearts-and-minds campaign was beginning to gather momentum.

The mounting difficulties that now beset the 221st Security Division's hearts-and-minds campaign were born partly of problems that had assailed Eastern Army propaganda efforts from the start. As early as autumn 1941, Einsatzgruppe B had stressed that the partisans were disseminating propaganda far more effectively than the Germans were.[85] One of the factors hampering distribution had been a lack of available aircraft; the 221st itself had had to wait until late October before acquiring the services of a solitary ex-stunt plane. This aircraft, moreover, had had to spread itself between propaganda distribution and the reconnaissance duty that constituted the bulk of its activities. A further obstacle, of which the 221st's Intelligence Section had been painfully aware, had been that Ortskommandanturen and Feldkommandanturen, constantly moved around as they were, were never able to cement constructive relations with the population.[86]

Though the Eastern Army had gone some way to solving these problems by the summer of 1942, Einsatzgruppe B was still far from satisfied. The 221st Security Division's Intelligence Section, meanwhile, was constantly stressing the need for effective supply and distribution of newspapers, Wehrmacht reports, and other Russian-language material.[87] Youth propaganda made particularly little headway. Not only did youth feel robbed of their prospects by the hardship and upheaval that the war had inflicted; because they had no memory of anything other than the Soviet regime, they were especially susceptible to Soviet indoctrination.[88]

By the autumn of 1942, ever-larger areas were falling under the influence of the partisans and their own brand of psychological warfare. And the miseries the German occupation was inflicting upon the populace had created a rich source of resentment for the partisans to tap.

To start with, growing animus was heaped on the native auxiliary police and German-appointed native civilian administrators. The population saw the auxiliaries' policing methods, such as arresting people without trial, as a vicious echo of Stalin's day.[89] It saw native administrators, with much justification, as venal, self-seeking, corrupt, and prone to abuse their position to advantage themselves, their families, and their friends.[90] Cause for yet further anger was the often-Neanderthal disposition of the Hungarian troops stationed in the 221st's area. "As a general rule," the division reported, "they beat up all road menders and foremen, arrest people with German work passes, and often beat up the inhabitants of entire villages. The [population's] willingness to work is suffering greatly as a result of all this."[91]

But all this paled next to the ghastly impact, worsened by increasingly voracious German requisitioning, of hunger. The ever-higher quota levels set by the Economic Inspectorate Center were a recipe for hardship and bitterness of the worst kind.[92] Winter's approach brought the prospect of even more grievous food shortages. The wretched desperation to which hunger could reduce the population made an indelible impression upon some German soldiers who witnessed it. Such, for example, were the images recounted in a letter by Lieutenant Emerich Pohl:

Tattered, half-starved shapes creep about here and there along the roads . . . In the night they dig planted seed potatoes out of the ground. Yesterday a boy was caught carrying a big parcel under his arm, which turned out to contain an old fur. When asked what he was doing with it, he explained he was taking it home to eat, by singeing the hair off and boiling the skin in water long enough for it to taste palatable.

If you let yourself think humanely, this misery can really get to you. But when you remember that everything's so scarce in the homeland, that the soldier at the front is undergoing every privation, then you think—well, better the Russians starve than we.[93]

Hellmut Prantl, an NCO of Sonderkommando 7a, the main Einsatzgruppe unit operating in the 221st's area during 1942, described the situation there in chillingly succinct terms: "Human life's unimportant here. A woman'll shoot her own husband for a bit of bread, a child'll inform on his parents just to get something to eat."[94]

Disillusionment at German agricultural "reforms" intensified the bitterness. By early October, the 221st's Intelligence Section was reporting that farmers' early enthusiasm for the reforms was evaporating rapidly, and that many feared that the scale of the requisitions would soon push them below subsistence level.[95] Within weeks, requisitions were combining with the impending winter to stoke a mood of black apprehension across the population.[96]

Similarly poisonous by now was popular loathing of labor service, especially over the compulsory recruitment of young girls. The 221st's Intelligence Section reported in early November that "wild rumors" (in reality, probably accurate ones) were circulating about the treatment of Russian girls working in the Reich: that they were forbidden to go out, had no leisure time, and were falling foul of illness, malnutrition, and a work burden that was driving them into the ground.[97] By now, civilians were going to ever-more-desperate efforts to escape labor service. "Just how averse the population is to the idea of compulsory labor service," observed the Intelligence Section, "how great the fear of being deported to Germany, is clear in the cases of girls getting themselves pregnant, or getting their doctors to lie for them in this respect, or getting married . . . everything they can possibly do to avoid being sent to Germany." Another increasingly popular option, with both men and women, was self-mutilation. By December, rumors that all single women below the age of thirty-five were to be deported to the Reich were rife. Fear and resentment of such strength, and on such a scale, were manna to a partisan movement itself intent on securing the population's cooperation. Its own membership swelled as men and women fled labor service to join it.[98]

Finally, there was now growing rage over German antipartisan measures. The indignation is captured in a report compiled in late

October by the Klintsy-based Feldkommandantur 528 (V). The 221st Security Division expected the Feldkommandantur to employ propaganda skillfully to persuade the population of the "necessity" of evacuating all able-bodied men from the partisan-endangered parts of its jurisdiction. Yet with the men of the villages fearing for the well-being, indeed the lives of the families they would be leaving behind, the Feldkommandantur held out no hope of their submitting to evacuation willingly. Of even greater concern to the Feldkommandantur was a plan hatched by Economic Staff East forcibly to snap up 1,500 men and 4,500 women from the Klintsy area for labor service. Selling this plan to the population on top of the "benefits" of forced evacuation, the Feldkommandantur pleaded, was beyond its powers of persuasion.[99]

Partisan efforts to secure popular support did not just exploit resentment. By autumn partisan propaganda was striking an increasingly nationalistic rather than ideological note. The partisans perceived, rightly, that such appeals were more likely to strike a chord.[100] They also contrasted the hardships the population had endured under the Soviet regime of old with the rosy future they now promised.[101] Inspiring a measure of fear in the population was equally important. By December 1942, in the increasingly large area they controlled or threatened, they often offered a simple choice: "They threaten to shoot those members of the population working for the Wehrmacht who do not cease such work and resign all their posts." Terror was spread by "murders of OD members and headmen and acts of vengeance against their families." In the endangered areas, mayors were fleeing to towns or villages occupied by German troops or, where that was not possible, were reduced to sleeping at a different address every night.[102]

By combining threats with enticements to "come over" in return for decent treatment, the partisans intensified attempts to persuade growing numbers of native administrators and auxiliaries to desert the Germans altogether.[103] On 29 November the 27th Security Regiment reported that partisans had twice contacted the OD leader in Mglin and urged him to come over to his own brothers. The mayor of Krasnogorki, meanwhile, had gone over to the partisans after they had captured him.[104] The desertion rate among *Hiwis* (unarmed native volunteers) and the rank-and-file OD, which had been creeping up already, leapt up in December.[105] It was fueled by rumors, often spread by former Hiwis and OD men themselves, that deserters could expect the partisans to treat them well. It was also fueled, more fundamentally, by the fact that Hiwis and OD men already harbored a host of grievances ripe for exploitation. Hiwi disgruntlement at the poverty of their supply was fueling defections as early as August. The manifold defects that plagued the OD, in clothing and equipment particularly, soon drove many of its number to similar action.[106]

Another inducement to cooperate with the partisans was the 221st Security Division's ongoing failure to locate and destroy them.[107] By December it was growing increasingly difficult to organize civilians living in fear of partisan reprisals to carry out official directives.[108] The accommodation they subsequently decided to reach with the partisans could be far from unwilling. A report by pro-German informers operating east of Chechersk described the attitude of much of the population there: "'Oh, leave the partisans be, they've done us no harm. Whereas the Germans are after our chickens, our eggs, everything . . .' In short, the population cannot be trusted."[109]

Yet the 221st's very lack of success in preventing this propartisan drift also helps explain why, at this stage, the effort of its own hearts-and-minds campaign was still being intensified. Though the campaign clearly was encountering setbacks, the division's continued failings in mobility and means of coercion probably helped convince division-level officers that their only option was to sustain and indeed intensify cultivation.

In any case, it still at least appeared that the battle for hearts and minds was far from lost. The 221st's Intelligence Section reported that the population's worsening mood notwithstanding, German propaganda was on the whole still well received.[110] Einsatzgruppe B drew a similar conclusion for the whole Army Group Center Rear Area.[111] The catastrophic climax of the battle of Stalingrad, in which, in February 1943, more than twenty encircled German divisions would be destroyed and nigh-on a million Axis troops lost, still lay ahead, and the outcome of the Russo-German War seemed far from settled. Though the situation was to change drastically during 1943, the omens on the ground for the Eastern Army's hearts-and-minds effort in the last months of 1942 did not, at least to German eyes, look unremittingly dismal.

At all points in 1942, then, a thread of continuity linked the 221st Security Division's antipartisan effort. Often, brutality resulted from the fear and frustration prompted by the hardships of antipartisan warfare. But the *particular* circumstances the 221st faced drove it in what was, by normal Eastern Army standards, a comparatively constructive and enlightened direction.

Crucial as well as conditions in shaping this approach, however, was the fact that the 221st's division-level officers were able to see the wisdom of it. Not all units, even in similar circumstances, were so perceptive. One such unit whose attitude was markedly harsher as a result was the 203d Security Division.

The 203d did show some sense over antipartisan warfare. In June 1942, for instance, the division's Operation Friendship, a propaganda undertaking that deployed loudspeaker vans and a Russian farmer giving upbeat talks on his experience of Germany, prompted many partisans to desert.[112] For July's Operation Cockchafer, the 203d's operations officer, Major Schmidt, explained that "attempts are being made to move inhabitants hiding out in the forests back into their villages, for they have nothing to fear providing they have not participated in partisan activities. It has become clear that the pointless slaughter of livestock or the unjustified burning of villages and shooting of inhabitants, as is often the wont of [SS] and police units, only succeeds in driving the inhabitants into the arms of the partisans."[113] The civilians under the thumb of the 201st Security Division in the Vitebsk-Polotsk region would have been grateful for such an attitude there.

But at other times the 203d assumed a markedly harsher stance. It neither criticized increasingly harsh higher-level guidelines—a contrast with the 221st's December 1942 attack on deserter policy—and often saw no need to curb its own troops' brutality. While the 221st, during the Yelnya-Dorogobuzh operations, had warned its troops against excess, the 203d's Administrative Section tersely remarked in August 1942 that it was scarcely avoidable "that many people killed in cleansing operations are not actually partisans."[114] The 203d's Operations Section, despite having urged restraint during Cockchafer, was by November displaying a more merciless persuasion. Major Schmidt's disquiet at the ravages the troops were committing, arising as it did out of concern for discipline and "uncomradeliness" rather than for military-civilian relations, comes across in cold utilitarian terms: "Reports constantly come in that properties are being vandalized or pillaged outright by members of units stationed in the area. These actions are highly uncomradely, for they can cause a dearth of sufficiently equipped accommodation for troops who have been sent to the rear to recover from particularly harsh front-line combat. They also contravene orders and indeed are acts of plunder. I shall ensure that reports are submitted on any similar cases in future."[115]

The language, too, is far less urgent than Lieutenant Beck's warning against excesses in the Yelnya-Dorogobuzh operations. It also fits the image of anti-Slavic derision conveyed in a report issued by Schmidt in October 1942. In this report, Schmidt's overall argument that the Germans should offer the population concrete hopes and goals was combined with contemptuous, derogatory observations of his own. "If we could offer some kind of goal to aim for then we could conduct a successful propaganda effort. It should nevertheless be remembered that the Russian has absolutely no love for the Germans, and never will. He feels, maybe unconsciously, that he is inferior to the Germans. This inferiority complex has been strengthened by Bolshevik influence."[116] That Schmidt was more than merely paying lip service to accepted racial stereotypes here is indicated by the fact that such sentiments appear in none of the 221st's official communiqués during 1942. Paying lip service to such stereotypes, then, was not necessarily a common motivation.

All this may suggest that racial contempt, guerrillaphobia, and general harshness colored the 203d's attitude decisively. It may, on the other hand, suggest something less dramatic, but perhaps even more unsettling: that the immediate, intense pressures the 203d Security Division faced simply rendered it indifferent both to the suffering it was inflicting and to the swelling popular bitterness that ultimately would cripple its own ability to control its jurisdiction even further. The tone of the division's directives, certainly, sounds contemptuously dismissive of the population's suffering rather than *virulently* anti-Slavic. Either way, the fact that its own recorded dead amounted to just 15 percent of recorded partisan dead between the beginning of July and the end of October, in contrast to 35 percent for the 221st, indicates that the attitude was widespread throughout the division.[117]

There was nothing particularly onerous about the 203d's situation to instill such a harsh mentality. Only a month separated its Operations Section's pleas for restraint in Cockchafer from the Administrative Section's terse comments about the "inevitability" of civilian deaths; yet there is no sign that the population's propensity for supporting partisans increased in that time.[118] Even by November, amid bitterness at economic misery and dwindling faith in German ability to combat the partisans, it still reported that the population was "generally not unfriendly."[119] Crucially, at both points—midsummer and midautumn 1942—the 221st was of a like mind.[120] The divisions' troops were stretched to similar extents and faced very similar levels of partisan activity.[121]

The question, then, is why the 221st behaved so differently. The key division-level figures who shaped hearts-and-minds policy were the divisional commander, the operations officer, and, most immediately, the intelligence officer. Lieutenant Beck's thorough prosecution of it is partly explained by the simple fact that, as intelligence officer, it was his direct responsibility. For this reason alone, he was likely to take constructive engagement more seriously than an operations section or a quartermaster's section, which, preoccupied as they respectively were with operational and economic matters, would have had correspondingly less time for and appreciation of the subtleties of hearts-and-minds campaigning. It was the 221st's Operations Section, after all, which had urged villages of less than 100 percent guaranteed loyalty to be flattened by bombardment, had issued serial directives impelling the troops to a hardbitten, pitiless prosecution of antipartisan warfare, and had then, after all this, disingenuously left the troops to decide the meaning of "necessary ruthlessness" themselves. Correspondingly, intelligence sections could be relative oases of enlightenment even in units with such a brutal track record as the 707th Infantry Division. In August 1942 the 707th's intelligence officer, in response to reports that "in certain villages, underground rumors spread by the partisans cause the villagers to flee into the woods whenever German troops approach," urged better treatment of prisoners and deserters and "impeccable conduct by the troops toward the civilian population."[122]

But there were also other reasons why Beck was so disposed to moderation. That some officers prosecuted antipartisan warfare with a measure of sense and restraint may have been due in part to an old-fashioned sense of decent soldierly conduct, to more civilizing peacetime values, or even to russophilia.[123] They were hardly likely to express themselves in such terms, but this was not their fault. An officer genuinely motivated by compassion would have been foolish to put his case in anything other than pragmatic terms.[124] For one thing, arguably, acquiring a reputation as too much of a soft touch was inadvisable within an institution embedded in the workings of a state as ruthless as the Third Reich. Such a reputation was not necessarily life-threatening, but it might harm promotion prospects. This potential, for many officers, may have been sufficient disincentive. Moreover, moral objections simply were far less likely to be acted upon, if at all, than were pragmatic arguments.[125]

All this notwithstanding, it would be wrong to assume that every pragmatic argument located in the official files masks humane motives. Lieutenant Beck's case certainly affords no such rosy interpretation. This, after all, was a man whose treatment of Jews and Red Army commissars in 1941 had been anything but decent, and whose opprobrious description of Soviet prisoners of war hardly marked him out as a russophile.

Rather, Beck's determination to pursue such an extensive hearts-and-minds effort was purely pragmatic. His bile-spewing description of Soviet POWs at Bialystok may have been a means of "getting things off his chest" before holding his nose and getting down to the necessary business of cultivating the population, rather than surrendering to his natural inclination to terrorize it.

Such pragmatism almost certainly shaped Beck's positive assessment of the population's mood during 1941, and his early appreciation of the necessity of cultivating partnership with it.[126] The Army Group Center Rear Area's Intelligence Section maintained in late 1941 that "any preferential treatment of Russians in German service means that the population's mood is influenced very positively by its own compatriots,"[127] and Beck drew similar conclusions in his own end-of-year report. "The conduct of the German soldier and propaganda of deed," he wrote, "have shown themselves to be the most effective propaganda methods."[128]

But Beck's agenda would never have got as far as it did without the assent of the division's two most important figures, its commander and operations officer. The 707th Infantry Division, for one, is a clear and harrowing example of the influence these offices could wield.

During the Yelnya-Dorogobuzh operations, some of the exhortations made by General Pflugbeil and his successive operations officers, Majors Brenner and Friedrich, to the troops did contain callous echoes of the 707th. This fact is hardly surprising. Not only was General Pflugbeil, as his conduct of 1941 had demonstrated, a very ruthless officer, but the operations also highlighted defects in the division's fighting power, which he and his operations officers were centrally responsible for overcoming. Thus a career-driven desperation for results—results that, in Pflugbeil's case at least, came too late—may have added to the compulsion to urge a new degree of ruthlessness from the troops.

But even Pflugbeil, it seems, was not *so* infected by poisonous ideology and tunnel-mindedness that he failed to see that a measure of cultivation was important also. That he and his operations officers were ready to accept it gave Lieutenant Beck the freedom *he* needed to implement it.

The readiness with which *these* officers embraced hearts-and-minds measures probably reflected the success of the division's cultivation of the population in 1941. Officers who were amoral yet pragmatic were quite capable of engaging the bulk of the population while waging a murderous, terroristic campaign against refugees and Red Army fugitives. Even Major Haupt's pronounced anti-Slavic proclivities did not prevent the division as a whole from pursuing this aim.

In November 1941 the Operations Section reported that armed civilians already constituted nearly half the security forces in the 221st's area. The 221st also expected its Feld- and Ortskommandanturen, and its regiments, to be proactive in OD recruitment. Recruitment had been more extensive than originally intended, the division reported, because the division had seen the OD's value in relieving pressure on the division's own troops by guarding supply dumps, protecting crops, procuring meat, and securing supply routes. OD knowledge of the area had been invaluable as well.[129] The 221st also enjoyed more success than some in its recruitment of eastern troops from the prisoner-of-war population. Army Rear Area 582, by contrast, had declared that the POWs' dislike of Bolshevism was matched only by their unreliability, asserting in December 1941 that "no prisoner enters the Wehrmacht's service out of idealism. The reason he's prepared to is his terror of the POW camp, and the prospect of a better life alongside German troops."[130]

Successes such as these possess a self-reinforcing dynamic. This dynamic was clear in the similarly sensible measures the 221st Security Division employed in the Yelnya-Dorogobuzh operations. Success begat success; Lieutenant Beck's end-of-operations report of 16 June 1942 claimed that in many villages "the population . . . willingly declared itself to the German troops, supplying valuable information about the movements and intentions of the partisans. It supported the Wehrmacht in every way, and in places provided militias for active combating of the partisans."[131] The fact that the report urged the units assuming responsibility for the area to continue operating in a similar vein is also significant; indeed, continuation of such a constructive line was effective in the long term in stifling support in the Yelnya-Dorogobuzh area.[132] Clearly, under the circumstances, partial failure did not faze Beck.

Beck's commitment to cultivation was even stronger in the Gomel region. And here, too, measurable successes were achieved. Among other things, the Intelligence Section claimed it had been able to explain and justify some potentially highly unpopular measures such as requisitioning meat and detaining civilians for security checks.[133] That the partisans sometimes found themselves in an uphill struggle in their own efforts to persuade the population to "come over"—partisan-inspired rumors that the Red Army had broken through at Bryansk and Orel, for instance, reportedly fell on largely deaf ears—also testifies to the 221st's success.[134] Almost certainly, the Intelligence Section talked up its achievements somewhat. Nonetheless, the achievements were tangible. Had they not been, the sheer seriousness of the situation would have compelled the Intelligence Section to give a stronger indication of it—as would indeed increasingly occur during 1943.[135]

Personnel changes at the division's top level in the early summer of 1942, if anything, reduced tendencies to terror further. Neither the Operations Section—commanded from July by Major Hellmuth Kriebel—nor the new divisional commander himself, General Lendle, issued any directives as merciless as those for which their predecessors in the Yelnya-Dorogobuzh operations had been responsible.

By now, divisional command as a whole apparently felt even greater unity of purpose. All division-level elements, it seems, were increasingly aware of their year-long record of success in maintaining constructive relations with the population, and of the fatal damage atrocities could wreak upon those relations.

The contradiction-riven Eastern Army security effort of 1942 both exuded brutality on an enormous scale and displayed emergent signs of a saner approach to antipartisan warfare. The forces that drove the former possessed a terrible potency. Germany's increasingly worrying strategic situation gave the already-pitiless National Socialist aims of the campaign in the east a new momentum. This momentum translated into an increasingly wholesale attempt to subjugate and exploit the Soviet Union as brutally and thoroughly as possible in the name of the Reich's war effort. The antipartisan campaign, like all aspects of the occupation, felt the effects.

Yet the 221st Security Division, a field-level formation that, only months earlier, had practiced the terroristic, nazified maxims of Wehrmacht security policy so enthusiastically, became a strong advocate of a more conciliatory approach during this period. The particular conditions the 221st faced, in both the Yelnya-Dorogobuzh and Gomel regions, compelled such a course. Such were they that, compared to some fellow security divisions, the 221st now lacked both the inclination for antipartisan brutality and the means to dispense it. That said, its perceptions, perceptions shaped by individual factors, departmental agendas, and, most importantly, institutional environment, decided it for this course even more surely. For they were the perceptions of men who, even if they retained a harsh National Socialist faith, were still sensible enough to draw certain lessons from what their own division had experienced of the partisan war already.

Looked at another way, however, the 221st Security Division's cultivation effort assumes a less impressive appearance. For genuine though it was, its effectiveness was hampered from the start by the wider dynamics of Nazi occupation policy, and by the division's own failings in men and material. This issue warrants consideration, for it illustrates the malaise that would-be conciliators in the Eastern Army's antipartisan campaign suffered more widely. And in the 221st Security Division's case, these weaknesses in its cultivation effort would in 1943 contribute to that effort's failure and subsequent reversal.

The division may have held its own antipartisan ruthlessness in check during 1942, but there was a limit to how far it could do the same against the brutal voraciousness of wider occupation policy. Though the population had not necessarily warmed to the partisans as yet, the combination of failed agricultural reform, food requisitioning and starvation, and the press-ganging of native Russians for labor service in the Reich were not a combination that any German hearts-and-minds effort was likely to find easy to sell. As if this were not enough, the 221st Security Division's own shortcomings blighted its cultivation effort further. Eminently sensible though hearts-and-minds measures in antiguerrilla warfare are, the French and British antiguerrilla experts writing earlier in the century were quite clear, on the strength of long experience, that they are most effective when combined with *measured* force: specifically, a certain degree of armed presence to remind the population of potentially unpleasant alternatives to cooperation. They might have added, for the 221st Security Division's benefit, that armed presence also was essential to convince a population fearful of choosing the wrong side that the division indeed could combat the partisans, and protect the population against their vengefulness. Instead, by often forcing supposedly static garrisons to move from pillar to post, scattering the 221st's troops in far-flung outposts along the railway lines, precluding the long-term stationing of German troops in villages within partisan striking distance, and generally preventing the 221st Security Division from maintaining that sufficient degree of armed presence among the population on an at least semi-permanent basis, the same overstretch that compelled the division to pursue cultivation simultaneously undermined that cultivation.

Nor was the 221st able to implement the political component of the equation urged by General Gallieni, the turn-of-the-century antiguerrilla guru of French North Africa, who had stressed the combined use of politics *and* force in such warfare.[136] Politics, too, requires manpower, as well as administrative acumen, and the 221st lacked both.

It was all very well, for example, for the commander of Second Panzer Army to urge his troops to avoid "indiscriminate slaughter."[137] Such advice simply required restraint. Genuinely viable constructive engagement, encompassing rigorous propaganda directed at both population and potential partisan deserters, together with the comprehensive measures in housing, economics, education, and the other sinews of the "organization of the country and its inhabitants" of which Gallieni had written, required administrative ability, resources, and effort.[138]

During the Yelnya-Dorogobuzh operations, the 221st's highly mobile, temporary presence in the region freed it from worrying about establishing the administrative apparatus it would have needed in the event of a longer-term occupation. The measures it enacted— decent day-to-day treatment of the population, enticement of deserters, bribery—were intended to facilitate the short-term aim of defeating a particular partisan group. Such measures required correspondingly less time and fewer resources.

Long-term tenure in the Gomel region posed very different requirements. Here, an effective ordering of the population's social and economic life was essential to viable long-term occupation. Instead, the shortage of German administrative personnel imposed by the size of the Feld- and Ortskommandanturen made the 221st excessively reliant, like all security divisions, on native administrators and auxiliary police of at best highly variable quality. The execrable reputation for corruption, thuggery, and incompetence that many of these shabby characters gained across the population reflected their unsuitability for the job. In this respect, too, the 221st Security Division's constructive engagement effort rested on rotten props.

Essentially, the 221st Security Division's hearts-and-minds campaign was not a well-resourced enterprise combining cultivation measures with measured force to optimum effect. Rather, it was an effort severely compromised by both the message it had to sell and its own concrete shortcomings. Lieutenant Beck may have seen its value as early as 1941, but in 1942 the division as a whole pursued it simply because, given its circumstances, cultivation was the only means of providing it with some kind of respite. All of which helps explain the signs, already gathering by late 1942, of this effort's ultimate failure: while the 221st Security Division's constructive engagement effort might still be slowing the process of accommodation between partisans and population, that process clearly was gathering pace.

In any case, with Operation Zugspitze, which the 221st Security Division executed in its northeastern sector in February 1943, the longer-term portents for the division's behavior assumed more ominous form. The ban on burning villages, which the division had imposed for the second Ankara operation, was lifted for Zugspitze. Behind this decision, probably, was a mixture of security-related and economic motives. For one thing, the 221st may have felt after Ankara II that it needed to exploit more fully the opportunities provided by winter. Winter, after all, was when snow tracks and frozen swamps rendered the task of hunting partisans and penetrating their arboreal strongholds easier. It was also when the particular harshness of the partisans' living conditions made them especially vulnerable to attacks on their supplies.[139]

There may also have been pressure from above. The 221st's critique of deserter policy had, perhaps, fueled higher-level perceptions that the division was taking constructive engagement a little too far. In a climate that, for now at least, was marked by a mood of ruthlessness initiated at the very highest level, some countering of such perceptions may have been necessary. The Zugspitze directive certainly would have met this requirement.

Most fundamentally, however, the irrepressible tide of rising partisan activity was creating a sense of impotent, brutalizing frustration that was finally beginning to cancel out moderation.

6

Locusts in Field Gray

From early 1943, the increasing likelihood of ultimate German defeat accelerated the growing accommodation between population and partisans. A situation even more ideal for a burgeoning and increasingly active partisan movement emerged. Thus was the German security effort in the Army Group Center Area assailed by a surge in activity from partisans better equipped, better trained, and, most important, better supported by the population than ever before. The 221st Security Division's response would lead, by the summer of 1943, to a policy that would put its relatively enlightened direction of 1942 into reverse: a policy to lay waste "pro-bandit" regions and turn them into "dead zones."

The Red Army's offensives in the winter of 1941–42 had already tarnished the Eastern Army's aura of invincibility. The events of the winter of 1942–43 shattered it. While the German thrust southward into the Caucasus had continued unabated throughout the autumn of 1942, the fury of the fighting amid the rubble of the shattered city of Stalingrad had exacted a horrible toll of lives and resources on both sides. The German Sixth Army's failure to capture the city completely was followed, during the second half of November, by its own encirclement by the Red Army. On the nineteenth of that month, the Soviets launched a winter counteroffensive that, in a matter of days, had entombed the Sixth Army in the "Stalingrad pocket." They then swept down on the rear of the German forces in the Caucasus, forcing them to turn tail and flee westward before they, too, were cut off. The fate of the Sixth Army itself is well known: enveloped by the Red Army, forbidden by Hitler to break out to unite with the German forces to the west, it succumbed to cold, hunger, disease, and a final Red Army assault in January 1943. As the vestiges of the Sixth Army staggered off to captivity and, in most cases, death in the prison camps of Siberia, the Eastern Army, like the Reich in its entirety, began facing up to the hitherto-unthinkable possibility of ultimate defeat.

Spring did provide respite, stabilization at the front, and, indeed, limited German success in a counteroffensive that recaptured the city of Kharkov. Thus were Hitler and the High Command able to contemplate a renewal of offensive action, if only one that, in view of the shifting balance of manpower and resources to the Soviet Union, was designed simply to give the Soviets a bloody nose, stabilize the Eastern Front, and release troops to face the impending Anglo-American assault on western Europe. For Operation Citadel, intended to destroy the Kursk salient that straddled the gap between Army Groups Center and South, the Germans further thinned their manpower along the rest of the front and amassed all the armored attacking power that the Reich's factories could produce and the Eastern Army could muster.

In the event, prior warning and the increasing strength and sophistication of Soviet military operations enabled the Red Army to assemble such a volume of troops and fortifications in the Kursk salient that Citadel was dead in the water before the first Tiger tank started to roll. When the Germans pressed ahead anyway, the cream of the Panzer divisions was annihilated. Though it wasn't necessarily obvious at the time, this "death ride of the Panzers," the destruction of the Reich's last source of offensive potency in the east, and the immense Red Army counterattacks against the weakened sectors of German front in the Bryansk and Orel regions that followed it had sealed the Eastern Army's doom.

Such cataclysmic events, together with simultaneous defeats at the hands of the western Allies in North Africa and the Mediterranean, had a pivotal effect on the partisan war. All of them intensified both Germany's strategic plight, and the concomitant readiness of the Reich's elites to rape the Soviet Union of its economic and human resources in the name of "total war." This new degree of rapacity could only alienate the population and drive it even more firmly into the arms of the partisans. And this development in turn rendered the German occupation still more incapable of balancing the need for economic exploitation with those of viable, long-term pacification and engagement. Nor, given unfolding events at the front, was there much point in the population's supporting the German occupation anyway.[1] Meanwhile, committing so many increasingly precious troops to both offensive and defensive action on the battlefronts continued to starve the Eastern Army's antipartisan effort of the necessary quality and quantity of manpower and equipment.

For all these reasons, partisan growth in the Army Group Center Area mushroomed in 1943. The partisan movement in Belorussia, the Germans estimated, grew from 57,000 in January 1943 to 103,600 in September. Across the German rear as a whole, numbers swelled from 130,000 to 250,000.[2]

An alarmingly extensive portion of the Army Group Center Rear Area now slipped beyond German control.[3] Three main areas within the general area of Army Group Center were firmly in partisan hands: the Bryansk forests, the Polotsk-Lepel districts, and around Bobruisk. Though the partisans had yet to secure a majority of rear-area territory, the population of the "twilight zones" caught between both sides was increasingly willing to support them. The Germans themselves increasingly fell back on the towns and cities and the areas immediately surrounding them. By August 1943, Army Group Center was reporting that only 23 percent of its area could be considered "pacified." Thirty-one percent was endangered by the partisans; a full 46 percent was under complete partisan control.[4] The partisans themselves, thanks partly to an increasingly favorable front-line situation that allowed the Red Air Force to increase the supply of instructors, technical expertise, and weaponry, became better trained, organized, and equipped.[5]

All this took place at a time when the quality and quantity of the German forces ranged against them continued to fall well below the level of what was needed. The deterioration in the 221st Security Division's situation, and its increasing impotence in the face of it, mirrored the wider picture. So wanting was its fighting power, so debilitating the overextension from which it was suffering, that it was increasingly unable either to combat surging partisan activity or to deploy its troops in partisan-endangered areas for any meaningful stretch of time.

The minor operations it executed in early spring brought little respite. Even where they were partially successful, these areas, too, were soon infested with partisans again. Forced recruitment, in some areas extended up to fifty-five-year-olds, enabled the partisans to establish entirely new groups. Instructors were being parachuted in, and Soviet officers had assumed control of partisan training and leadership.[6] With their territory's inexorable growth, the partisans were bearing down on railway lines, highways, and strongpoints with ever-greater force and frequency. April, the 221st's Operations Section reported, saw "the unrest in the entire divisional area [reach] dangerous proportions. Everywhere, valuable economic installations—depots, dairies, distilleries, and so on—were attacked and in places burned down. Raiding and plunder of villages and murder of village headmen and other pro-German inhabitants became the order of the day. The inadequacy of the force available severely restricted the division's attempts to combat this mushrooming threat."[7]

Mushrooming was indeed the word. There were 131 clashes with the partisans during May 1943, in contrast with just 59 during February. In April and May alone, partisan attacks on villages rose in number from 140 to 308, sabotage acts from 87 to 233. All this ensued just after the 221st had had to relinquish three of its battalions to duties elsewhere.[8]

The mounting strain exacerbated the decline in the division's fighting power. Moreover, mobile antipartisan operations combined with the unrealistic demands of passive security further restricted opportunities for the training that might yet at least have slowed that decline.[9] As training levels sank, so did discipline and morale. Lieutenant André, an Operations Section officer inspecting security posts along the Gomel-Dovsk-Cherikoff railway in April, reported that strongpoints were being left unfortified and uncamouflaged, that the squads available for their defense were too small, and that the troops manning them sometimes chose simply to vegetate in their living quarters rather than guard the bridges as they were supposed to.[10] Another cause for consternation was the widening gap in the quality of German and partisan equipment. Reports multiplied of partisan groups that were not only numerous but also, thanks to the Red Air Force's supply efforts, increasingly well armed. The 45th Security Regiment, one of the 221st's subordinate units, described the inevitable results: "Many times our railway patrols have come to grips with enemy mine-layers, but on every occasion the bandits have been equipped with machine-pistols and our own troops have not. For this reason, despite the fact that the actions are often fought at extremely close quarters, it is never possible to establish the enemy's losses. In the darkness, directly after the moment of surprise has gone, the rifleman hardly ever has the chance to fire a second shot. The regiment wishes to stress the psychological effects of all this upon the troops."[11]

Nor could the division find solace in its Ordnungsdienst (OD) units. Despite significant improvements in their equipment, they fell far short of what was needed to keep pace with the expansion to which the 221st, whose reliance upon them was increasingly pressing, was subjecting them. Unsurprisingly, OD morale was sinking further, OD desertion to the partisans rising correspondingly. Desertion was being fueled not only by the worsening situation at the front, and all the fearful apprehensions of Soviet vengeance against collaborators that came with it, but also, more so even than in 1942, by partisans' cultivation of captured OD men.[12]

The OD's increasingly miserable showing in the service of the Reich was attested to by the German officers who witnessed it. Feldkommandantur 528 (V), for one, did little to conceal its rising anger at its eastern auxiliaries. In one instance, it reported, after a Sergeant Gebauer of the military police had been killed leading an OD squad against partisans, the squad had failed to pursue the partisans immediately. Their excuse had been that they had felt too shaken by the death of Gebauer, to whom they had been devoted, to be capable of decisive action.[13] More alarming still was a report from the first battalion of the 8th SS Police Regiment. An officer of this unit, which was operating in the 221st's still especially vexatious northeastern sector, had been ordered to build a strongpoint in Bazun and man it with OD. But when the OD men accompanying him had been thus instructed, they had simply waited for the detachment from the battalion itself to depart, and then disappeared one by one.[14] By June the OD's evaporating reliability was meeting with sneering contempt from Feldkommandantur 516 and the Feldkommandantur in Gomel also.[15]

With a shortfall, in the face of snowballing partisan activity, of five battalions since February, the 221st Security Division's impotence was emphasized in a report of 11 June.[16] The division was not entirely powerless; in that month it at least managed to prevent the number of partisan attacks on the railways from increasing. But with interminable spells of guard duty and other rigors of passive security pushing the troops' endurance to the limit, such successes were bought at mounting cost. The division predicted further imminent deterioration at the beginning of July. "While the average age of other security regiments many not be so high, or the signs of strain so clear, as they are in the case of Security Battalion 242," the Operations Section reported, "the sudden loss of a strongpoint is always possible under current conditions. Everything boils down to the fact that . . . there is no prospect of reinforcement. This means first that the demands [on the division] are always increasing, and second that there is often no possibility of leave."[17]

In part, the division's response to its plight did sustain its hearts-and-minds effort of 1942. It was not alone in this respect. Indeed, a December 1942 conference of high-level representatives of the

Army High Command, the Armed Forces High Command, and Rosenberg's Eastern Ministry in Berlin had already made a higher-level case for constructive engagement.[18] In April 1943, Colonel Gehlen of Foreign Armies East forwarded proposals for better treatment of partisan deserters. Three months later, "Basic Order No. 13a," issued by the Army High Command, directed that partisans deserting outside a combat situation be given preferential treatment, and that partisans surrendering in the course of combat be accorded the same treatment as prisoners of war. Units in the field persisted with their propaganda efforts, and some increasingly advocated a degree of self-government for the occupied territories.[19] The more powerful, rapacious, and terroristic dynamics of the German occupation ultimately would render these efforts fruitless, but the individuals who made them were not yet deterred. In the antipartisan effort itself, meanwhile, the spread of partisan territory would by late 1943 lead to the foundation of fortified "strategic hamlets" peopled by pro-German collaborators.[20] For the 221st itself, the memory of its earlier hearts-and-minds success and the languishing position it still occupied on Army Group Center's list of manpower priorities made continuation of some form of cultivation even more compelling.

Thus did the 221st's cultivation effort that spring not only encompass employment of tried and tested methods, but also echo the call for more fundamental change in higher-level policy.[21] Beck's report for May asserted that while many civilians still felt cause to fight the partisans, their willingness could be harnessed effectively only if a nationalist Belorussian government, similar in form to the governments in Burma and Manchuria installed by the Japanese, were formed in the very near future.[22] Beck combined his call for reform with a withering assault on propaganda tactics that employed practically meaningless, cliché-ridden slogans such as "the battle against Bolshevism,"[23] and signaled his despair at the effects of the ruthlessness and exploitation of occupation policy in general. "The enormous moral credit that the German Wehrmacht possessed at the time of the invasion has almost completely evaporated," he wrote, "and belief in German victory destroyed. This is due to our mistaken perception of the Russians, and in particular, our tendency to draw no distinction between Russians generally and Bolsheviks specifically."[24]

The division's ongoing commitment to a relatively humane policy was particularly pronounced over Operation Csobo, a Hungarian-led operation that took place in its jurisdiction at the beginning of July. Initially the joint directive that the 221st's Operations and Quartermaster's Sections issued for Csobo adhered to the cold, calculating principle of determining the "reliability" of villages, and therefore their fate, on the basis of their economic worth. Requisitions, it ordered, must be restricted to quota level only in the villages that were to be spared. Quickly, however, this last part of the order was changed to cover *all* villages.[25] Following this, the Operations Section contacted the division's liaison officer with Hungarian VIII Corps with more sweeping instructions: "The division requests that the Hungarian troops refrain from any evacuation, destruction of villages, or reprisal action in the course of the operations. The division wishes to point out that the general burning of villages and measures directed against the population are strictly forbidden by order of the army group commander."[26]

The Hungarians ignored this instruction, slaughtered 900 people during the operation itself, and then complained about the 221st's excessive leniency to Army Group Center:

> In the course of Csaba [*sic*] it has been necessary to annihilate entire villages within the operational area and resettle their inhabitants. From communication with the 221st Security Division it has become clear, however, that the divisional command, as the senior field command, is opposed to this policy. I must urgently emphasize that only the most radical pursuit of this policy will prevent the partisans and inhabitants from pouring back in a very short space of time and polluting the area once more.[27]

The dreadful death toll the Hungarians exacted, and their commander's indignation at the questioning of such methods, may partly reflect the fact that Hungarian security units were if anything even more poorly equipped on the whole, and therefore even more likely to lash out in frustration than were their German counterparts. Certainly, the particularly pitiful condition of many Hungarian units fueled their brutal behavior in the Army Group South Rear Area during 1942.[28] That said, the 221st's fighting power, with all the hardships the division had undergone, was by now probably little better than that of the Hungarians. In any case, the Hungarians' fighting power is unlikely to have been so much worse that it explains fully the vast difference between what the 221st wanted from the operation and the scale of the death toll the Hungarians delivered. Moreover, the 221st's restraint on this occasion contrasted not just with the Hungarians but also with one of its own subordinate units; a report by the third battalion of the 45th Security Regiment had earmarked twenty-two "bandit-friendly" villages for destruction in the course of Csobo.[29] All this testifies to the fact that, increasingly severe though its own circumstances now were, the 221st's division-level officers remained better able than many to see that restraint was warranted.

All that said, this conciliatory spirit was increasingly challenged during 1943. Overall, the 221st Security Division's prosecution of antipartisan warfare became markedly harsher. Operation Zugspitze had signaled it. The quite grotesquely named Operation Easter Bunny, which the 221st executed in the middle of its jurisdiction at the end of April 1943, reiterated it with awful clarity.

Easter Bunny took place in a region that particularly exasperated the 221st. During April the partisans had stepped up their attacks on the railway system there with particular force.[30] Easter Bunny was an operation, like many others by now, that explicitly targeted the partisans' source of supply. The division-level green light to burn villages enabled the units involved, as in Zugspitze, to carry out requisitioning on a scale that left nothing behind.[31] In the event, although Easter Bunny involved fewer units than either Ankara operation, it requisitioned more than twice as much livestock as either.[32]

Yet Easter Bunny was merely the harbinger of a brutal new phase in the 221st Security Division's antipartisan campaign. This new ruthlessness was not just a frustrated, desperate response to increasingly intractable conditions. Also crucial in fueling it was the realization, which division-level officers increasingly seem to have shared, that constructive engagement no longer countered those conditions effectively.

If the 221st's extensive hearts-and-minds campaign of 1942 already had contained seeds of failure, failure is what it increasingly faced in 1943. Both popular anti-German ire and the partisans' prevailing exploitation of it were building. Seizure of villagers for labor service in the Reich intensified. As a result, not only were "most civilians earmarked for labor service fleeing their villages," but "the effects of 'good news' from the Reich," presumably letters or public talks by eastern workers on leave, had "all but dried up."[33]

More important still was the rising specter of Soviet victory. "The population sees the increasing activity of the Red Air Force and the growing number of bombing raids," the Intelligence Section reported, "and the rumors of increasing difficulties at the front grow stronger. These rumors eclipse all others."[34] The overall effect was to focus civilian minds on the likely situation not just if, but when, the Germans were eventually driven out.[35] The presence of tens of thousands of troops from the Italian Eighth Army during February helped the 221st Security Division not one iota. These troops had staggered into the division's area after being trounced in the winter battles in southern Russia, and their morale and discipline were dangerously low. They marauded and seized Russian houses and accosted Russian women and girls, but also, and most worryingly for the 221st, they spread defeatist talk that fueled the growing perception that the hour of Soviet triumph was at hand.[36] At the end of April, the Intelligence Section reported that "the successes of the Red Army and the rising partisan activity in the rear areas, skillfully exploited and exaggerated by enemy propaganda, have almost totally destroyed the population's belief in the victory of German arms."[37] The observations of Economic Detachment Vitebsk, stationed farther north, would have resonated greatly with the 221st's officers.

The governing principle in the population's behavior, the detachment asserted, was that "loyalty lies where the power lies."[38] It must have been clear to the officers and men of the 221st that this principle was now working firmly against them.

All this meant that partisan success in winning over ever-greater swathes of the population, by whatever means, could only increase. While terror wrought upon collaborators remained a central tool in the partisans' armory, their cultivation of the wider population was increasingly inventive. Not wishing to antagonize the population in their immediate vicinity, they conducted their press-ganging sprees as far from their home base as possible. In fact, far from plundering neighboring villages, they increasingly sought to supply them. Such requisitioning as the partisans did carry out in these villages was inflicted on the families of German-appointed administrators or OD men. Overall, the partisans were now seeing that surly, press-ganged civilians made far less effective recruits. Instead, through their deeds, they must win willing volunteers.[39] Corporal Meynecken, a soldier of the 221st Security Division who managed to escape partisan captivity, described what he had seen of the results:

The population of every village was in a good mood. Everywhere the bandits were welcomed and fed, and so far as I could see this was all done willingly and without any pressure from the bandits themselves. The bandits had brought two accordions with them, which they brought out at every village they rested in for the villagers to dance to. The villagers didn't seem at all intimidated when they chatted with the bandits. The bandits, too, seemed in a remarkably good mood. I was made to watch while they danced to harmonica music.[40]

Hearts and minds also were being lost among eastern units.[41] The partisans were launching ever-more-strenuous efforts to reeducate captured members of the OD, the eastern battalions, and the native civilian administration:

Hand-written, printed leaflets targeting the OD and other native units have been found, encouraging the reader to desert with his weapon, appealing to his national honor and also employing the standard scare tactics depicting the grisly revenge that the already advancing Red Army will inflict upon all OD men. There is particular emphasis on "fantasy totals" of German dead, as well as the names of OD deserters who are praised for enticing more of their comrades to desert with their weapons. Of particular note were a number of personal hand-written letters by bandit chiefs to mayors and other civilians, threatening them with the most dire consequences if they continued working for the Germans. Leaflet raids and distribution have been reported in all districts; lately they are being distributed in the marketplaces.[42]

The division's own response looked increasingly desperate. The Operations Section tried bribery. "In order to give some substance to the constant announcements of a reward system for the OD," it announced on 6 July, "a representative of Section VII is to be responsible in every larger operation for ensuring that the belongings of bandits and bandit accomplices are secured for distribution to the OD."[43] The division had already started "rewarding" OD personnel and headmen with requisitions seized in antipartisan operations. But reports show that the sheer magnitude of the OD problem was beyond the 221st's powers to solve.[44]

By early summer the partisans were establishing illegal printing presses in towns such as Novosybkov, and seducing the population with cut-price salt and textiles. Their influence was especially strong among the youth of the region. "Youth is especially receptive to partisan propaganda," the Intelligence Section reported, because it saw the terroristic, exploitative straitjacket of German occupation as "robbing it of all prospects in life."[45] It described partisan propaganda as "skillful and up-to-date, [exploiting] all the latest developments as far as it can."

Even in areas still ill disposed toward the partisans, the 221st's powerlessness to combat them guaranteed its own troops a decidedly cool reception. Thus reported the 930th Security Regiment:

> The population is in two minds about the troops . . . On the one hand, they know they have nothing to fear from German soldiers; on the other, heavy propaganda activity by the bandits arouses great distrust of the troops, especially in those areas that have felt little of our presence. The fear of being named a traitor by one's neighbor and turned over to the partisans is hindering people from giving precise statements about bandit movements. It was also clear that of all the headmen whom we came across, none could name or wanted to name anybody suspected of helping the partisans. It is obvious from this that no headman feels that his life is safe.[46]

Indeed, with partisan influence spreading inexorably and German influence receding, German-appointed native administrators were covertly shifting allegiance in ever-greater numbers. "Time and again," the Intelligence Section reported, "official directives are followed only if the force is there to impose them." Practically speaking, this increasingly meant never.[47]

And by now, faced as it was by an increasingly ominous partisan threat, the 221st's lack of men and material was undermining its hearts-and-minds effort more directly. With both Red Air Force and partisan attacks on the railways increasing, propaganda supply was being severely disrupted.[48] The propaganda staffs themselves were stretched intolerably. During March most of the propaganda staff in Gomel, assigned to particular antipartisan operations as they were, were quite unable to organize any general talks and displays for the population. During April, in the course of one of the desperate cleanouts of potential manpower to which the Reich increasingly was resorting, it had to relinquish thirteen of its younger men for duty elsewhere.[49] "In its current state," it was soon reporting, "this unit is unworthy of the title 'propaganda staff.'"[50] Nor was the propaganda staff in Klintsy spared; much of its propaganda material went up in smoke when its headquarters was bombed.[51]

In July the 221st Security Division tried to saturate its area with its biggest output of propaganda literature yet. Its propaganda troops distributed 178,000 newspapers and magazines, 60,050 brochures, 250,000 placards, and 813,700 leaflets, provided school and youth propaganda with the newspaper *Skolnik* and the teachers' journal *Schule und Erziehung*, and supplied picture books for kindergartens.[52] All of this was pointless: across the board, the portents of ultimate failure were clear. The cause of the pro-German army raised by the renegade Russian general Vlasov, in the 221st's jurisdiction as across the Army Group Center Rear Area, fell completely flat.[53] The level of voluntary popular participation in the "celebrations" of the anniversary of the German invasion, the "day of liberation" of 22 June, was pathetic. "Voluntary participation," the Intelligence Section reported, "was incredibly weak. 'We can't see what there is to celebrate,' the people said. 'For us, it's a day of mourning.'"[54]

Those potentially more hawkish elements within the 221st, the Operations and Quartermaster's Sections, must by now have been doubting the efficacy of hearts-and-minds measures seriously. Granted, they may still have felt ready to accept a measure of cultivation, but mounting desperation and frustration probably buttressed the belief that it was now time, in the absence of any better ideas, to see if intensified coercion might bring results where cultivation clearly was failing to. General Lendle, too, in sanctioning the hardening of policy embodied in the orders for Easter Bunny, was by now probably increasingly persuaded to coerce a little more, cultivate a little less.

In other words, even if the overall effect on the 221st was not as dramatic as it might have been, the pressure of the emergent situation the division now faced was creating a bridge for the return of at least some of the markedly harsher attitudes of old.

As it was, the apparent conversion of that onetime bastion of constructive engagement, the Intelligence Section, was indeed dramatic. In July 1943 Captain Beck—following his promotion in May

—showed a newfound enthusiasm for such harsh antipartisan measures as the evacuation of villages. "Evacuating villages in the bandit areas has a detrimental effect upon the bandits," he wrote. "It prevents them from filling their ranks with the inhabitants, and the supply of food, which came primarily from the inhabitants of the evacuated villages, is no longer possible. When the bandits are prevented from harvesting and exploiting the best land, this affects their supply severely, and impairs their mood greatly."[55]

More strikingly still, Beck's ideological fervor came to the fore for the first time in two years. It was clearest of all in the content of the propaganda the Intelligence Section was now distributing to potential partisan deserters. Back in June, the Intelligence Section had contemptuously dismissed anti-Bolshevik sloganeering as a rallying call to the population. It was precisely this kind of claptrap, however, to which the Intelligence Section now resorted in its efforts to entice partisan deserters. A supplement to the Intelligence Section's report for January–August 1943, compiled in November, asserted that "the Jews and Bolsheviks are mercilessly leading millions of your brothers, fathers, and sons to certain death, in order to save their own miserable skins. Russian lives and Russian blood count for as little now as they did before the war. So long as life is treating him well, the Jew-Bolshevik is unmoved by the worst sufferings of the people."[56]

It was not that Beck had given up on cultivation. But desperation, it seems, was driving him to means of cultivation that held a deep personal resonance for him—an unreconstructed appeal to anti-Bolshevism and anti-Semitism—and blinded him to the likelihood that they were doomed to fail as well. Omer Bartov argues that from 1943, as the situation became more hopeless, the troops' ideological convictions were strengthened by their need to feel that their suffering was in a noble cause.[57] Beck may well have been undergoing a similar process.

A final inducement to a more ruthless kind of antipartisan warfare, and a massive one, was economic calculation.

By the spring of 1943 neither the 221st Security Division nor Economic Detachment Gomel could ignore the damage that partisan

activity was wreaking upon the economic life of the division's jurisdiction. "As far as agriculture is concerned," the detachment's Agricultural Section reported, "the security situation has deteriorated
again. By night the entire region becomes the partisans' area of operations. From every forest, fires burn and rockets climb into the air to
light the way for the Red Air Force."[58] The March report of the Economic Inspectorate Center singled out the 221st's area as one of special concern: "In Economic Detachment Klintsy's area the security
situation has worsened further . . . bands of several hundred, sometimes over a thousand, rove through the region paralyzing all economic activity and destroying dairies, tractor stations, and depots."[59]
Supply of food and labor from the region, at a time when the Reich's
need for both was increasingly pressing, was thoroughly incapaci-
tated. What the Reich was denied, moreover, the partisans gained.
The inexorable spread of partisan territory could only heighten the
situation's urgency.

In May, as partisan activity increased, Economic Detachment
Klintsy grew more pessimistic still. The most endangered areas were
Chechersk, Buda-Kochelevskava, and Klimov; in Klimov particularly, fearful reports of plunder and murder were flooding in daily.[60]
Moreover, bombing raids were killing many agricultural workers,
unsettling the rest, and causing production to tumble even further.[61]
By now, the 221st's Operations Section reported, partisan activity
had caused collection of agricultural products and taxes to fall, and
only supply points in the major towns could be defended.[62]

And the 221st had even more direct reason to worry: all this
threatened its own troops' food supply. The rear security forces were
already being deprived to favor their front-line colleagues. In mid-
April the Army Group Center Rear Area fixed the daily ration for
fresh potatoes at a maximum of 500 grams.[63]

In the 221st's jurisdiction, the debilitation was clearest among the
men of the 183d Security Regiment.[64] At the beginning of July the
regimental commander, Colonel Alfred Kessler, reported that "the
men don't understand why they are being supplied at this time of
year with dry vegetables, which are neither nourishing nor appetiz-

ing." The resulting food was atrocious even if it had been prepared by an expert—which in most cases, because most outposts lacked a proper cook, it had not. Normally the troops received four pieces of bread daily on which to spread 15 grams of fat. "This, as I have already reported, is barely enough for a single slice of bread. Of course, it's possible in theory to spread 15 grams over four slices. But you can hardly see it." Kessler stressed that the troops' morale, already damaged by the fact that their families lived mainly in one of the most heavily bombed areas of the Reich, was endangered even more acutely by hunger. Most ominously, he pointed out, the troops saw their food situation as no better than that which had presaged the collapse of morale in the German Army in 1918.

Pitilessly utilitarian logic suggested only one solution to this malaise: a dead zones policy. The all-embracing plunder and devastation of "bandit areas" that such a policy would encompass was unlikely to offset economic losses completely, but it would offset them to some extent.

Finally, of particular import to the burgeoning needs of the German war economy, dead zones policy could also yield a new source of forced labor. This, given the Reich's ever-more-desperate need for eastern workers and the increasing ineffectiveness of all other attempts to provide it, was a pressing consideration indeed. The 221st's Intelligence Section later reported that "despite every conceivable propaganda effort by the division itself, the population's resistance [to labor service] was so strong that the recruitment in July 1943 of the 1925–1926 year groups was a total failure in most areas of the division's jurisdiction."[65] Economic Detachment Klintsy's Agricultural Section was asserting as early as June that "forced labor recruitment is having an extremely bad propaganda effect," and arguing that, "so as to show the peaceful areas that they may work under German protection, it would be better to carry out labor recruitment in unpacified areas."[66] The drive for eastern workers was stepped up by a directive issued by Sauckel, the Reich plenipotentiary for labor, on 21 July. From 1 August, it ordered, the greater portion of the

Army Group Center jurisdiction, encompassing both the Army Group Rear Area and the rear areas of Army Group Center's individual armies, was to be combed weekly for an additional 3,800 workers.[67]

The immediate push to a dead zones policy in the 221st's jurisdiction, though, seems to have come from developments on the ground. Mounting partisan attacks on economic installations in July finally compelled the 221st to recognize the full danger that the "bandit areas" posed:

> In the farthest corner of the extensive bandit territory around Korma, Krasnopolye, and Chechersk, the farmers are forced under threat of reprisal to thresh grain immediately after harvest, and hand nearly all of it over at the partisan airfield in Osinovka. The bandits, then, are not just restricting themselves to destroying economic concerns through attack and sabotage; increasingly, they are trying to deny the crops to the occupying troops . . . Bandit-ruled territory has been progressively isolated from neighboring areas, and the movement of civilians within it restricted with draconian methods, with the result that whole tracts of the divisional area have been cut off. Our own propaganda effort has been largely expelled from such areas. These areas constitute a severe danger, because enemy forces, including airborne troops, are able to gather within them.[68]

For the 221st, plagued by rising partisan activity, economic chaos, and its own dwindling ability to counter either, the appeal of a policy cultivating select parts of its territory and evacuating and devastating the rest would have been clear.

The decision to restrict its hold to only parts of its jurisdiction was not the only thing that allowed the 221st Security Division to direct its troops to devastate the rest. Relief from newly arrived Hungarian forces at the beginning of July released the troops the 221st needed to execute such devastation.[69] Partly in anticipation of this reinforcement, the division announced what it called a "galvanizing of the bandit war" on 25 June.[70]

Dead zones policy did not necessarily mean unleashing a frenzy of barbarism. Put coldly, the indiscriminate killing of potential workers was of no use to anybody. With Economic Detachment Klintsy's Agricultural Section and later Army Group Center itself urging heightened priority for seizure of labor, then, the officers commanding the 221st Security Division's operations that summer would have been acutely aware of the need to keep their troops on some kind of leash. Thus did the 25 June directive, which covered several envisaged operations, order requisition of crops and livestock up to quota level, evacuation and burning of "villages serving as bandit bases," seizure of able-bodied men for labor service, and propaganda measures to "explain and justify" the measures to the population and entice forced partisan recruits to desert.[71] What it envisioned, in other words, was a uniform, systematic execution of dead zones policy, with no room for unbridled brutality. On 4 July, for instance, the division ordered "evacuation, reprisals, and destruction of villages only with division's authorization" in an operation to be carried out by the 183d Security Regiment.[72] The low number of partisans whom the 221st recorded killed in combat during July and August indicates that it did indeed impress its troops with the need for some element of restraint. During July, the apparent height of the 221st's dead zones policies, only seventy-two partisans were recorded as killed in combat by the division's troops as opposed to the division's sixty-four dead.[73]

Yet the fact that the division's troops didn't unleash an unfettered bloodbath themselves during these operations does not detract from a fundamental truth: the overwhelming reality of dead zones policy was dreadful. For one thing, many "suspects" caught during the operations almost certainly were then exposed to the tender mercies of the Einsatzgruppen or the Wehrmacht's own Secret Field Police. Death at the hands of either was a distinct possibility. "Suspect, non-able-bodied elements," mainly women, children, and the elderly, whose suspect status could combine with their "economic uselessness" to doom them, would have been particularly vulnerable. And the number of such "suspect" elements was potentially enormous; so influential and widespread was the partisan movement by now that huge swathes of the population could scarcely avoid helping it in some way or other. Though there is no actual record that the 221st issued a directive that, as elsewhere in the Army Group Center Area, envisioned the wholesale transfer of "useless" people to the Einsatzgruppen or Secret Field Police, this absence does not mean that such a directive was not issued. It is possible, then, that the 221st's dead zone operations initiated a horrendous degree of killing even if it wasn't necessarily committed by the division's troops themselves.

And the 221st's troops, though they may not have been party to mass killing themselves, were certainly party to mass destruction. Thus could Economic Detachment Klintsy report that, between 1 and 11 July, "Mglin district has largely been evacuated and burned to the ground. Over the next few weeks, the remaining crops there will need to be gathered . . . Likewise in the district of Slinka, twelve villages have been burned down in the course of a military operation."[74] The 221st had even more personal reason to desire the wholesale requisitioning such destruction facilitated; increasingly, the need to keep the OD sweet demanded it. Thus did the orders for Operation Summer Festival, for instance, direct the troops to distribute some of the requisitions among "deserving" headmen and OD personnel.[75]

This litany of mass requisitioning, wholesale destruction of villages, evacuation, uprooting and effective enslavement of much of the population, and liquidation of the rest, shows more than anything else how far the 221st's divisional level came to favor the whip over the sugar during 1943.

The turning tide of the entire war had disastrous ripple effects for the Eastern Army antipartisan campaign during 1943. For one thing, defeats at Stalingrad and Kursk and against the western Allies magnified both the acuteness of Germany's strategic situation and the readiness of her elites to ransack the occupied Soviet Union in the name of "total war." But as well as eroding crucial popular support by "unleashing the locusts," the changing fortunes of war eroded it further by obliterating any lingering belief among the occupied population that the Soviet Union might lose the war. As popular support fueled partisan numbers and effectiveness, moreover, the increasingly dire situation at the front continued to deprive the security divisions of men and material.

For the 221st Security Division, these combined developments rendered constructive engagement increasingly ineffective. Soviet victories and general German rapacity made the product it had to sell even less viable and attractive than before. The ongoing, indeed worsening, thinning of the troops across its jurisdiction continued to hamstring its ability, so crucial to complementing hearts-and-minds measures, to maintain a sufficiently permanent presence among enough of the population enough of the time. Indeed, by now great swathes of the 221st's jurisdiction, like the entire Army Group Center Rear Area, were so firmly under partisan control that the division could not even attempt to "engage" their populations anyway. For the division simply was no longer in charge. And by now, shortages in manpower and resources, in the shape of increasingly skeletal propaganda staffs and unreliable supply of propaganda material, were also hitting the constructive engagement effort more directly.

Moreover, the veritable explosion of partisan activity from the spring of 1943 and, in particular, partisan control of agriculture and labor created an urgency for which the longer-term, "softly softly" approach of constructive engagement could offer no immediate solution anyway. Partisans, and the local populations that were seen to support them, needed to be hit hard and hit fast. The "plunder operations" that resulted, of course, forced the division to reduce its efforts in the spheres of wider pacification and engagement even more. In 1943, however, the main priorities were not long-term pacification and engagement, but immediate exploitation and short-term damage. Relations with the population almost certainly were crippled even more comprehensively by the fact that the plunder operations themselves, even if they did not result in extensive bloodshed, had a horrendous effect on the targeted regions and populations.

The perceptions of individual officers, of course, continued to play a role. It is significant, in this context, that the 221st Security Division did not give up on constructive engagement. The increasingly intractable situation may have caused a resurgence of its old harshness, but the resurgence was not as pronounced as it might have been. It is clear, then, that even in the brutalizing context of 1943, the longer-term lessons it had drawn from past cultivation successes had not been forgotten entirely. But such was the urgent immediacy of the situation in 1943 that, overall, a dramatic reversal of its 1942 policy, however brutal, destructive, and ultimately counterproductive it might be, seemed the only means of alleviation.

What the policies of both years had in common was that, overall, they were adopted less as well-thought-out, well-resourced *solutions* to the problem of security than as desperate measures to stave off its worst effects.

7

Fear in the Forest

During 1942 and 1943 the 221st Security Division commanded a succession of regiments and battalions, together with a generally static lineup of Feld- and Ortskommandantur garrisons. The need to pacify, engage, and exploit, which the 221st's division-level officers were charged with fulfilling during this period, the situation those officers contended with, their perceptions, and the impetus to cultivate or coerce that this combination of factors generated, all influenced their subdivisional units also.

But what distinguished the subdivisional level from the divisional level and united its component formations was an experience of antipartisan warfare that was even more direct and personal. They underwent an ordeal markedly more intense, and markedly more brutalizing, than anything their division-level colleagues experienced.

Sensations of isolation, dread, and hatred, and the barbarized mentality these sensations could fortify, are conveyed with an unsettling strength of feeling in letters from common soldiers across the spectrum of the Eastern Army's security forces.

"These are dangerous swine," wrote Corporal Erich Stahl of Guard Battalion 542, "and no soldier is safe from them. The danger is there wherever you go and wherever you stay . . . and you only breathe out when you've come back from your post unhurt . . . If the

moon's not out, you stay awake at your post like an ox."[1] Private
Hans Schröder of the 389th Infantry Division described on 19 June
1942 how "two of our comrades in first company tragically lost their
lives . . . Though we kept watch, a partisan still was able to creep up
to one of our houses. A grenade chucked in through the window, and
it was done . . . We took revenge straight away, and rightly. I used to
think one should act humanely, but this subhumanity just isn't worth
it." As to the form of revenge for "this cowardly act against our two
comrades, twenty civilians were made to dig their own graves, and
were then shot."[2] Corporal Hans Waigel, serving on antipartisan operations with the 4th Panzer Division, recalled that he and his comrades were "assigned to catch a sixty-five-year-old partisan woman,
who absconded in the middle of the night. Had we caught her, I'd
have spared a bullet and beaten her brains out instead."[3] He also described an incident in which two Russians caught with what they
claimed was bait for fishing were shot for ferrying supplies to the
partisans: "The other day, our patrol caught an old man and a six-
year-old sprog with a supply of salt and potatoes. They claimed they
were using it to catch fish, but they had something else in mind
entirely. We didn't keep them prisoner long, but set them free—
through death. I personally haven't had the pleasure of shooting anyone yet, but would do so with joy."[4]

The experiences of the 221st's lower-level units, and the brutalization to which those experiences contributed, developed in four
phases during 1942 and 1943. The Yelnya-Dorogobuzh operations
of the spring of 1942 committed the 221st's substandard formations to fast-moving combat, in atrocious conditions, against partisans largely trained and equipped to military standards. During the
period of largely static security in the Gomel region that summer
and autumn brutality ebbed somewhat, but units at an increasingly
low level of discipline and morale were then thrown into an unrelenting series of arduous midwinter operations in the thickly forested, partisan-infested territory to the 221st's northeast. Finally, the
spring and summer of 1943 saw the 221st's lower-level units in the
vanguard of the burgeoning terror that was the division's emerging

dead zones policy. It also saw the physical and mental demands imposed on them by chronic overextension foster attitudes often far harsher than the division-level conception of antipartisan warfare. These conditions, although they can never justify the outrages committed, can at least begin to explain them. By reinforcing the harsh mentalities of some of the officers who commanded the units, they created a fertile seedbed for a brutality drawing no distinction between partisans and population.

Some aspects of the occupier-occupied relationship, of course, were *not* brutalizing. As with any aspect of National Socialist ideology and its effect across society, military or civil, anti-Slavism was not universal among German soldiers.[5] And in an occupation of such duration, barriers were bound, for some, to be eroded anyway. Though never on the scale that the rose-tinted postwar recollections of Wehrmacht veterans claimed, fraternization on a daily, personal level between occupier and occupied did take place. Indeed, Hitler and Himmler estimated, to their considerable alarm, that German soldiers had fathered roughly one million illegitimate babies in the first year of occupation alone.[6]

Social relations between the 221st Security Division's troops and the population do not seem to have extended this far. One reason may be that most of the troops were well over thirty and that many had wives and families. Another reason was that the men of the ostensibly static garrisons, men who might have had more opportunity than most to develop relations with the population around them, were in fact frequently moved around, and the majority of the rest of the division's troops spent most of their time in far-flung outposts along the railway lines. Even so, the division frequently had to warn the troops about the dangers to security posed by excessive fraternization.[7] Clearly, then, fraternization was taking place, and day-to-day contact with the population was not always marked by fear.[8] It is conceivable that both officers and men who held a less than negative impression of the population would have restrained themselves somewhat in antipartisan warfare.

In any case, selective reading of the record of the 221st Security Division's subordinate units indicates that they often behaved with a certain amount of restraint. Over neither execution of prisoners nor killing of "partisans in combat" did the death tolls they inflicted approach the colossal dimensions of the butchery that such units as the 201st and 286th Security Divisions and, above all, the 707th Infantry Division perpetrated. And it was not just more limited opportunity, important though that factor was, that reduced their propensity for brutality. For a number of their mobile operations, highly conducive to greater killing, were also prosecuted with considerable restraint. Perceptions of the population that tempered brutality were almost certainly at work here. So too was the influence of a division-level policy that, even in 1943, continued, for the sake among other things of day-to-day relations with the population, to urge a degree of moderation. More pragmatically, finally, the need to curb the kind of brutality that could damage soldierly discipline also would have been in many officers' minds.

The division's files also cite specific examples of lower-level restraint. On 19 December, the first day of Operation Ankara, the first battalion of the 8th Police Regiment, subordinate to the 36th Security Regiment during the operation, exercised notable restraint when it discovered that the village of Guta, which it had just entered, clearly had been serving as a partisan base. "It was clear from the agricultural stockpiles in Guta," the battalion recorded, "that the village was being used as a bandits' strongpoint. Of the thirteen men present, the eight able-bodied ones were therefore arrested."[9] While these eight unfortunates could expect little mercy, the battalion at least chose not to carry out an indiscriminate massacre. Such restraint appears even more remarkable given that the battalion's arrival in Guta immediately followed its total failure to intercept the partisan group that was active in the area. This was a failure it could have chosen to cover, as units often did, with a large body count of "partisans killed in combat."

A second incident during Ankara, attributed to no particular unit, took place on 20 December. "A flask of [gun]powder," the 36th Security Regiment reported, "was found in a house in Sinovyevka. Ammunition detonated when the house was burned down by order of the regiment. A sawn-off shotgun and a hunting rifle were found in the ruins, which despite a thorough search beforehand had not been found. The owner of the house admitted that her husband was with the partisans and had left the ammunition behind after his last visit. The woman was shot, and her children handed over to the village headman."[10]

The personal consequences of this severity were tragic. But wholesale massacres had been committed for less. Even in the face of strenuous conditions and pressure for results, then, restraint—however relative, and however meaningless, on an individual level, for families such as this—was not beyond lower-level units.

But the conditions of the partisan war were not an incubator of human kindness. The immediacy and intensity of the conditions units faced from the Yelnya-Dorogobuzh operations onward could also drive them to markedly more ruthless action. In doing so, they acted as a particularly strong conductor for the ruthless attitudes, ideological, militaristic, and other, that had permeated Wehrmacht antipartisan doctrine and underpinned both the criminal orders of 1941 and their sometimes even-more-severe successors of late 1942. Even without these influences, however, the combination of danger, fear, frustration, and extreme discomfort that such conditions could generate possessed considerable brutalizing power in its own right.

Against the 278 men the 221st Security Division lost against the trained, dangerous Yelnya-Dorogobuzh partisans between March and June 1942 were 806 enemy "killed in combat" and another 122 partisans shot after capture. For a security division, overstretched and overburdened as it was at the best of times, 278 dead was a grievous loss. But the claim that the 221st's inadequate formations inflicted losses three times as high on a partisan enemy containing a great many trained and equipped military personnel in its ranks is hardly credible. The suspicion that a great many of the recorded partisan dead were in fact unarmed civilians is raised by this disparity alone. The fact that only 51 machine guns and 150 rifles were captured from more than 900 enemy dead confirms this likelihood virtually beyond doubt.[11]

Six times, moreover, the division's subordinate units committed atrocities on a grander scale. Each time, more than twenty "partisans" were recorded killed at little or no loss to the division's units. Between them, these atrocities killed at the very least 293 "partisans," possible many more, at a cost to the division of 7 dead and 20 wounded.[12] These massacres not only account for a great many of the "partisans" the 221st credited itself with having killed. They also provide an insight into how and why the killing of noncombatants took place on such a scale during the operations.

The particular conditions the 221st Security Division experienced during the Yelnya-Dorogobuzh operations—second- and third-rate manpower operating in appalling weather, with often-inadequate transport, against a numerous enemy largely trained, organized, and armed to full military standard—provided fertile ground for lower-level brutality. Admittedly, the 221st's superior combat troop elements had removed one potential source of brutalization, their mocking memory of Blitzkrieg triumphs past, when they had left for the front in December 1941. But brutalization born instead of frustrated impotence was all the more likely in the situation the 221st's remaining units now faced.

An officer need not have possessed the "criminal orders mentality" particularly strongly to be brutalized by such conditions. For one thing, a kind of brutalizing career pressure existed for territorial unit officers also. They might never see front-line action even if they wanted to, but if they failed to perform as rear-area officers they faced the prospect of enforced retirement and, with it, a feeling of personal failure. Frustrated by the obstacles posed by their situation, and pressured for visible and immediate results in the shape of dead partisans, such officers probably would have felt less concern about preserving relations with the population.

Further, the mere fact that the enemy in the Yelnya-Dorogobuzh region were still classed as "partisans" would have led officers who subscribed to the Wehrmacht's institutional guerrillaphobia to hold them in contempt. By extension, they would have reacted viciously to any assistance, real or imagined, rendered to the partisans by the population. And nowhere was distrust of the population sharper, or its potential for brutalization greater, than among the lower-level field units, which not only felt the pressures of the situation most keenly but also interacted with the population daily.

And on this occasion, the interaction is unlikely to have broken down barriers. For one thing, the mobility of the operations prevented troops from settling down in one location, thus perhaps establishing a degree of trust with the population, for any extensive period. Even more fundamentally, in German eyes, the Yelnya-Dorogobuzh population must have appeared particularly shifty. In the areas of the region they controlled, the partisans had actually reestablished Soviet forms of government.[13] Though this phenomenon was to become widespread throughout the Army Group Center Rear Area during 1942,[14] the particular partisan strength in the Yelnya-Dorogobuzh region made it especially prevalent there. The region's population, therefore, probably was already more prone than most to be forever looking over its shoulder, weighing the advantages of siding with the Germans against the advantages of keeping faith with the Soviet regime, and attempting to avoid the wrath of either.[15] Inevitably, many German field officers and their men would have viewed it with particular distrust.

Certainly, there were clear instances of this distrust. On 24 April one of the 221st's battle groups, Group Illig, came across 113 refugees who had drifted into the division's jurisdiction.[16] The refugees hardly constituted a serious security threat—they consisted of 7 men, 47 women, 59 children, and a cow—but they were handed over to Einsatzgruppe B all the same.[17] Suspicion of and contempt for the population may have been exacerbated by anti-Slavism. Such harsher guidelines as the 221st's division-level departments issued during the operations, such as the Operations Section's order to shell suspicious villages on sight, legitimized brutality even further.

And it was units that, on top of this atmosphere of distrust and contempt, felt the strain particularly acutely, that often went on to behave with particular brutality.

Only one of the six larger atrocities of the Yelnya-Dorogobuzh operations was perpetrated by men from one of the 221st's weakest units.[18] But this fact probably stems from the reality that such units, held over for static security duty as they were, had little opportunity for brutality.[19] As it is, the case of that particular unit, Territorial Battalion 545, provides a striking illustration of how particularly pressured conditions could tip a unit "over the edge."

Territorial Battalion 545 possessed all the ingredients of a third-rate formation. Relegated mainly, by dint of its combat inadequacy, to static security duty, its lack of fighting power and its need to appear effective may well have tormented its officers. An "engagement" of 30 May 1942, in which units of the battalion on a mobile operation claimed to have killed twenty-five partisans in the village of Dorogonino at no loss to themselves, is a textbook example of what was more likely a massacre of civilians dressed up as a combat encounter. The battalion's depiction of the engagement as a hard-won battle, involving house-to-house fighting against stiff partisan resistance, would have fitted the purposes of "presentation" admirably.[20] That the battalion did not slaughter more of the village's inhabitants that day suggests even more strongly that its actions stemmed from a calculated desire to conceal its impotence, and not from a wild, spontaneous outburst of frustration.

Other units, though they benefited from higher fighting power, had had to participate in particularly punishing action against the partisans. Territorial Battalion 230, which on 8 April 1942 demolished four villages and claimed to have killed sixty-two partisans at a cost to itself of three dead and six wounded, had recently had to attack the partisans around Yelnya.[21] The attack, during which the battalion had undergone a fierce encounter near Baltutino on 28 March in which it suffered nine dead and four wounded, had been blighted by unspeakable weather conditions, impassable roads, and a collapse in transport and supply.[22]

Cycle Squadron 213's conduct was even worse. On 12 May 1942 it killed more than seventy people, razed three villages to the ground, and claimed that up to another seventy had burned alive in the conflagration.[23] The battalion captured a minuscule number of partisan guns, and itself suffered not one casualty.[24] Here, too, the experiences it had just undergone may have fueled its propensity for such outrages. From 30 April to 3 May the squadron had been part of a battle group, Group Illig, that had borne the brunt of a particularly fierce Soviet counterattack and sustained losses of thirty-five dead, ninety-four wounded, and fifteen missing.[25]

On their own, the undeniable hardships these units had endured seem a very poor excuse for such indiscriminate butchery. But on top of all the other manifest pressures and prejudices that influenced units' behavior during the Yelnya-Dorogobuzh operations, their potential to provide the final push is clear.

The record of brutality, between June and October 1942, among subordinate units in the Gomel region is less extensive. But such self-control should not be viewed too rosily. For one thing, in comparison with mobile operations involving extensive use of artillery, a static security effort with hamstrung mobility offered little opportunity for brutality. Nevertheless, it does seem that the more measured division-level attitudes were shared at the lower levels also. For when mobile operations did take place, notably during July and August, they were not marked by horrific body counts. Though the records are incomplete, it seems that the four main mobile operations of August—South, Crow, Triangle, and Quadrangle—resulted in the deaths in action of fewer than 120 "partisans" at a cost to the 221st of 36 dead. By contrast, the recorded death toll for the 203d Security Division's three main operations of the summer—Potsdam, Cockchafer, and Eagle—was 321 partisans killed in action at a cost to the 203d of 28 dead.[26]

Moreover, the larger-scale atrocities the division's troops committed were neither as numerous nor as bloody as those of the Yelnya-Dorogobuzh operations. Next to the body count of around 300 dead in the Yelnya-Dorogobuzh operations, the larger-scale atrocities in the Gomel region during the 221st's first six months there—June 1942 to January 1943—produced fewer than 200 verifiable dead. "Relativizing" very high body counts, both of which consisted, after all, of individual human beings, may at first appear unsavory if not obscene. Yet in any assessment of the 221st's subordinate units, the latter figure is important both for its level and for its composition. Of these 198 individuals, 70 were killed by the Order Police, 24 by an Ordnungsdienst (OD) unit, and only 85, for certain, by the division's own troops. Of these in turn, a further 65 almost certainly were killed by the 45th Security Regiment, a particularly ruthless unit, and one to which attention turns later. In other words, across the division's own *army* units as a whole, the proclivity for brutality dropped greatly.[27]

But the division's new situation had potential to nurture viciousness also; the still-significant overall gap between recorded German and recorded partisan dead demonstrates this potential clearly. All told, the period between the 221st Security Division's arrival in Gomel in mid-June and the end of the year saw it inflict 981 "partisan" dead against the loss of 234 among its own German and native units.[28] Deteriorating manpower, and the inability to get to grips with actual partisans as a result of overextension, seem to have stoked the fear, frustration, "pressure to perform," and the tendency to substitute terror against the population for antipartisan action that could spill into open brutality.

It was units in the field that had to cope most directly, among other things, with the throttling consequences of poor training. Though a directive the 221st Security Division issued on 25 1942 June ordered commanders down to company level to ensure that training was being conducted properly,[29] training troops scattered in small groups across such a vast area was a burdensome task at best. Security Battalion 706, for example, was so overstretched that the only troops available to patrol its territory were drivers and clerks. Its third company alone was responsible for seventy kilometers of rail track.[30] Moreover, many security division officers, mainly because of their age, clearly were not up to the job.[31] Yet the onus on lower-level units to master these labyrinthine problems themselves was enormous; both General von Schenckendorff and the 221st's divisional command still held lower-level officers personally responsible for their units' defects. For the 221st Security Division, the Operations Section complained at the start of August that numerous officers were failing to execute their orders with "proper thoroughness and application."[32]

Be it via fear, frustration, the need to cover for failure, or the perception that the partisans could be combated only by terrorizing the population, the officers whom the pressure of circumstance and pressure for results probably brutalized the most were the garrison commanders of the Feld- and Ortskommandanturen. If security troops often were the "last scraps," these officers very often were the last of the last. Indicative of this circumstance is the June–December 1942 report of the 221st's personnel officer. It recounted that the division's replacement officers from the west had been so far below the standard necessary for service in Russia that most had been assigned to "relatively quiet" postings as Feld- and Ortskommandanten. This example certainly corresponds to the view of Gerald Reitlinger, who described the "typical" rear-area military official as "an officer whose career had failed, a captain or major in late middle age who had been given an unpopular task because of his incompetence."[33] Their particularly advanced age made them especially unequal to their duties.

The units at their disposal, moreover, had to administer large areas with a level of manpower that, even by normal security division standards, was particularly lacking. This was certainly a problem for Feldkommandantur 550, in the 203d Security Division's jurisdiction, which on 24 July reported that "there are good grounds for doubting that Ortskommandantur Lyuban is up to the task of carrying out its duties with the care and application that Russian conditions demand. It is staffed by one sergeant, one senior private as clerk, and one interpreter."[34] Back in the 221st's area, the cumulative effect of these stresses may well have fueled the "incident" of 6 September 1942 in which the Ortskommandantur in Roslavl reportedly killed twenty-eight partisans in combat at no loss to itself.[35]

In the Gomel region also, even though the length of the division's tenure there enabled the troops to build up some sort of relationship with the population, mounting suspicion was inevitable as well. The 27th Security Regiment felt that its every move was being reported to partisan intelligence, and concluded that partisan eyes and ears must be everywhere.[36] Nor, with the partisans making every effort to install moles as village headmen or OD leaders, could the Germans trust even apparently loyal civilian administrators. One Intelligence Section report recounted that an elderly partisan informer had deliberately been left behind in the Soviet retreat of 1941 because the partisans had assumed, correctly as it turned out, that his "dignified bearing" would fool the Germans into giving him an administrative post.[37] Trust was not facilitated, of course, by the fact that many troops indeed still did not interact with the population long enough for certain bonds of trust to be created. The state of affairs whereby supposedly static village- and small-town garrisons were frequently moved around, and an increasing number of troops was scattered along the railways lines in isolated outposts, was a constant throughout almost the whole of the division's period of security in the Gomel region.

Finally, the corrosive effect on inhibitions of institutional mentalities, personal prejudices, and criminal orders would not have hindered the brutalization these conditions could stoke.

All told, however, the tendency to terror among the 221st's subordinate units remained relatively subdued at this time. But the new pressures of the mobile operations of the winter of 1942–43 ended this state of affairs.

The two Ankara operations, conducted in the 221st's particularly troublesome northeastern sector, and the Limpet II operation, in which units of the 221st, collectively designated Group von Geldern, were committed against partisans in Army Rear Area 532's jurisdiction, were the setting for this harsh reversal. Although the directives the 221st Security Division issued for its winter operations urged self-control, the severity and brutalizing potential of conditions in the field left the participating units with little inclination to comply. Together, the operations exacted a reported body count of nearly 300 partisans killed in action. The Secret Field Police and the division's own troops shot another 234 "partisans and partisan accomplices" after capture. Across the three operations, the 221st's units themselves lost 19 dead.[38]

There were three directions, probably, from which this brutality came. In the first place, the new extremes of ruthlessness "against women and children also," urged by Hitler's 16 December directive, on top of the criminal orders of the previous years and the institutional attitudes that underpinned them, probably encouraged it. In terms of concrete conditions, there was the pressure, so common to large-scale operations, that the task of having to cleanse massive areas in a brief period with inadequate manpower created. But Limpet II, bloodiest of the three operations by a long way—the units that executed it inflicted a body count of "partisans killed in combat" as high as both Ankara operations combined—saw both pressure of circumstances and higher-level incitement to ruthlessness at their most direct.

At first glance, the conditions in which Limpet II was conducted seem no worse than those of the Ankara operations. The level of manpower committed to it was no lower, the size of the area it encompassed no greater, than those of either Ankara operation. The timetable for Limpet II, scheduled over a fortnight, was positively generous. Though the operation was hindered by meter-deep snow, outdated maps, insufficient manpower, and an active partisan group with a strong hold over the population, so too were the Ankara operations.

But there was a major difference: Security Battalion 791, the first battalion of the 8th SS Police Regiment, the third battalion of the 638th (volunteer) French Infantry Regiment, and Eastern Battalion 604 had just been through the experience of both Ankara operations. This unrelenting, monthlong commitment to mobile operations seems to have reduced them to a serious state of exhaustion, ineffectiveness, and indiscipline by the time of Limpet II. Eastern Battalion 604's loss during Limpet II of its commander, Major Chegelov, who was described as having been "the soul of his unit," was apparently the final straw that compelled the 221st to pack the battalion off for four to six weeks' retraining as soon as the operation ended. The 36th Security Regiment's after-action report on Limpet II accused the first battalion of the 8th SS Police Regiment of unprofessional judgment, wild imaginings, and "overreaction."[39]

Discipline and morale in the French battalion, though a volunteer unit, was especially poor. Many of its officers and NCOs seem to have been rogues and adventurers rather than "ideological warriors," and morale suffered because many soldiers felt demeaned as antipartisan fighters, preferring to be at the front with their sister battalions. The French troops were also concerned about relatives being held as prisoners of war in France, and about the hardships their families were experiencing—fears that had grown more acute after the Anglo-American invasion of French North Africa in November 1942.[40] Such low morale and discipline earned them the hatred of the civilian population through a level of plundering that, even for this operation, was particularly incessant and unbridled.[41] The reports' deafening silence on the conduct of the regular Eastern Army troops who took part in the operation may well have been cover for the fact that their conduct had been appalling also.

Further, in units at such a pitch of fecklessness and frustration as the battalions the 221st committed to Limpet II, the requisitioning order for the operation was especially likely to encourage brutality. Executed as it was not in the 221st's area itself, but in the rear of the Second Panzer Army to the northeast, Limpet II was characterized by a requisitioning policy more pitiless than the one the 221st was prosecuting that winter. The relevant directive told the units taking part that, to a large extent, they would have to forage for their own food, albeit with some regulation, during the operation.[42] But the most chilling instruction is one that stands in total contrast to the 221st Security Division's advice on treatment of deserters of 3 December 1942. The 221st urged that partisans who surrendered during or after an operation, providing they brought their weapons with them, should be spared alongside those who had deserted before.[43] But the instructions for Limpet II directed that "whoever tries to give himself up in the course of battle because he sees no other way out is still a bandit." It defined bandits, moreover, as "anyone, be it man, woman, or child, who confronts the troops with a weapon, who has assisted the bandits, scouted for them, or guarded for them."[44] Given that this was a partisan-infested area in which most of the population would have had no choice but to assist the partisans in some way, this description could have applied to almost anyone. Taken together, these instructions were a green light for pillaging and extreme excess and violence.

Most of the "plunder" operations of 1943 were noticeable for the lack of actual blood that was shed, despite their horrendous general nature, in the course of them. The reason for this comparative restraint, it seems, was that these operations were more tightly controlled by a divisional command that appreciated that the orderly requisitioning and procurement of labor were of the most urgent importance. The conduct of individual, isolated units away from the main operations, however, was harder to control. And it was also during 1943 that overextension and isolation, declining fighting power, rising partisan activity, and the increasingly alarming supply situation lowered the general threshold of brutality among such individual units further. The swelling death tolls the 221st's subordinate units inflicted not in the major operations, but in the "smaller" atrocities they perpetrated, are a clear sign.

Nearly 200 "partisans" had perished in such encounters between mid-June and the end of December 1942, at a cost to the Germans and their allied native units of 10 dead. But much of this death toll had been inflicted not by the 221st itself, but by associated Order Police and OD units. In any case, the equivalent figures for January–August 1943 dwarfed this disparity. Granted, such "engagements" did exact a marginally higher toll of the 221st—19 dead, 19 wounded, and 9 missing—during those eight months. But the toll of native dead they inflicted was awful. More than 300 "partisans" were reported killed, up to 150 more "killed or wounded."[45] Terror against the population, then, was spiraling.

But it was again primarily the division's weakest units that inflicted this terror. The native auxiliaries of the OD, whose hand in these atrocities was as extensive as it was bloodstained—its tally comprised seventy-two dead "partisans" at the loss of three fatalities itself—certainly fell into this category.[46] Lieutenant Gäuger, of the second company of Security Battalion 791, described an action in January in which, though thirteen German and thirty-three OD men had participated, the German troops would have been far more effective on their own. The OD's incompetence had resulted directly in the loss of an antitank gun, and Gäuger claimed that "in the firefight that ensued, the combat value of the OD was precisely zero."[47] Sometimes the OD was probably just a convenient whipping boy for German units anxious to conceal their own inadequacies. But the pathetic levels of training and equipment that crippled it must have massively affected its fighting power—with brutalizing implications.

But the case of Security Battalion 242 illustrates the barbarizing effect of arduous conditions and ebbing fighting power most vividly. Its record speaks for itself: well over 350 "partisans" killed or wounded, for the loss of 15 dead and 13 wounded, in two separate engagements.[48]

It would be wrong to assume that a base of institutional guerrillaphobia, anti-Slavic contempt, and general harshness, intensified by Nazi ideology, did not play some part in fueling this extreme brutality. But it also would be wrong to underestimate the singular barbarizing potency of the brew of distrust, fear, frustration, and desperate need for visible antipartisan success that this particular battalion's conditions imposed on it.

Even by the increasingly dismal standards of the conditions Eastern Army security units endured, Security Battalion 242's situation was atrocious. The area of the 183d Security Regiment, to which it was subordinate, spanned the northwestern corner of the divisional jurisdiction. Because this sector contained none of the major rail routes that crisscrossed the rest of the jurisdiction, the 221st Security Division viewed the partisans there as less threatening, numerous and active though they might be, to the vital maintenance of supply to the front. The 183d's area, then, remained far down its list of priorities, and only a single battalion was assigned to it. Security Battalion 242 was the unlucky unit.

In terms of reinforcements, rations, and equipment, the battalion was neglected consistently. Anguished situation reports describe the state of impotence and fear to which Security Battalion 242, in an area increasingly slipping from German control, was consequently reduced. By 10 May 1943, a week before the first massacre, civilian laborers reportedly were no longer turning up to help deforest the area on either side of the railway tracks; the Germans and the OD in effect had to drag them there. A day earlier, German sentries had been murdered on duty.[49] Meanwhile the OD itself was becoming increasingly disobedient and unreliable. One occasion that made this clear was the killing of Corporal Nickel, of Security Battalion 242's third company, on the night of 13–14 June. Nickel was inspecting the OD barracks in Yanovka when the building suddenly came under partisan attack. To the third company, it was clear that the attack had taken place with the connivance of OD men: Nickel, a special hate figure for the OD, had been shot in the back.[50]

Fear almost certainly was stoked not only by the partisans' gathering strength, but also by the devious methods the partisans reportedly were using all over the 221st's jurisdiction. February brought reports of female Russian agents posing as kitchen personnel and poisoning the troops' food or throwing strychnine down wells.[51] That month also, partisans managed to tune into the same wavelength as one of the division's regiments. The exchange that followed was recorded by the division's Intelligence Section: "At the end of the conversation an unknown voice called down the line: 'Thanks for the chat! Yours, the partisans.'"[52] The partisans, it was later reported, were also erecting dummies with guns in the middle of the forest;

German troops approaching them had opened fire and given their position away.[53] In June the Intelligence Section reported an increase in partisans wearing German, Slovak, Hungarian, or pro-German Cossack uniforms. The same report stated that the partisans were making false telephone calls to lure German troops and OD men out of their strongpoints.[54]

In the pressure-cooker situation Security Battalion 242 was facing, however, the mounting dread such developments fueled would have been especially severe. The battalion's troop morale seemed in danger of going into free fall. "The troops' pride and confidence," the battalion reported, "are suffering because their paltry numbers, inadequate weaponry, and low mobility prevent them from delivering the bandits a powerful blow . . . The current strained situation is creating demands that cannot be met in the long term."[55]

The first time this pressure translated into the indiscriminate massacre of civilians was 17 May. On this day the battalion reported an "engagement" in which its troops, at no loss to themselves, had killed around 65 partisans and wounded up to another 150.[56] Such a yawning gap in casualties clearly indicates what had actually taken place. If the battalion's desperate situation were not remedied, moreover, its troops were likely to bloody themselves thus once more.

Nor was any remedy forthcoming. By late May the battalion's situation was worse in every respect:

Last night, quite by accident, the Ortskommandantur in Propoisk uncovered a plot by some auxiliary volunteers, who until then had been reliable, to murder their officers and then, with the OD and bandits massing before Propoisk, to annihilate the other Germans there . . . without any prospect of reinforcement, the battalion's strength continues to dwindle and its tasks grow more difficult and numerous. Things cannot continue as they are. The men on watch are being pushed to the limits, and every man down to the lowliest private is afraid in the face of the danger that grows more threatening all the time. No one can explain or understand why our side is so weak and inactive; this is a condition the German Army has never before experienced.

The companies can no longer spare any men for the training courses that have been ordered . . . the last replacements arrived in September 1942.[57]

Food supply in the 183d Security Regiment's jurisdiction was appalling as well. For soldiers on the ground, hunger blighted not just fighting power, but also basic health. "If you're in the army back in the Reich, and have money, you can at least buy bread," wrote Corporal Ludwig Birkenfeld of Supply Battalion 563. "But here in the forest, where is there anything to be had? Our alleged descent from apes is no help, for there are no bananas or coconuts among the firs and pines."[58]

By mid-June the battalion was in a pathetic condition. It had lost forty-seven dead, fifty-three wounded, and six missing. Two-thirds of these losses had been sustained since February 1943. Its reinforcements consisted of one man and two NCOs, and even these were of shoddy quality.[59] And this in an area now infested with as many as 3,000 partisans, armed to a large extent, it was reported, with machine guns.[60] Perhaps the only surprise is that the battalion did not inflict another bout of indiscriminate butchery before 29 August.

The barbarizing possibilities of such crippling conditions become clearer by contrast with a unit that did *not* suffer from them.

No Eastern Army security unit had it easy at any time during the campaign in the Soviet Union, still less by 1943. But the 930th Security Regiment enjoyed manifold advantages over Security Battalion 242.[61] In April and May 1943, Security Battalion 242 was able to commit more men per kilometer of rail and road than the 930th was.[62] But any overall advantage it might have enjoyed was more than offset by the poor quality of its troops, the poor quality *and* unreliability of the OD on whom it increasingly depended, and the fact that the 930th could call on twice as many troops to patrol the interior.[63] The 930th's sector, though of special concern to the 221st because of its rail routes and proximity to the front, was considerably less infested with partisans than Security Battalion 242's.[64]

The 930th's easier circumstances translated into a less ferocious form of antipartisan warfare. This is not to say that the 930th did not inflict great misery. Its execution, in February, of Operation Zugspitze saw the burning of nine "bandit villages" and the shooting of 141 "accomplices" by the Secret Field Police.[65] A sharp rise, in March, of partisan sabotage along the railways in the 930th's area caused the regiment to call, on 8 April, for ruthless execution of a no-man's-land order by which any Russian civilian found on either the track or its environs was to be shot on sight.[66] And increasingly intractable circumstances—the loss of regimental personnel to duties elsewhere in April, and an increase in partisan rail sabotage in May—hardened the regiment's attitude further. It culminated in summer directives ordering the widespread razing of "bandit" villages.[67]

In human terms, this is a harrowing picture. One shudders to think of the misery and loss of life it inflicted. But the 930th never actually spurred its own troops to the potentially far worse *unbridled* killing of civilians. There is no indication, in the records of the 221st Security Division or the 930th itself, of the kind of indiscriminate slaughter Security Battalion 242 perpetrated.

The pattern that emerges from this bleak examination is clear: the more a unit felt afflicted directly by its situation, the more vicious its response.

But circumstances were not the only brutalizing force at work. Other examples of the indiscriminate killing by various regiments and battalions highlight particularly lethal attitudes among certain commanders.

The destruction of four villages and killing of 62 alleged partisans by Territorial Battalion 230 on 8 April 1942, and Cycle Squadron 213's even more destructive tally of three razed villages and up to 140 "partisans" killed on 12 May, were undoubtedly the work of units under pressure. But the 221st's divisional command judged them as numbering among its more effective formations.[68] Conditions alone, then, are unlikely to have driven their brutality. Scrutiny of their officers suggests additional explanations.

For Cycle Squadron 213, Colonel Alfred Illig, the officer who commanded the battle group to which it belonged, may have played a brutally influential hand. Illig, born in Leignitz in eastern Germany in 1894, may have been inculcated with anti-Slavism to a stronger degree than fellow officers born farther west. Speculative though this sounds, it does in fact conform to a wider pattern in officers' behavior, one that will be considered further later.[69]

And it may be no coincidence that still another of the Yelnya-Dorogobuzh massacres was the work of the regiment that Illig regularly commanded. On 27 April 1942, at the height of the Yelnya-Dorogobuzh operations, a unit of the 44th Territorial Regiment reported that it had killed thirty partisans, at a loss to itself of just one man, in a cleansing operation in the swampy, wooded area east of Baltutino. Once more, the recorded disparity between partisan dead and partisan weapons captured—an antitank gun and four grenade launchers, together with a horse—indicates something far more murderous.[70] Here, the vicious legacy of the Free Corps also echoes. For the particular unit that almost certainly was responsible for this atrocity was Territorial Battalion 974, whose own commander, Lieutenant-Colonel von der Groeben, was an ex–Free Corps man.[71]

Territorial Battalion 302, which on 1 June 1942 reported killing at least forty partisans, at a cost to itself of two dead, was not the 221st Security Division's most inferior unit either.[72] Nor had it undergone particular hardship during the Yelnya-Dorogobuzh operations. Indeed, stationed until recently in the jurisdiction of the 286th Security Division, it had previously enjoyed an altogether quieter existence. Probably the decisive factor in the butchery of 1 June was the fact that the battalion was subordinate to Colonel Hans Wiemann's 45th Territorial Regiment. This formation—renamed in summer 1942 as the 45th Security Regiment—provides a detailed, extensive, and unsettling example of how the ruthless proclivities of certain officers could drive the brutality of their units.[73]

Several orders from the Gomel region during the second half of 1942 show the singularly suspicious, contemptuous regard in which Wiemann held the population. Such were his orders for a pacification operation around Novosybkov in late June: "Security and pacification measures are to be executed ruthlessly. Partisan suspects and any civilians who are possibly in contact with the partisans are to be dealt with using the utmost harshness. If the population does not voluntarily participate in the antipartisan effort [through information and reconnaissance] then it is to be treated as suspect."[74]

The last two sentences in particular say a great deal about Wiemann. To urge utmost harshness against anyone possibly in contact with partisans, and to throw suspicion of such contact automatically on anyone not voluntarily participating in the antipartisan effort, was to sanction and encourage a degree of coercion and suspicion so indiscriminate that it could extend to anyone. Such unrefined, blanket hostility toward the population was absent from any directive issued by any of the 221st's other subordinate regiments during 1942. It also went completely against the spirit of the more measured, differentiating treatment the division itself was urging. When it came to actual mass killing during these operations, the 45th did hold itself in check. But the longer-term effect of these exhortations upon the mindset of its subordinate units and troops seems to have been considerable. Sure enough, the months from September through December 1942 saw the 45th embark on a drive of pyromania and killing significantly in excess of anything the 221st's other subordinate regiments committed.

On 11 October, on the basis of a report by German intelligence troops that partisans had been gathering in the area, Wiemann's troops burned down the villages of Hatki and Pechi. Hatki included eight houses with strong walls, and twenty-one "bunkerlike" cellars; because these might conceivably be of use to the partisans, the 45th's pioneers blew them to pieces. The rest of the village, along with Pechi, went up in flames, and the entire population of both villages was arrested.[75] On 21 October, ostensibly to prevent partisans from gathering there, the 45th destroyed the village of Osinovka also.[76]

It added to this catalogue of devastation with two mass killings, on 12 September and 28 December, that harvested sixty-five "partisan" dead at a cost to the 45th of three killed and seven OD men missing.[77]

All the 221st Security Division's subordinate units were under strain during the second half of 1942, but none lashed out with the ferocious regularity of the 45th. This pattern would intensify during 1943.

The worst example of the extraordinary ruthlessness that characterized the 45th Security Regiment, as well as the best documented, was April 1943's Operation Easter Bunny. The pitiless mindset of Wiemann and his fellow officers was not the only thing that powered the division's butchery drive in that operation. Yet, when all the diverse forces that contributed are examined, the importance of that mindset is clear.

In the course of the operation, at a cost to themselves of only 5 dead, the 45th Security Regiment and its subordinate units recorded the deaths of 250 partisans in combat with only 34 small arms captured. These disparities dwarfed the equivalent figures in all the 221st's other mobile operations that year. The 45th claimed that 70 partisans had been killed by antitank guns, but even if this was true, a massive shortfall remained. Indeed, the recording of 250 partisan dead but just 34 guns captured seems to confirm that the vast majority of dead were noncombatants. The regiment's further claim that the partisan dead/partisan weapons disparity arose from the fact that the partisans had transported many of their weapons away seems dubious; it was unlikely that partisans who presumably wished to break out of the regiment's cordon would have allowed themselves to go weaponless.[78]

At first, some blame for the operation's brutality seems to fall on the 221st Security Division itself, and in particular on the green light it gave to destroying villages during the operation.[79] Yet such economically determined destruction of villages, callous in the extreme though it was, was a *systematic* process. Villages might be razed to the ground. The able-bodied population might be evacuated, perhaps for forced labor. "Economically nonviable" individuals might be handed over en masse to the Einsatzkommandos or Secret Field Police. But such a process did *not* involve killing civilians indiscriminately and then passing them off as partisans fallen in combat.

Other possible explanations, also, leave questions unanswered. The pressures of the large-scale operation mechanism—second- or third-rate troops in insufficient numbers, charged with cleansing an area within an unrealistic time scale—certainly affected the troops who carried out the operation. Security Battalion 242 (again), two of whose companies were on loan to the 45th, was despondent about its lack of mobility and the advanced age of its officers.[80] The forces committed to the operation fell short of what an effective encirclement required, and troops committed by the 203d Security Division had to be returned to it halfway through the operation.[81] Yet the pressures of time, distance, and manpower that overshadowed Easter Bunny's conduct were no more formidable than those of the Ankara operations of the previous winter—and in these two operations, only thirty-two partisans, reportedly, had been killed for certain.[82]

Only a breakdown of the operation itself sheds further light on precisely what caused such carnage.

The killing seems to have been concentrated in two days. That on 29 April, which took place in a forest three kilometers west of Lossov, seems to have been the work of Luftwaffe troops.[83] The level of killing would certainly fit the Luftwaffe field divisions' usual reputation in antipartisan warfare. But the action that took place two days earlier around the village of Kamenka was not. It is here that the brutal hand of Colonel Wiemann becomes apparent.

There was a major clash in the forest near the village, with a surprise German attack on a partisan camp, before the Germans moved on Kamenka itself. "The village of Kamenka," the 221st's Operations Section reported, "had been built up as a well-stocked supply base, primarily with livestock and horses. All of these fell into the hands of the troops."[84]

The requisition the 45th's troops carried out in Kamenka was reported as "total." All the produce and livestock seem to have fallen into the hands not of the requisition staff from Economic Detachment Gomel, but of the troops themselves.[85] A letter from Corporal Werner Scheibe described a similar operation carried out by the 12th Panzer Division: "At midday, after a long journey, we reached the bandits' territory and encircled it. I for one saw very few actual partisans, and certainly only a few were caught. So instead we destroyed the villages that they'd used as their base, and snapped up all the provisions we found there. We led a proper Wild West robbers' existence . . . but it was a lot of fun. Loads of chickens, sheep, cows, and pigs were slaughtered. We've been enjoying several fat and easy days since then."[86]

Troops in such a ravenous, violent frame of mind were unlikely to treat civilians with restraint. Thus many civilians in Kamenka itself, or in the forests round about, may well have perished in this process. But why the troops were allowed "first go" at the pickings in Kamenka in the first place, when no order to that effect had been issued by divisional command, remains unclear. A ruthless regimental directive or, at the very least, the pervasiveness of the 45th's institutional ruthlessness may well have been decisive.

The fanaticism of Colonel Wiemann, and possibly of other officers of the 45th Security Regiment, therefore provides the missing part of the explanation for Easter Bunny's brutality. The files for the operation itself clearly show this mindset at work. Easter Bunny was the only one of the 221st Security Division's 1943 antipartisan operations for which the regiment commanding even mentioned the German bogeymen of old, the Soviet commissars, in its after-action report. It was the commissars, the 45th claimed, who had been a driving force behind the partisans' "ferocity." "Under pressure from the commissars," the regiment reported, "the enemy fought doggedly and bitterly." The commissars, it claimed, had been shooting any partisans trying to flee.[87]

In 1941 such explanations for Soviet combat ferocity had been common. This certainly was not the case by 1943. No other report has been unearthed from the spring or summer of 1943 that attributed ferocious partisan resistance mainly to the threats and merciless exhortations of the commissars. A clear demonstration of just how rare and how at odds with reality the 45th's comments were comes from the contrast they present with those of General Hermann Hoth. Though Hoth issued a particularly ruthless ideological general order to his troops in the autumn of 1941, and was also at the forefront of efforts to radicalize conduct of the Commissar Order, even he recognized that the Russians were not fighting primarily out of fear of their commissars.[88] By 1943 there was if anything greater reason to draw this conclusion.

And if the vast disparity between German and partisan dead is any guide, there was hardly any genuine partisan resistance in Easter Bunny anyway. All this says much about the dynamic that drove the 45th. Either the officer who wrote the report was so ideologically paranoid that he actually believed what he was writing, or he was intent on currying favor with a regimental commander who did indeed perceive the world in such terms.

It was this *ideologically* colored ruthlessness, permeating the officers' collective mindset and taking brutality beyond the point where the concrete pressures of the situation alone would have taken it, that drove the 45th Security Regiment throughout 1942 and 1943. The same dynamic probably inspired the 45th's memo for the Hungarian-led Operation Csobo in July, which, in total violation of the 221st's call for a moratorium on the razing of villages during the operation, earmarked twenty-two such villages for destruction.[89]

Colonel Wiemann's personal file, though necessitating a certain reading between the lines, yields numerous clues as to what influences shaped his conception of war in the east.[90] Born in 1885 to a Saxon landowning family, Wiemann spent the years 1915–1918 on the Eastern Front. Experience of "primitive" eastern living conditions during a formative time in his life may have reinforced an animosity toward "eastern races," animosity that, in view of the fact that he hailed from the traditionally more anti-Slavic eastern part of Germany, may have marked him already.

If Wiemann's anti-Slavism was firmly in place by 1918, his experience of the next two years was very likely to have intensified his anti-

Bolshevism. On the signing of the Treaty of Brest-Litovsk in March 1918 and the launch of General Ludendorff's final offensives against the allies in France, Wiemann was transferred to the Western Front. While he was there, he would have experienced the trauma of the autumn of 1918, when, Ludendorff's attacks having long petered out and with the German Army in retreat, Bolshevik subversion allegedly pushed the morale and combat effectiveness of many of its units to collapse. Wiemann's role in the bloody suppression of the left-wing revolts of 1918–1920, meanwhile, was as extensive as it was direct; in March 1919 he was appointed battalion commander in the government security forces in Bremen, and eight months later he was working for the security police in that city.

In the 1920s and early 1930s, finally, Wiemann was manager of a building firm that fell victim to the economic crisis in 1931 and was liquidated in 1932.[91] A resulting sense of personal humiliation and contempt for the economic failings of the Weimar Republic could have strengthened his ideological proclivities even more lethally.

Wiemann, then, was not a product of the "turnip patch" from which many rear-area officers came. His background and experiences made him prime "ideological warrior" material.

Colonel Julius Lehmann, who up to the end of April 1943 commanded the 930th Security Regiment, was an officer whose apparent *lack* of ideologically founded ruthlessness helped foster a significantly different kind of antipartisan conduct. Lehmann was born in the Kandel–Rhine Palatinate region of western Germany in 1899.[92] Thanks to this geographical accident of birth, Lehmann may have been less subject to the pronounced anti-Slavism so prevalent in eastern Germany. Coming into the Kaiser's army only in April 1917, his exposure to the barbarizing conditions of World War I also was less far-reaching than Wiemann's. His seventeen-month stint on the Western Front—he never saw action in the east—ended with his capture by the British in September 1918. Perhaps most important, the timing of his capture meant that, unlike Wiemann, Lehmann did not participate in the Time of Struggle. Granted, his status as an officer during the Weimar years bound him to an anti-Bolshevik, antidemocratic organization. But it also ensured that, unlike Wiemann, such National Socialist enthusiasm as he did feel was not bolstered by the demoralizing, debilitating experience of unemployment.

Nor did the other three of the 221st's regimental commanders—Colonels von Geldern-Crispendorff, Hegedüs, and Luckmann—display a great deal of harshness. As late as May 1935, according to his personal file, Geldern-Crispendorff had still not got round to joining the Nazi Party.[93] In March 1943 his superiors described his attitude to antipartisan warfare as "not yet harsh enough."[94] Indeed, the colonel's impressive command of foreign languages and his experience as a military diplomat in Tehran during the first two years of the war mark him out as a man more likely to have regarded other countries and cultures with respect rather than with disdain.[95] Likewise Colonel Hegedüs, an ethnic German born in Hungary in 1889, seems to have been similarly underenthused. A divisional report of February 1943 spoke of "too much theory, not enough practice" from him, and described him as an average officer at best.[96] His command of a front-line unit in the opening weeks of Barbarossa had ended in ignominy.[97] Similarly, Luckmann, another subject of the former Austro-Hungarian Empire, was described as a rather weak personality lacking in toughness and independence.[98] Hegedüs and Luckmann, certainly, typify far less the ideological warrior of the Wiemann mold than the archetypal "failed front-liner" rear-area officer.

Reports by the 221st's divisional command and other units under which they served describe all three officers, along with Lehmann, as "reliably National Socialist in character."[99] But this may have been a stock phrase, used by the compilers of such reports to avoid making the officer in question look politically suspect in any way. It is certainly one that appears regularly in officers' personal files. The division's judgment of Wiemann, by contrast, described him in markedly stronger terms as a "convinced bearer and conveyor of the National Socialist worldview."[100] Considering how Wiemann is likely to have influenced his regiment's prosecution of antipartisan warfare, this is an extremely telling comment. Even if Wiemann himself didn't always issue direct orders to the effect, his efforts to instill National Socialist belief in his subordinates seems to have infected his regiment's conduct at all levels.

The final indication of this influence is the account by Captain Dresdner, commander of the regiment's eleventh company, of how his total distrust of the population shaped his unit's execution of an operation in May 1943. "The population of the forest villages," Dresdner wrote, "or of the villages at the edges of the forest, is working without exception with the bandits. It is immaterial whether this cooperation is voluntary or coerced; it alone is sufficient reason to deal the partisans a decisive blow by evacuating the population and burning down the villages in these areas."[101]

Subordinate officers may or may not have shared Wiemann's worldview actively. But their sense of careerism, intensified by the dynamic of the National Socialist leadership principle, may have been enough on its own. Winning their commander's approval would have been all the incentive they needed to display the ruthlessness integral to that view, convey it to their own troops, and assure those troops' participation in amassing what was, by the 221st Security Division's standards, a singularly appalling record of butchery and destruction.

The dreadfulness of the examples cited in these pages does not detract from the point, made at the beginning of this chapter, that over antipartisan warfare specifically, even if not over treatment of the population generally, the majority of the 221st Security Division's units behaved reasonably correctly the majority of the time. To a considerable extent, a relative lack of opportunity for brutality may well have determined this state of affairs. But it is also likely that at least some of division-level command's attitudes, attitudes more measured than they might have been even in 1943, influenced the division's regiments, battalions, and garrisons.

Clearly, though, the potential for and frequent practice of brutality were there throughout the period. The mobile operations of

1942 and early 1943 afforded opportunities for brutality, even if the economically driven operations later in 1943 were kept on a tighter rein. Smaller-scale encounters, meanwhile, offered prospects for brutality outside the main operations.

The attitudes of individual officers, shaped perhaps by their own life experiences, clearly played a role in determining how readily a unit responded to such opportunities. But most of these atrocities were committed by units whose commanders do not seem to have been fanatical. Almost certainly, much of the brutality that was meted out by the division's German units was founded on that bedrock of anti-Slavism, institutional guerrillaphobia, careerism, and general harshness embodied in the criminal orders of 1941 and 1942. But the fact that several of these atrocities were committed not by German troops, but by the 221st's native OD units, reveals that the most common factors at work were the stresses and strains that, at this level, were felt particularly painfully.

These stoked frustration at the increasingly "demodernized" state in which units found themselves, fear and contempt of actual or perceived partisan ruthlessness, distrust of and contempt for the population, and the desperation of troops simply out of their depth. By 1943, in response to worsening circumstances, an increasingly dangerous partisan movement, and certain higher-level orders encouraging ever-greater viciousness, the tendency was growing stronger.

Much of the brutality of the 221st Security Division's subordinate units was symptomatic, then, of a wider malaise in the antipartisan campaign. For the higher-level directives that shaped its overall course not only encouraged officers and men to think excessively ruthlessly. Most immediately, by underresourcing them so chronically, higher directives increasingly *drove* them to exercise such ruthlessness.

If the division's reports are anything to go by, these atrocities were never as grave a threat, overall, to relations between occupier and occupied as were blanket, rapacious economic policies such as food and labor requisitioning. But the concerns expressed over such operations as Limpet II and Easter Bunny show, along with the array of similar concerns expressed in these pages, that the extremely debilitating effect such atrocities could have was appreciated. For the division's long-term relations with the population, the fact that the brutalizing dynamics at work were often more powerful than calls for restraint was disastrous. Upon the survival and well-being of the population itself, of course, the effects were even more direct and devastating.

Conclusion

REAP AS YOU SOW, 1943 AND 1944

Archival holes render impossible any investigation of the 221st Security Division beyond August 1943. At this point, as the entire Army Group Center front line was pushed back by the impact of the Red Army's Bryansk and Orel counteroffensives, the division's jurisdiction moved westward for the first time in more than two years. But how far the brutalizing trend in its behavior continued is unknown. Also unknown is how far the 221st discriminated between different parts of its jurisdiction, between those segments of the population to be cultivated, above all for the strategic hamlets, and those targeted for further merciless treatment in the name of military and economic expediency.

What is known, however, is the ultimate fate of the Eastern Army security effort during late 1943 and 1944.

The first half of 1943 had already demonstrated both the completeness of the German failure to overcome the partisans, and the new level of organization and effectiveness the partisans themselves enjoyed. In 1944, as before, the persistence of harsh Wehrmacht attitudes, the ruthless, rapacious dynamics of Nazi occupation overall, and an urgency to the situation on the ground that often precluded a longer-term cultivation approach, all conspired to prevent the antipartisan effort from breaking free of the ambiguity that had shackled it to counterproductive ruthlessness. This phenomenon continued despite the fact that, at higher levels at least, some more strenuous efforts at engagement finally were being made. The Armed Forces High Command's May 1944 directive on partisan warfare advocated that partisans captured in civilian clothes or uniform be treated as prisoners of war, the exception being those disguised in uniforms captured from the Germans or their allies. The importance of fair treatment of the population was stressed.[1] Yet the directive also stressed that in the event of "particularly malicious acts," local German commanders could shoot prisoners and the populations of implicated areas. Reinhard Gehlen's provisions for the lenient treatment of prisoners may thus have saved thousands of captured partisans and "suspects," but the scope for brutality was still immense.[2]

The effects, as before, were clear across the board. Operations such as Spring Festival, which the Third Panzer Army executed in the Polotsk-Uschatschi sector in spring 1944, may have shown an awareness of the importance of treating the population with restraint, and employed measures such as the "relocation to safety" of the ill, elderly, mothers, and children under ten years old.[3] Even so, 7,011 "partisans" were killed, 6,928 prisoners executed. While the figure of 300 German dead indicates that some of these "partisans" were indeed armed and dangerous, the gap is still huge.[4]

The establishment of strategic hamlets, populated by "pro-German civilians" (essentially, those whom the Germans, in increasingly chaotic conditions, were able to entice with material inducements) was another aspect of antipartisan warfare that contained a markedly brutal dimension alongside a conciliatory one. The plan, first initiated in October 1943, was to establish the hamlets in areas under German control. But by late 1943 the notion of an area fully under German control was history. Once more the Einsatzgruppen came into their own, screening prospective inhabitants, weeding out "suspect elements," and in places, at the behest of the Eastern Army or SS commander on the spot, shooting them.[5]

In any case, all this activity increasingly resembled rearranging the deck chairs on the *Titanic*. With German abandonment of territory not just inevitable but increasingly imminent, overall control of day-to-day administration slipped from German control ever more conclusively. Such was Army Rear Area 559's report from Smolensk, one of the first cities to be abandoned to the advancing Red Army, in July 1943: "Absolute lawlessness, corruption, and immorality hold sway everywhere, even on the part of the police, such that there is no place for the population where they can seek justice or to which they can bring their complaints. The only people who live well and comfortably are those who engage in black marketeering or indulge in prostitution, as well as those who in one way or another were appointed by the German authorities."[6]

Meanwhile the damage wrought by partisans on supply and communication in the German rear increasingly throttled the front-line troops' ability to fight.[7] This development came at a time when the front-line situation was growing ever more desperate; Soviet superiority in men and material in the air and on land was growing close to overwhelming. Eastern Army strength, meanwhile, was being sapped by growing demands for manpower from other theaters; the summer of 1943 saw the western Allies invade Sicily and southern Italy, and increasingly mass their forces for an assault on the northern French coast.

Thus did a Soviet offensive launched against Army Groups Center and South just two weeks after Kursk succeed in throwing Army Group Center back to the River Pripet, crossing the Dnepr, and isolating the German forces in the Crimea. In the process it recaptured areas of vital economic importance to the Reich's war effort.[8] Elsewhere the Soviets pushed the Germans back 160 kilometers west of Leningrad and reached the eastern end of the Carpathian Mountains.

Desperate attempts to scrape together enough manpower to stem the Soviet advance meant, of course, that Eastern Army security troops increasingly found themselves dispatched to the front. This development rendered the partisans' task even easier. Partisan successes between the summer of 1943 and the spring of 1944 were manifold. On 2 and 3 August 1943, timed to coincide with the start of the German retreat to the River Dnepr, they detonated 8,422 mines along rail lines behind Army Group Center's sector of the front. Another wave of partisan rail sabotage in the autumn of 1943 effected wholesale desertion to the partisans among the eastern units guarding the rail lines. September 1943 saw the Bryansk Forest partisans play a major role, through their attacks on German supply, in easing the Soviet advance into the sector. Thus were Red Army units able to sweep through the area unopposed. In January 1944 partisan activity and sabotage in the German rear helped cut off the whole of Army Group North.[9]

When the retreating Germans discarded territory, the process was cruel and chaotic. Mounting desperation lent German conduct a further ruthless edge. In Army Rear Area 582, all "useless" members of the population—the elderly, ill, handicapped, and women with large numbers of children under the age of ten—were abandoned to impede the Soviet advance, while the rest, with minimal food supply, were herded in vast columns westward where the Reich could wring the remaining vestiges of economic use from them.[10]

Desperation also overwhelmed restraint in the scorched-earth policies the Germans enacted:

All the installations and equipment in the abandoned area of possible use to the enemy are to be destroyed: accommodation [houses and bunkers], machines, mills, windmills, wells, hay- and strawstacks. Houses are without exception to be burned down . . . wells to be rendered useless by destroying drawing equipment and throwing in refuse [corpses, cow dung, petrol], hay- and strawstacks and stocks of any description to be set alight, farming machines and their linkages to be blown up, ferries and small boats to be sunk. Engineers will destroy bridges and block the roads with mines.

It is the duty of every single soldier to ensure that the area abandoned to the enemy will be useless for any military or agricultural purpose in the foreseeable future.[11]

Even in retreat, the Germans were harried by partisans. The Bryansk Forest in September 1943 was just one area in which German efforts to create a wasteland were hindered massively when the partisans mobilized the population to repair as much of the damage as possible and thus ease the Soviet advance.[12]

In 1944, both in the rear and at the front, disintegration accelerated and finally climaxed. On 22 June the Soviets launched Operation Bagration against Army Group Center. By mid-July they had advanced more than 300 kilometers and removed 300,000 troops from the German order of battle. Army Group Center's security divisions, thrown into the front line or simply caught up in the chaos when the front line collapsed, were even more outnumbered and outmatched than other Eastern Army divisions. They were annihilated.

Less than a month later the Soviets launched similarly ferocious assaults in the north and south. Throughout these offensives the partisans were active not only in disrupting German supply and communications but also, increasingly, aiding Red Army units in cutting off and destroying German units.[13] Over the next three months the Red Army drove Army Group North out of the Baltic states, trapped the rest of it in the Courland Peninsula, and reached the East Prussian border, the River Vistula below Warsaw, and the Hungarian border along the Carpathians. Its armies swept out of the Soviet Union into eastern Europe and the Balkans. The Third Reich, now also facing an Anglo-American advance on its western border, had but months to live.

Erich Hesse describes the last months of the war on Soviet soil as the Germans went from being partisan hunters to the hunted themselves:

> The Soviet troops thrust relentlessly through the partisan areas that had appeared constantly in the German reports of the previous three years. Where the partisans were of suitable quality, the Red Army absorbed them. For those that were left remained a more fitting task: in the areas where the Soviet offensive had

rolled through, they hunted the thousands of fugitive German soldiers who, in the smallest of groups, sought an escape route to the west. Through weeks and months the hunt went on for men who, no longer resembling a military force, and driven by hunger and fear, knew that capture by the partisans meant a cruel death.[14]

National Socialist Germany's war against the Soviet Union aimed not at mere military victory, but at the complete destruction of the state's political and economic basis, and the decimation, subjugation, and exploitation of its people. This conception, set against all the precepts of effective, conciliatory occupation policy, was bound to engender bitter popular resistance. Given the Wehrmacht senior officer corps' support for this conception, and its singularly brutal tradition of antiguerrilla warfare, the ruthlessness of its campaign against that resistance was preordained before the first shot of the eastern campaign was fired. Ideological convictions shared with National Socialism, naked careerism, a propensity for professionalized violence, and singularly virulent guerrillaphobia all characterized the senior officer corps, and all merged in its conception of antiguerrilla warfare. Ideology provided the real concrete. The National Socialist ideology to which so much of the senior officer corps adhered further legitimized the use of violence in antipartisan warfare. It also encouraged such violence to be directed against the "ideological" enemies—Jews, Communists, eastern races—who aroused long-standing, widespread ire within the officer corps. Furthermore, it inspired officers to display brutality in antipartisan warfare as a means of advancement. That inveterate ruthlessness invested this combination, at the eastern war's outbreak, to such an extent also reflected developments that progressively brutalized and corrupted the officer corps through the 1930s and into the early years of World War II. On the eve of the invasion of the Soviet Union itself, a ruthlessly pragmatic incentive invested the entire undertaking of security in the east with further violent potential. The incentive came from the Wehrmacht leadership's belief that only terror would enable its security forces to meet the challenge of occupying a vast, inhospitable region with manpower and resources as paltry as those that the Wehrmacht leadership had allocated to the task.

This train of thought spawned the criminal orders the German Eastern Army took with it into the war against the Soviet Union. That conflict held a position of pivotal importance in four spheres: in the course of World War II; in the National Socialist regime's military plans, imperialist ambitions, and ideological worldview; in the life experiences of the eleven million or so Germans who served in the Wehrmacht; and in the extent of the culpability of those eleven million in war crimes. The outrages perpetrated in its course may have been less systematic than those of the Holocaust of European Jewry, but in the degree of death and suffering they spawned, they certainly rival it. The Wehrmacht's culpability was not all-encompassing, but it was enormous nonetheless. It is no surprise, given all the forces that had shaped its doctrine, that the German Eastern Army's antipartisan campaign was one of the most brutal aspects of that culpability.

Even so, if the severity of the *doctrine* behind the campaign was entrenched from the start, its full *application* in the field was not inevitable. From confident beginnings to wretched demise, the brutality of the antipartisan campaign ebbed and intensified at different times and, at the level of prosecution by middle-level field units, in different places. The backdrop to these developments was the wider dynamics of the eastern war and, indeed, of World War II itself. But it was middle-level field units that prosecuted the campaign, and wider developments were not the most immediate determiner of how they prosecuted it. More immediate were how those developments affected a particular unit, and to what extent ruthless attitudes, absorbed from the Wehrmacht and other sources, colored the mentality of the officer who commanded it. The diverse conditions in which antipartisan warfare in the Soviet Union was fought molded the first; the diverse perceptions of the thousands of individuals who made up the officer corps' middle level molded the second.

There is every reason to suppose that the conduct of units that were involved in other aspects of the war in the east—the treatment of Soviet prisoners of war, of Jews, and of other groups; the wider subsumption of the Soviet people and economy to the German war effort; and training, indoctrination, and combat at the front line— was determined by a similar set of ingredients. In any case, all these ingredients—institutional mindsets, wider developments in both the eastern war and the war in general, individual perceptions, and conditions in the field—conditioned the Eastern Army's antipartisan campaign on the ground. The dreadfulness of this campaign overall, and the levels of death and human misery it spawned, are indisputable. What remains to be answered is *the extent to which* the causes and degree of the brutality damn the middle-level officers as willing tools of a criminal regime.

The period of antipartisan conduct that presents the most damning spectacle is that of 1941. This was a period in which all three of the security divisions in the Army Group Center Rear Area—the 221st, 286th, and 403d—victimized Jews, colluded to the hilt in the mass murder of Jews and other groups by the SS and Order Police, and eventually infused their own security effort with a murderous ferocity even more remarkable for the fact that no partisan enemy to speak of even existed yet. That the 1941 campaign invites such condemnation lies in the fact that, of all the three periods focused on here, it was in 1941 that the violence of German methods outweighed the actual partisan threat most strikingly.

There were reasons for this brutality, not all of them to do with the ruthlessness that saturated both Wehrmacht security doctrine and the criminal orders that embodied it. The practical pressures such an ill-resourced security campaign faced were exacerbated as the eastern campaign stalled and dragged. Units at subdivisional level underwent particularly immense strain as the year progressed. In turn, these pressures played a direct role in driving cooperation, over even the most heinous of crimes, with the SS and police, and the escalation, from late summer, of the Eastern Army's own efforts against all potential sources of *future* partisan activity.

But all that aside, only a particularly ruthless mindset, one that the criminal orders had reinforced, could have contemplated reacting to that strain as brutally as it did. Nothing else explains the fact that, at this stage, the security divisions showed far less interest in winning the partisan war through cultivation, instead of terror, than they did later on.

It is necessary again to note Rolf Elble's reminder of the difficulty of judging the Wehrmacht, comprising as it did more than eleven million individuals, as an entire organization.[15] The caution applies to security divisions also. That *every* officer and man of all three of the 1941 security divisions was equally culpable in this abhorrence, if indeed culpable at all, is unlikely in the extreme. What can be stated categorically is that both the divisional and regimental officers of the 221st Security Division were implicated gravely. So, too, if the selected examples examined in these pages are any guide, were their divisional-level colleagues, and at least to some extent their regimental level colleagues also, in the 286th and 403d.

Individually, these officers displayed a mix of motives. Overall, however, they displayed the combination of ideology, military harshness, and personal ambition, that legacy of decades of institutional brutalization, that the criminal orders made explicit. And overall, the results were horrific.

Even had the antipartisan campaign ended in December 1941, the record of all three divisions would have been damning. The spate of immensely destructive large-scale operations carried out in the Vitebsk-Polotsk region during 1942 and 1943 condemns the senior officers of the 286th Security Division, like those of the newly arrived 201st, during those two later years also. But 1942, in contrast to 1941, saw a genuine continuum of brutality in the antipartisan campaign, ranging from extreme ruthlessness by the 201st and 286th, through the less ferocious albeit still very harsh approach of the 203d, to the relative sanity and restraint displayed by the 221st. The 221st, above all other Army Group Center security divisions, recognized that a situation in which understrength German forces faced genuine, widespread partisan activity necessitated a new, conciliatory approach both to the population and to potential partisan deserters. It recognized, in other words, that the *engagement* dimension of occupation administration had assumed new importance.

Though its division-level officers had the sense to see this, however, the 221st had not undergone some moral transformation. The single most important factor that governed the behavior of the 221st and its fellow security divisions was their particular situation. It was not just how difficult a division's situation was that was important, but the form that difficulty took, as well as how far that situation *enabled* it to respond to those difficulties brutally, that determined how far the conditions of 1942 tempered or stoked brutality. It was pragmatism in the face of a lack of ruthless alternatives that prompted officers like General Pflugbeil and particularly Lieutenant Beck to implement a more conciliatory antipartisan campaign.

And the shelflife of such constructive engagement was limited. The appetite of Germany's increasingly desperate war economy hardened National Socialist conceptions of occupation in the east and subjected the occupied population to a regime of rapacity and terror that even the most conciliatory officer could do only so much to alleviate. And of course, it was very hard for any propaganda campaign to sell the "benefits" of German occupation to a population that was undergoing such an ordeal. Such effective constructive engagement as a security division was able to achieve also was limited by the shortcomings, imposed by higher-level decree, of its own manpower and administration. In 1941 pacification through terror had been beyond the 221st Security Division. It is no surprise that in 1942 the more-complex demands of implementing the mutually supportive combination of effective yet measured force with constructive engagement ultimately were beyond it also.

But however calculating their motives, and however limited their long-term viability, restraint and cultivation were significant features of the 1942 antipartisan campaign. The fact that the 221st, one of the four security divisions in the Army Group Center area that year, practiced it extensively, and a second, the 203d, practiced it partially, does not compensate, in the general scheme of things, for the horrific results produced by the mobile operations of the 201st and

286th Security Divisions. But for the civilians on whom such conduct was visited, the difference could be crucial to whether they perished or survived.

The pivotal importance of conditions in the field is further demonstrated by the effect they had on the 221st Security Division in 1943. For in 1943, the pressures the 221st faced brutalized it also. Though its ruthlessness during 1943 never attained the heights of brutality reached by the 201st and 286th, the strains accumulating by that point put the cause of cultivation back decisively.

It was not simply that pressures on the 221st became onerous to the point where further brutalization was inevitable. Rather, a decisive break was reached when the inability of constructive engagement to cope with those demands became clear. The message it was trying to sell now looked even more unattractive than ever—it consisted of an occupation regime of ever-greater ruthlessness and rapacity, practiced by an army that in any case clearly was losing the war. The inadequacy of the human and material resources at the hearts-and-minds campaign's disposal, both directly and indirectly, had worsened. It had failed to prevent the partisans from increasing their support, numbers, and effectiveness. All this made it more likely that the division would lurch, if nothing else out of desperation, toward a harsher expedient.

It was not just the degree of pressure that increased, however, but its nature also, in the shape of the ever-greater importance, in an increasingly desperate situation both locally and for the Reich itself, of exploitation. This exploitation heightened the imperative to de-emphasize what was, in any case, an increasingly ineffective policy of constructive engagement and longer-term pacification. Instead, it prioritized an approach that aimed simply to hit the partisans and the growing propartisan population fast, and hit them hard.

Throughout this period, meanwhile, the closer, more-intense antipartisan warfare experience of the 221st Security Division's lower-level regiments, battalions, and garrisons contributed to brutalizing them frequently and increasingly. Certainly, there was a bedrock of institutional ruthlessness, nurtured by a series of higher-level directives, for that experience to tap. But it was the harshness of conditions that, more often than not, played the greatest role in converting that ruthlessness into the perpetration of atrocities. The tragic consequences inevitably undermined the efficacy of constructive engagement even further.

Conditions, then, were not the root cause of German brutality, but at all three stages of the campaign they played a pivotal role in either intensifying or moderating it.

Yet despite the importance of situation, officers were not slaves to it entirely. That the 221st Security Division pursued cultivation more energetically than some units in a similar situation supports this conclusion. The effects not just of conditions, but of officers' own inclinations, then, are crucial to any assessment of middle-level officers' conduct. The picture of the officers of the 221st Security Division that emerges contains various shades of gray. Even this, however, is to understate its complexity.

A decidedly dark shade was displayed by that group that, clearly, did not need even especially difficult circumstances to unleash its inherent ruthlessness. Colonel Illig and Lieutenant-Colonel von der Groeben, officers who, even though their units had not been undergoing particular hardship, assailed the population of the Yelnya-Dorogobuzh region mercilessly, seem clear candidates for this group. Clearest candidate of all was the 45th Security Regiment's Colonel Wiemann, a man whose exploits, were it not for the light they shed on the brutalizing potential of the life influences that shaped him, would not bear thinking about. All three stand out, together with the 350th Infantry Regiment's Colonel Koch in 1941, as officers whose ruthlessness surpassed the expectations, and even went against the wishes, of divisional command.

Considerably removed from these officers was a group that, though it might prosecute antipartisan warfare with some ruthlessness, still showed a significant and consistent degree of moderation. Those regimental commanders of late 1942 and early 1943 whose conduct showed comparative restraint—Colonels Lehmann, Luckmann, Hegedüs, and von Geldern-Crispendorff—belong to this group. General Lendle, whose assumption of command of the 221st Security Division in June 1942 contributed to the refinement of its more enlightened policies, belongs to it also. True, the consistency of his moderation weakened in 1943, but it is surely significant that, under his command, the division continued to conduct itself that year also with significantly more restraint than it might have done.

Such a small sample is not, of course, the stuff of firm conclusions. But the contrast in behavior is unmistakable. So too is the contrast in characteristics. Of the former group, at least three, and possibly the fourth, Lieutenant-Colonel von der Groeben, were born in eastern Germany; of the latter, none.[16] There is reason to suppose, then, that the former group was infected particularly strongly with the anti-Slavism so pronounced in that region. None of the former group were continuing officers during the interwar period; of the latter, four were continuing officers—Lendle and Lehmann in the Reichswehr, Hegedüs and Luckmann in the Austrian federal army. It is not far-fetched to argue that officers who spent most of the Weimar years living and working not among brother officers, but among Germany's beleaguered middle class, could have had their ideological conviction strengthened even further from that source also. It was the German middle class, after all, that formed the bed-rock of National Socialist support during the late 1920s and early 1930s.

Conversely, it is not far-fetched to surmise that officers who continued to serve in the Reichswehr during the interwar years, while almost certainly absorbing some of its institutional ruthlessness, may also have imbibed something of its more decent traditions.[17] The fact that Hitler needed, before and upon his assumption of power, to impress certain elements of the officer corps with a "stress upon decency, morality, order, Christianity, and all those concepts which went with a conservative idea of the state" shows that in 1933 such concepts still retained some currency within the officer corps.[18] One might argue that the 1944 attempt, by high-ranking officers, to blow Hitler up indicates that they still retained a certain currency a decade later. Though the constraints of the institution to which Lendle and his ilk belonged prevented them from expressing themselves in such terms, it is possible that values such as these did indeed broaden their view, and moderate their conduct of antipartisan warfare somewhat. The fifth "moderate" officer, Colonel von Geldern-Crispendorff, was of aristocratic stock, and was therefore perhaps less susceptible to National Socialism in any case. It should be remembered that even as late as 1935 he had yet to join the Nazi Party.[19]

But if the 221st Security Division is any guide, it was a third group of officers who, overall, had the most decisive effect on troop conduct. These are best described as "self-styled pragmatists." The self-styled element is important.

Unlike most of the aforementioned fanatics or moderates, these were not regimental officers, but division-level officers. Division-level remits, unlike those at regimental level, encompassed not just execution of orders in the course of day-to-day security and antipartisan operations. They also encompassed all the wider areas with which an occupation administration may have to deal—pacification, engagement, and exploitation. These tasks were complex, multifaceted, and interacting. That division-level officers may have been fanatically or moderately inclined, then, was less important than the fact that, if they were to fulfill these tasks from day to day, they had to consider all interrelated aspects of the occupation situation systematically. Probably more fundamentally important than their personal inclination, particularly for those in the various division-level departments directly responsible, was the fact that fulfilling these tasks was their job.

It was from this systematic consideration of circumstances, more than from their preexisting personal inclinations, that their conduct emerged. And the fact that circumstances changed meant that their conduct could change also. For this reason did officers like General Pflugbeil and Lieutenant Beck introduce a considerable amount of cultivation in 1942, in place of much of the ideologically colored terror they had favored in 1941—even though Beck, whatever else may be said of him, seems also to have recognized the importance of a degree of cultivation early on.

But this brand of pragmatism contained a considerable self-styled element. It was a self-styled pragmatism in that, although the officers who practiced it may have wished to view it as a sensible, constructive response to their situation, it fell far short of such a positive description in reality. Granted, it did contain a measure, particularly in Beck's case, of genuine farsightedness. But the divisional level as a whole seems to have subscribed to pragmatism less as a considered, viable, long-term approach to the problem of security than as a desperate response to immediate circumstances. Indeed, lack of resources and manpower and the alienating effects of wider occupation policy hampered its long-term viability anyway. In view of what motivated it, it was not necessarily the kind of genuine pragmatism that enabled officers to see the real "bigger picture" of the effect of both the antipartisan campaign specifically and Nazi occupation policy generally. Given the inclinations of men who, like Pflugbeil, were convinced Nazis, the likelihood that they indeed did fail to see the bigger picture is strong. Even Beck's farsightedness, when conditions reached a certain point in 1943, was superseded by a reversion to blinkered ideological type.[20]

The sources on the other Army Group Center security divisions are too patchy to permit any firm conclusions. The scale of brutality in the antipartisan policy that units such as the 201st and 286th Security Divisions practiced suggests not only that harsher conditions, crucial though they were, were at work. It also suggests that foresight, and for that matter basic humanity, were in these divisions crowded out by National Socialist conviction even more than they were in the 221st. What united all the security divisions, however, were middle-level officer contingents that, drawn from diverse backgrounds as they were, would have contained some mix of fanatics, moderates, and self-styled pragmatists. Both diverse conditions and diverse perceptions, then, channeled the sources of ruthlessness that emanated from above in different ways, and to different degrees.

Explaining the role played by "ordinary men" in National Socialist Germany's war of extermination, a war of singular destructiveness and immense scale, is an important undertaking. Recognizing the diversity of the Eastern Army's antipartisan campaign, as well as its dreadfulness, aids this process. It is worth adding finally, however, that if recognizing diversity aids historical explanation, then recognizing the ruinous, devastating nature of the forces that shaped the Eastern Army's antipartisan campaign *overall* holds even greater current import.

None of the prominent international powers of today would succumb to the degree of degenerative brutality with which the National Socialist conception of the war in the Soviet Union infused the Eastern Army's antipartisan campaign. Through both the ruthlessness of its wider occupation policy and the underresourcing of its security forces, this policy hamstrung officers' ability to enact a measured, multifaceted, effective antipartisan campaign. National Socialist ideology, meanwhile, synthesized and hardened the prejudices of all too many officers, inclining them to the kind of ruthlessness guaranteed to undermine the essential maintenance of workable relations between occupier and occupied.

Quality troops in sufficient numbers, equipped to overcome not only guerrilla warfare's physical challenges but the equally important challenge of securing popular cooperation, are essential to the successful and *humane* prosecution of any antiguerrilla campaign. It is also essential that the wider occupation regime, in all its forms, be geared to fostering such cooperation. History since 1945 shows that these lessons have been widely learned. It is to the credit of counterinsurgency commanders and occupation administrators operating in often difficult, complex situations that this is the case. Yet that same difficulty and complexity must not prevent the conduct of antiguerrilla warfare in general from incorporating those lessons even more fully. The German Eastern Army's antipartisan campaign, though an extreme example, provides manifold instances of where failure to learn such lessons may lead.

APPENDIXES

ACKNOWLEDGMENTS

ABBREVIATIONS AND TRANSLATIONS

NOTES

BIBLIOGRAPHY OF PRIMARY SOURCES

INDEX

Appendix A

LARGER ANTIPARTISAN OPERATIONS CARRIED
OUT BY THE 221ST SECURITY DIVISION,
DECEMBER 1942–APRIL 1943

Name	Period	Sector	Partisan dead	No. of partisan small arms taken	German & allied dead	Main 221st Security Division units participating	Main livestock seized
Ankara	12/19–12/24/42	Northeast	See Ankara II figures	No figures	See Ankara II figures	36th Security Regiment (commanding); 8th SS Police Regiment, 638th (French) Infantry Regiment, Eastern Troops (one battalion each)	74 cows; 122 sheep
Ankara II	1/18–1/20/43	Northeast	For Ankara I & II: 150 (32 counted); 41 "accomplices" shot	No figures	For Ankara I & II: 5	As above	66 horses; 53 cattle; 70 sheep
Limpet II	1/20–2/7/43	Kletnya forest (Army Rear Area, Second Panzer Army)	441 to whole operation, of whom 342 to 221st's troops	81 to whole operation, of which 51 to 221st's troops	14	As above, plus Security Battalion 791	244 horses; 79 cows
Zugspitze	2/3/43	Southeast	141 "accomplices" shot by Secret Field Police	No figures	0	930th Grenadier Regiment (commanding)	200 cows; 140 sheep

Easter Bunny	4/26–4/30/43	Central	250	34	5	45th Security Regiment (commanding), Security Battalion 242 (two companies); Luftwaffe battle group	88 horses; 160 cattle; 200 sheep

Sources: Ankara: KTB, 6/18–12/31/42, Sich.-Div. 221 Ia, 12/22/42, file 29380/1, T-315/1678, NA; Betr.: "Unternehmen Ankara. Gefechtsbericht, 12/19–12/24/42," p. 1, Sich.-Rgt. 36 Ia, 12/26/42, file 36509/11, T-315/1685, NA. *Ankara II:* KTB, 1/1–6/1/43, Sich.-Div. 221 Ia, 19/1/43, file 36509/1, T-315/1682, NA; Sich.-Div. 221 Ia, 1/16/43, p. 1, file 36509/11, T-315/1685, NA; Betr.: "Unternehmen Ankara II. Gefechtsbericht, 1/17–1/21/43," Sich.-Rgt. 36 Ia, 1/25/43, file 36509/12, T-315/1685, NA. *Limpet II:* Betr.: "Unternehmen Klette II," Sich.-Div. 221 Ia, 2/12/43, file 36509/4, T-315/1682, NA; Betr.: "Unternehmen Klette II. Gefechtsbericht," Sich.-Rgt. 36 Ia, 2/9/43, file 36509/12, T-315/1685, NA; Betr.: "Regimentsbefehl für die Sicherung des bei Ankara u. Klette II befriedeten Raumes," 2/9/43, ibid. *Zugspitze:* Betr.: "Unternehmen Zugspitze," Gren.-Rgt. 930 Ia, 1/18/43, file 36509/17, T-315/1686, NA; "Bericht über Verlauf und Ergebnis des Unternehmens Zugspitze," 2/8/43, ibid.; Betr.: "Erfassung beim Unternehmen Zugspitze," Gren.-Rgt. 930 Ib, 2/9/43, ibid. *Easter Bunny:* Betr.: "Bericht über Unternehmen Osterhase," Sich.-Div. 221 Ia, 5/2/43, file 36509/13, T-315/1685, NA.

Appendix B

The definition of "atrocity" as recorded in the table is any case in which more than 15 partisans are recorded as killed and in which the German losses appear too low to reflect genuine combat. The smallest ratio between partisan and German losses in the table is approximately 7.5:1. References to partisans burned to death are not intended to refer to deliberate acts of immolation (though this may sometimes have happened). Rather, these partisans are supposed to have perished in burning buildings in the course of battle.

The use of artillery and/or tanks in the actions of 4/8, 4/27, 5/12, 5/30, and 6/4/42 may account for a significant amount of the disparity between recorded German and recorded partisan dead on these dates. However, so minute or even nonexistent were German losses that it also seems likely that much of the disparity is still explicable in terms of the deaths of noncombatants. After all, the combined recorded partisan dead for these five actions was 199 at the very least and was probably nearer 300, whereas German dead amounted to just 4. Moreover, while no figures for captured weapons are recorded for any of these five instances, the massive overall disparity between recorded partisan dead and recorded partisan weapons captured during the Yelnya-Dorogobuzh operations as a whole is an even stronger indication that a massive number of noncombatants perished. Incidents in the table for which the sources do not provide further information are not analyzed in the text.

Date	Unit	Recorded "partisan" dead
4/8/42	Territorial Battalion 230, with artillery and tanks	62; German losses: 3 dead, 6 wounded
4/27/42	44th Territorial Regiment (probably Territorial Battalion 974), with artillery	30; German losses: 1 dead, 1 wounded
5/12/42	Cycle Squadron 213, with tanks	71; 60–70 estimated killed in burning village; German losses: 0
5/30/42	Territorial Battalion 545, with artillery.	25; German losses: 0
6/1/42	Territorial Battalion 302	40, probably more killed in burning village; German losses: 2 dead, 8 wounded
6/8/42	No details	65; German losses: 1 dead, 5 wounded
7/25/42	No details	15; German losses: 0
9/6/42	Ortskommandantur Roslavl	28; German losses: 0
9/12/42	45th Security Regiment (probably Security Battalion 230)	At least 40; German losses: 4 dead
9/26/42	1st battalion, 8th Police Regiment	70–80; German dead: 2
11/14/42	Security Battalion 791	20; German dead: 0
12/28/42	Probably 45th Security Regiment	25; German/OD dead: 3, 7 OD missing
1/11/43	OD	24; OD dead: 0
2/14/43	Unknown	At least 30; German losses: 0
3/30/43	OD	15; OD losses: 2 dead
4/18/43	OD	25; OD losses: 0
4/22/43	Unknown	At least 83; German losses: 0
4/23/43	Unknown	22; German/OD losses: 1 dead, 4 OD wounded
5/5/43	OD	15; OD losses: 0

Date	Unit	Recorded "partisan" dead
5/17/43	Security Battalion 242	ca. 65; up to 150 reported wounded; German losses: 0
7/7/43	Unknown	20; German losses: 0
8/29/43	Security Battalion 242	150 killed or wounded; German losses: 15 dead, 13 wounded, 9 missing
8/30/43	OD	17; OD losses: 1 dead

Sources: KTB, 3/20–6/17/42, 221. Div. Ia, 4/8, 4/27, 5/12, 5/30, 6/1, 6/8/42, file 22639/1, T-315/1676, NA. KTB, 6/18–12/31/42, Sich.-Div. 221 Ia, 7/25, 9/6, 9/12, 9/26, 11/14, 12/28/42, 1/11/43, file 29380/1, T-315/1678, NA; KTB, 1/1–6/1/43, Sich.-Div. 221 Ia, 1/11/43, file 36509/1, T-315/1682, NA; KTB, 1/1–5/1/43, Sich.-Div. 221 Ia, 2/14, 3/30, 4/18, 4/22, 4/23/43, file 36509/1, T-315/1682, NA; KTB, 5/1–8/31/43, Sich.-Div. 221 Ia, 5/5, 5/17, 7/7, 8/29, 8/30/43, file 36509/2, ibid.

Acknowledgments

Grateful thanks are due to Professor John Breuilly, Department of Medieval and Modern History, University of Birmingham, who supervised the Ph.D. research from which this book originated; the Institute for German Studies, University of Birmingham, for giving me the opportunity to conduct that research; the Department of Medieval and Modern History, University of Birmingham, for the opportunity to support myself with teaching while writing this book; the School of Law and Social Sciences, Glasgow Caledonian University, for the current post that enabled me to finish it; Kathleen McDermott at Harvard University Press and the external reviewers there, for helpful advice on writing the book; and the German Academic Exchange Service, the British Academy, the German Historical Institute, and Royal Holloway College, University of London, for extra research funding. Thanks also to the following individuals, who freely gave advice or practical help: in Germany, Klaus-Jochen Arnold, Phil Blood, Henry Böhm, Bernd Boll, Bernhard Chiari, Wilhelm Deist, Cynthia Flör, Jürgen Förster, Stig Förster, Christian Gerlach, Christian Hartmann, Hannes Heer, Ulrich Herbert, Gerhard Hirschfeld, Martin Humburg, Johannes Hürter, Bernhard Kroener, Norbert Kunz, Bernd Lemke, Bernd Martin, Franka Maubach, Manfred Messerschmidt, Georg Meyer, Hans Mommsen, Klaus Moser, Georg Müller, Klaus-Jürgen Müller, Rolf-Dieter Müller, Rüdiger Overmans, Dieter Pohl, Christoph Rass, Wolfgang Remmers, Irene Renz, Volker Rieß, Florian Rohdenborg, Otmar

Schneider, Heinrich Schwendemann, Christian Streit, Gerd Ueberschär, Bernd Wegner, and Wolfram Wette; in the United Kingdom, Louise Allamby, Ian Farr, John Grenville, Jonathan Grix, Alexander Hill, Charlie Jefferey, Ian Kershaw, Lothar Kettenacker, Peter Longerich, Corey Ross, Theo Schulte, Nick Terry, and Wilfried van der Will; and in the United States, Truman Anderson, Omer Bartov, Colin Heaton, Tom Laub, Bryan Rigg, and Jonathan Steinberg.

Thanks also to those private individuals whom I contacted for further information on former Wehrmacht officers, who took the time either to write or to meet with me; and to the staff of the following institutions: Federal Archive, Aachen-Kornelimünster; Federal Archive, Berlin-Lichterfelde; Federal Archive, Koblenz; German Armed Services Office, Berlin; German Historical Institute, London; Imperial War Museum, London; Institute of Contemporary History, Munich; Military History Research Institute, Potsdam; Library of Contemporary History, Stuttgart; U.S. National Archive, College Park, Maryland; Wiener Library, London; Zentrale Stelle der Landesjustizverwaltungen, Ludwigsburg. On the archival front, I owe special thanks to the staff at the Federal Military Archive, Freiburg im Breisgau, for their unfailing patience and help.

Abbreviations and Translations

Abt.	Abteilung (section)
Anl.	Anlage (supplement)
BA-MA	Bundesarchiv-Militärarchiv (Federal Military Archive), Freiburg im Breisgau
Betr.	Betrifft (regarding)
BfZ	Bibliothek für Zeitgeschichte (Library of Contemporary History), Stuttgart
Chef der Sipo	Der Chef der Sicherheitspolizei und SD (Chief of Security Police and Security Service)
DDSt	Deutsche Dienststelle (German Armed Services Office), Berlin
EM	Ereignißmeldung (Event report)
Gren.-Rgt.	Grenadier-Regiment
Inf.-Div.	Infanterie-Division
Inf.-Rgt.	Infanterie-Regiment
IWM	Imperial War Museum, London
Kp.	Kompanie (company)
KTB	Kriegstagebuch (war diary)
LSR	Landesschützen-Regiment (territorial regiment)
MadbO	Meldung aus den besetzten Ostgebieten (Report from the Occupied Eastern Territory)
NA	U.S. National Archive, College Park, Maryland
OD	Ordnungsdienst (Order Service)
OKH	Oberkommando des Heeres (Army High Command)
OKW	Oberkommando der Wehrmacht (Armed Forces High Command)
Prop.-Abt.	Propaganda-Abteilung (Propaganda Section)
Qu.	Quartiermeister (quartermaster)
RHGeb.	Rückwärtige Heeresgebiet (Army Group Rear Area)
Sich.-Btl.	Sicherungs-Bataillon (security battalion)

Sich.-Div.	Sicherungs-Division (security division)
Sich.-Rgt.	Sicherungs-Regiment (security regiment)
TWCNMT	Trials of War Criminals, Nuremberg Military Tribunal
Voraus-Abt.	Voraus-Abteilung (Reconnaissance Section)
WFSt	Wehrmachtführungsstab (Wehrmacht Leadership Office)
WiKo	Wirtschaftskommando (Economic Detachment)

Notes

Introduction

1. Strictly speaking, the term *Wehrmacht* translates as "armed forces," referring not just to the German Army (Heer) but also to the Luftwaffe and the German Navy (Kriegsmarine). However, the debate surrounding its nature and conduct during the Third Reich is concerned mainly with the Army. This book accordingly distinguishes among the Wehrmacht, Luftwaffe, and Kriegsmarine.

2. On the German High Command's military and organizational performance during World War II, see Geoffrey P. Megargee, *Inside Hitler's High Command* (Lawrence: University Press of Kansas, 2000).

3. Wolfram Wette, "Erobern, zerstören, auslöschen. Die verdrängte Schuld von 1941: Der Rußlandfeldzug war ein Raub- und Vernichtungskrieg von Anfang an," *Zeit-Punkte*, no. 3 (1995), 17.

4. Theo J. Schulte, *The German Army and Nazi Policies in Occupied Russia* (Oxford: Berg, 1989), p. 32.

5. Manfred Messerschmidt, *Die Wehrmacht im NS-Staat: Zeit der Indoktrination* (Hamburg: R. V. Decker's, 1969); Klaus-Jürgen Müller, *Das Heer und Hitler: Armee und nationalsozialistisches Regime 1933–1945* (Stuttgart: Deutsche Verlags-Anstalt, 1969). See also Schulte, *German Army and Nazi Policies*, pp. 8–10.

6. Bernhard R. Kroener, "Strukturelle Veränderungen in der Militärischen Gesellschaft des Dritten Reiches," in Michael Prinz and Rainer Zitelmann, eds., *Nationalsozialismus und Modernisierung* (Darmstadt: Wissenschaftliche Buchgesellschaft, 1994), pp. 267–296, esp. 272–278.

7. F. L. Carsten, *The Reichswehr and Politics, 1918 to 1933* (Oxford: Clarendon Press, 1966), pp. 199, 200.

8. Ibid., pp. 119, 164.

9. Fritz Fischer, *Griff nach der Weltmacht: Die Kriegszielpolitik des kaiserlichen Deutschland 1914/18* (Düsseldorf: Droste, 1961), pp. 714–736; Vejas

Gabriel Liulevicius, *War Land on the Eastern Front: Culture, National Identity, and German Occupation in World War I* (Cambridge: Cambridge University Press, 2000).

10. Alexander B. Rossino, *Hitler Strikes Poland: Blitzkrieg, Ideology, and Atrocity* (Lawrence: University Press of Kansas, 2003), pp. 5–8.

11. Gerhard L. Weinberg, *Germany, Hitler, and World War II: Essays in Modern German and World History* (Cambridge: Cambridge University Press, 1995), p. 132.

12. Michael Geyer, *Aufrüstung oder Sicherheit: Die Reichswehr in der Krise der Machtpolitik 1924–1936* (Wiesbaden: Steiner, 1980); idem, "Professionals and Junkers: German Rearmament and Politics in the Weimar Republic," in Richard Bessel and E. J. Feuchtwanger, eds., *Social Change and Political Development in Weimar Germany* (London: Croom Helm, 1981), pp. 77–133; idem, "Etudes in Political History: Reichswehr, NSDAP and the Seizure of Power," in Peter Stachura, ed., *The Nazi Machtergreifung* (London: Allen and Unwin, 1983), pp. 101–123; idem, "Traditional Elites and National Socialist Leadership," in Charles S. Maier, ed., *The Rise of the Nazi Regime: Historical Reassessments* (Boulder: Westview, 1986), pp. 57–73.

13. Kroener, "Strukturelle Veränderungen," pp. 277–278.

14. Geyer, "Professionals and Junkers," p. 84.

15. Klaus-Jürgen Müller, *The Army, Politics, and Society in Germany, 1933–45* (Manchester: Manchester University Press, 1987), pp. 19–35.

16. On the appeal that the idea of the national community held in military circles, see Martin Broszat, "Soziale Motivation und Führer-Bindung im Nationalsozialismus," *Vierteljahreshefte für Zeitgeschichte* 18 (1970), 392–409; Manfred Messerschmidt, "The *Wehrmacht* and the *Volksgemeinschaft*," *Journal of Contemporary History* 18 (1983), 719–744.

17. Jeremy Noakes and Geoffrey Pridham, *Nazism, 1919–1945*, vol. 3: *Foreign Policy, War, and Racial Extermination*, 2d ed. (Exeter: University of Exeter Press, 2001), p. 31.

18. Kroener, "Strukturelle Veränderungen," pp. 277–278.

19. Broszat, "Soziale Motivation und Führer-Bindung," p. 401.

20. Kroener, "Strukturelle Veränderungen," pp. 274–276; Robert G. L. Waite, *Vanguard of Nazism: The Free Corps Movement in Postwar Germany, 1918–1923* (Cambridge, Mass.: Harvard University Press, 1952), chap. 2; Nigel H. Jones, *Hitler's Heralds: The Story of the Freikorps, 1918–1923* (London: John Murray, 1987), introduction, chap. 1.

21. G. J. Giles, *Students and National Socialism in Germany* (Guildford: Princeton University Press, 1985).

22. On anti-Semitism in the German officer corps before 1914, see Martin Kitchen, *The German Officer Corps, 1890–1914* (Oxford: Clarendon Press, 1968), pp. 37–48. Regarding the literature on longer-term anti-Semi-

tism in German society, see Michael Burleigh and Wolfgang Wippermann, *The Racial State: Germany, 1933–1945* (Cambridge: Cambridge University Press, 1991), pp. 359–360; Ulrich Herbert, "Extermination Policy: New Answers and Questions about the History of the 'Holocaust' in German Historiography," in Herbert, ed., *National Socialist Extermination Policies: Contemporary German Perspectives and Controversies* (Oxford: Berghahn, 2000), pp. 17–24. Despite its title, the chapter also covers English-language historiography.

23. Jonathan Steinberg, *All or Nothing: The Axis and the Holocaust, 1941–1943* (London: Routledge, 1990), p. 237 (brackets in original); Carsten, *Reichswehr and Politics*, p. 203.

24. Jürgen Förster, "Hitlers Entscheidung für den Krieg gegen die Sowjetunion," in Horst Boog et al., *Der Angriff auf die Sowjetunion* (Frankfurt am Main: Fischer, 1991), p. 48. Christian Streit attaches particular importance to anti-Bolshevism as an "integrating factor" in officers' support for the Nazis; *Keine Kameraden: Die Wehrmacht und die sowjetischen Kriegsgefangenen*, 2d ed. (Bonn: Dietz, 1997), pp. 50–59; idem, "Ostkrieg, Antibolschewismus, und 'Endlösung,'" *Geschichte und Gesellschaft* 17 (1991), 242–255.

25. Burleigh and Wippermann, *Racial State*, pp. 23–28.

26. Kroener, "Strukturelle Veränderungen," pp. 274–276.

27. Waite, *Vanguard of Nazism*, p. 23.

28. On impressions German soldiers gleaned of Russian primitiveness during World War I, see Peter Jahn, "Russenfurcht und Antibolschewismus. Zur Entstehung und Wirkung von Feindbildern," in Jahn and Reinhard Rürup, eds., *Erobern und Vernichten: Der Krieg gegen die Sowjetunion 1941–1945: Essays* (Berlin: Argon, 1991), p. 51; Liulevicius, *War Land*, pp. 151–156.

29. Johannes Hürter, "'Freischärler'—'Banden'—'Horden.' Erfahrungen späterer Wehrmachtsgeneräle mit irregulärer Kriegführung 1914–1920," paper presented at the conference of the German Committee for the Study of the Second World War, 6/29/01.

30. Hans-Heinrich Wilhelm, *Rassenpolitik und Kriegführung: Sicherheitspolizei und Wehrmacht in Polen und der Sowjetunion* (Passau: Wissenschaftsverlag Rother, 1991), pp. 147–148.

31. Liulevicius, *War Land*, chaps. 6, 8.

32. Streit, *Keine Kameraden*, pp. 50–59; Manfred Messerschmidt, "Harte Sühne am Judentum. Befehlslage und Wissen in der deutschen Wehrmacht" in Jörg Wollenberg, ed., *"Niemand war dabei und keiner hat's gewußt": Die deutsche Öffentlichkeit und die Judenverfolgung 1933–1945* (Munich: Piper, 1989), pp. 113–128; Steinberg, *All or Nothing*, pp. 236–241.

33. Wilhelm, *Rassenpolitik und Kriegführung*, pp. 147–148.

34. Helmut Krausnick, *Hitlers Einsatzgruppen: Die Truppe des Weltanschauungskrieges 1938–1942* (Frankfurt am Main: Fischer, 1985), p. 192.

35. On the impact of the experience of Free Corps service on German Army officers, see Broszat, "Soziale Motivation und Führer-Bindung."

36. Hürter, "'Freischärler'—'Banden'—'Horden.'"

37. Joachim C. Fest, *The Face of the Third Reich* (London: Weidenfeld and Nicolson, 1970), p. 237.

38. On the Wehrmacht officer corps' development and its evolving relationship with National Socialism between 1933 and 1939, see Messerschmidt, *Die Wehrmacht im NS-Staat;* K.-J. Müller, *Das Heer und Hitler;* idem, *The Army, Politics, and Society.* On its military and organizational development, see Megargee, *Inside Hitler's High Command,* chaps. 2–4.

39. Kroener, "Strukturelle Veränderungen," pp. 274–276, 279 ff.

40. Ian Kershaw, *The Nazi Dictatorship: Problems and Perspectives of Interpretation,* 4th ed. (London: Edward Arnold, 2000), chaps. 4–6.

41. Weinberg, *Germany, Hitler, and World War II,* p. 140.

42. For an introduction to Nazi foreign policy, see ibid., chaps. 6–11; Kershaw, *Nazi Dictatorship,* chap. 6 (on the historiographical debate).

43. Weinberg, *Germany, Hitler, and World War II,* chaps. 9–11; Rossino, *Hitler Strikes Poland,* pp. 5–8.

44. Rossino, *Hitler Strikes Poland,* p. 1, chaps. 2–4, p. 234.

45. Ibid., chaps. 3–4.

46. Omer Bartov, *Hitler's Army: Soldiers, Nazis, and War in the Third Reich* (New York: Oxford University Press, 1992), p. 66.

47. Rossino, *Hitler Strikes Poland,* pp. 115–120; Jürgen Förster, "Wehrmacht, Krieg und Holocaust," in Rolf-Dieter Müller and Hans-Erich Volkmann, eds., *Die Wehrmacht: Mythos und Realität* (Munich: Oldenbourg, 1999), p. 953.

48. Ian Kershaw, *Hitler, 1936–1945: Nemesis* (London: Penguin, 2001), p. 300.

49. Adolf Hitler, *Mein Kampf,* quoted in Alan Bullock, *Hitler: A Study in Tyranny* (London: Penguin, 1990), p. 650.

50. On the literature concerning how long-term Hitler's foreign policy goals were, see Kershaw, *Nazi Dictatorship,* chap. 6.

51. Bullock, *Hitler,* pp. 640–641.

52. On background to the motives that shaped the senior officer corps' attitude toward impending war with the Soviet Union, see Andreas Hillgruber, *Die Zerstörung Europas: Beiträge zur Weltkriegsepoche 1914 bis 1945* (Berlin: Propyläen, 1988), pp. 256–272; Förster, "Hitlers Entscheidung"; Rolf-Dieter Müller, "Von der Wirtschaftsallianz zum kolonialen Ausbeutungskrieg," in Boog et al., *Der Angriff auf die Sowjetunion,* pp. 141–

245; Weinberg, *Germany, Hitler, and World War II*, chap. 12; Megargee, *Inside Hitler's High Command*, chaps. 5–6.

53. Bartov, *Hitler's Army*, p. 129.

54. Rolf-Dieter Müller, "Das Reich der Herrenmenschen," *Zeit-Punkte*, no. 3 (1995), 21.

55. Weinberg, *Germany, Hitler, and World War II*, p. 160.

56. Streit, *Keine Kameraden*, pp. 50–59; idem, "Ostkrieg, Antibolschewismus, und 'Endlösung.'"

57. R.-D. Müller, "Von der Wirtschaftsallianz zum kolonialen Ausbeutungskrieg."

58. Kershaw, *Nazi Dictatorship*, pp. 154–160; Weinberg, *Germany, Hitler, and World War II*, chap. 14.

59. Megargee, *Inside Hitler's High Command*, chap. 6.

60. Weinberg, *Germany, Hitler, and World War II*, pp. 161–162; idem, *Germany and the Soviet Union, 1939–1941* (Leyden: Brill, 1954, 1972), chap. 8.

61. Jürgen Förster, "Das Unternehmen 'Barbarossa' als Eroberungs- und Vernichtungskrieg," in Boog et al., *Der Angriff auf die Sowjetunion*, pp. 514–515.

62. R.-D. Müller, "Das Scheitern der wirtschaftlichen 'Blitzkriegstrategie,'" in Boog et al., *Der Angriff auf die Sowjetunion*, p. 1187.

63. Kroener, "Strukturelle Veränderungen," p. 282.

64. Christian Gerlach, *Kalkulierte Morde: Die deutsche Wirtschafts- und Vernichtungspolitik in Weißrußland 1941 bis 1944* (Hamburg: Hamburger Edition, 1999), p. 870; Timothy P. Mulligan, "Reckoning the Cost of People's War: The German Experience in the Central USSR," *Russian History* 9 (1982), 45, 47.

65. Alexander Werth, *Russia at War, 1941–1945* (New York: Carroll and Graf, 1984), p. 722.

66. Joachim Hoffmann, "Die Kriegführung aus der Sicht der Sowjetunion," in Boog et al., *Der Angriff auf die Sowjetunion*, pp. 918–930); idem, *Stalins Vernichtungskrieg 1941–1945* (Munich: Verlag für Wehrwissenschaft, 1995), pp. 17–80, 216–248.

67. Jörg Friedrich, *Das Gesetz des Krieges: Das deutsche Heer in Rußland 1941 bis 1945. Der Prozeß gegen das Oberkommando der Wehrmacht* (Munich: Piper, 1993).

68. Daniel Jonah Goldhagen, *Hitler's Willing Executioners: Ordinary Germans and the Holocaust* (London: Abacus, 1997).

69. Studies of German society and popular opinion in the Third Reich include Ian Kershaw, *Popular Opinion and Political Dissent in the Third Reich: Bavaria, 1933–1945* (Oxford: Clarendon Press, 1983); Lutz Niethammer,

ed., *"Die Jahre weiß man nicht, wo man die heute hinsetzen soll"*: *Faschismuser-fahrungen im Ruhrgebiet* (Berlin: Dietz, 1983); Martin Broszat and Elke Frölich, *Alltag und Widerstand: Bayern im Nationalsozialismus* (Zurich: Piper, 1987); Detlev Peukert, *Inside Nazi Germany: Conformity, Opposition, and Racism in Everyday Life* (London: Penguin, 1993).

70. A concise introduction to the Nazis' rise to power and the nature of its electoral support is Conan Fischer, *The Rise of the Nazis* (Manchester: Manchester University Press, 1995).

71. On the impact of Nazi social and economic policy on different socioeconomic groups, see Kershaw, *Popular Opinion*, chaps. 1–3, 7; Peukert, *Inside Nazi Germany*, chaps. 6–7.

72. George L. Mosse, *The Crisis of German Ideology: Intellectual Origins of the Third Reich* (New York: Howard Fertig, 1998), chaps. 13–15; Burleigh and Wippermann, *Racial State*, pp. 359–360; Herbert, "Extermination Policy," pp. 17–24. On popular opinion toward Jews during the Third Reich, see Kershaw, *Popular Opinion*, chaps. 6, 9.

73. Liulevicius, *War Land*, chap. 8.

74. Manfred Messerschmidt et al., *Das Deutsche Reich und der Zweite Weltkrieg*, vol. 1: *Ursachen und Voraussetzungen der deutschen Kriegspolitik* (Stuttgart: Deutsche Verlags-Anstalt, 1979), pp. 25–106.

75. Kershaw, *Nazi Dictatorship*, chap. 8.

76. Fest, *The Face of the Third Reich*, p. 237.

77. Alexander Dallin, *German Rule in Russia, 1941–1945: A Study in Occupation Policy* (London: MacMillan, 1981), p. 507, quoted in Schulte, *German Army and Nazi Policies*, p. 32.

78. Peter Hoffmann, *German Resistance to Hitler* (Cambridge, Mass.: Harvard University Press, 1988); idem, *Stauffenberg: A Family History, 1905–1944* (Cambridge: Cambridge University Press, 1996); idem, *The History of the German Resistance, 1933–1945*, 3d ed. (Montreal: McGill-Queen's University Press, 1996).

79. On the need for a nuanced approach to the officer corps and the Wehrmacht generally, see Rolf-Dieter Müller, "Die Wehrmacht—Historische Last und Verantwortung. Die Historiographie im Spannungsfeld von Wissenschaft und Vergangenheitsbewältigung," in Müller and Volkmann, *Die Wehrmacht*, pp. 3–35.

80. Sources generated by NCOs and rank-and-file soldiers, by contrast, are private sources—letters, diaries, interviews, and so on—available to historians far less extensively. On the source-related problems with which a study of NCOs and rank-and-file soldiers has to contend, see Ben Shepherd, "German Army Security Units in Russia, 1941–1943: A Case Study" (Ph.D. diss., University of Birmingham, 2000), pp. 7–10.

81. Throughout the book, the name Belarus is used to denote the pres-

ent-day country. The name Belorussia is used to denote the Soviet Socialist Republic of Belorussia, which existed until the dissolution of the Soviet Union.

1. "Success Comes Only through Terror"

1. Throughout this book, *guerrilla* is used as a generic term for armed irregulars, whereas *partisan* is used in connection with the armed irregulars the Germans faced during World War II in eastern Europe and the Soviet Union.

2. Ian F. W. Beckett, *Modern Insurgencies and Counter-Insurgencies* (London: Routledge, 2001), p. 26.

3. G. H. Lovett, *Napoleon and the Birth of Modern Spain* (New York: New York University Press, 1965), pp. 675, 684, 693.

4. Thomas Pakenham, *The Scramble for Africa* (London: Abacus, 1991), p. 649.

5. Bruce Vandervort, *Wars of Imperial Conquest in Africa, 1830–1914* (London: University College London Press, 1998), p. 206.

6. Beckett, *Modern Insurgencies and Counter-Insurgencies*, pp. 32–36.

7. Byron Farwell, *The Great Boer War* (London: Penguin, 1977), pp. 350–351, 353, 392.

8. Geoffrey Best, *Humanity in Warfare: The Modern History of the International Law of Armed Conflict* (London: Weidenfeld and Nicolson, 1980).

9. John Ellis, *From the Barrel of a Gun: A History of Guerrilla, Revolutionary, and Civil Warfare from the Romans to the Present* (London: Greenhill, 1995), p. 148.

10. Beckett, *Modern Insurgencies and Counter-Insurgencies*, pp. 37–38, 42–47.

11. Ellis, *From the Barrel of a Gun*, p. 80.

12. Michael Howard, *The Franco-Prussian War* (London: Rupert-Hart Davis, 1961), p. 250.

13. Ibid., pp. 250–251.

14. Vandervort, *Wars of Imperial Conquest*, p. 198.

15. Mark Cocker, *Rivers of Blood, Rivers of Gold: Europe's Conflict with Tribal Peoples* (London: Pimlico, 1999).

16. Vandervort, *Wars of Imperial Conquest*, p. 202.

17. John Horne and Alan Kramer, *German Atrocities 1914: A History of Denial* (New Haven: Yale University Press, 2001), p. 169.

18. Ibid., p. 39.

19. Ibid., pp. 419, 435–439.

20. Ibid., pp. 94–113, 129–139.

21. Ibid., pp. 113–129, 153–161.

22. Ibid., p. 425.

23. Mark Mazower, "Military Violence and the National Socialist Consensus: The *Wehrmacht* in Greece, 1941–44," in Hannes Heer and Klaus Naumann, eds., *War of Extermination: The German Military in World War II, 1941–1944* (Oxford: Berghahn, 2000), p. 156.

24. Hans Umbreit, "Das unbewältigte Problem. Der Partisanenkrieg im Rücken der Ostfront," in Jürgen Förster, ed., *Stalingrad: Ereignis—Wirkung—Symbol* (Zurich: Piper, 1992), p. 133.

25. Alexander B. Rossino, *Hitler Strikes Poland: Blitzkrieg, Ideology, and Atrocity* (Lawrence: University Press of Kansas, 2003), pp. 203—216.

26. Ibid., pp. 86–87, 126–129.

27. Richard C. Fattig, "Reprisal: The German Army and the Execution of Hostages during the Second World War" (Ph.D. diss., University of California at San Diego, 1980), pp. 30–47.

28. "Richtlinien für die Ausbildung der Sicherungsdivisionen und der dem Befehlshaber des rückwärtigen Heeres-Gebiets unterstehenden Kräfte," pp. 1, 2, OKH Ia, 3/21/41, file RH 26-221/7, BA-MA.

29. For thorough, comprehensive treatment of the formulation and implementation of Eastern Army rear-area security in 1941, see Jürgen Förster, "Das Unternehmen 'Barbarossa' als Eroberungs- und Vernichtungskrieg" and "Die Sicherung des 'Lebensraumes,'" in Horst Boog et al., *Der Angriff auf die Sowjetunion* (Frankfurt am Main: Fischer, 1991), pp. 498–538, 1227–87.

30. Förster, "Die Sicherung des 'Lebensraumes,'" pp. 1227–28; Matthew Cooper, *The Phantom War: The German Struggle against Soviet Partisans, 1941–1944* (London: MacDonald and Jane's, 1979), pp. 37–40.

31. Ian Kershaw, *Hitler, 1936–1945: Nemesis* (London: Penguin, 2001), p. 356.

32. Erich Hesse, *Der Sowjetrussische Partisanenkrieg 1941–1944 im Spiegel deutscher Kampfanweisungen und Befehle*, 2d ed. (Göttingen: Muster-Schmidt, 1993), pp. 80–82. An indispensable (albeit not entirely accurate) "directory" of World War II German Army units, among other things listing composition, movements and categories, is the seventeen-volume work by Georg Tessin, *Verbände und Truppen der deutschen Wehrmacht und Waffen-SS im Zweiten Weltkrieg* (Osnabrück: Biblio Verlag, 1972–1997).

33. Haupt is not his real name. Federal German data-protection laws prevent naming of individuals who are still alive or have died within the last thirty years, or for whom no date of death or proof that they are still alive could be found, but who were born within the last 110 years. For this study, individuals for whom no date of birth could be established are also anonymized. Nor are photographs of anonymized individuals reprinted.

34. Not their real names. For an overview of the workings of German

military administration in the Soviet Union, see Alfred Toppe et al., "Kriegsverwaltung," PO33 (1949), in *Guides to Foreign Military Studies* (Historical Division HQ, U.S. Army Europe, 1954), BA-MA.

35. Burkhart Müller-Hillebrand, *Das Heer 1933–1945*, vol. 1 (Darmstadt: E. S. Mittler & Sohn, 1954), pp. 68–72; Bernhard R. Kroener, "Die Personellen Ressourcen des Dritten Reiches im Spannungsfeld zwischen Wehrmacht, Bürokratie und Kriegswirtschaft 1939–1942," in Bernhard R. Kroener, Rolf-Dieter Müller, and Hans Umbreit, *Das Deutsche Reich und der Zweite Weltkrieg*, Band 5/1: *Organisation und Mobilisierung des deutschen Machtbereichs, 1939–1942* (Stuttgart: Deutsche Verlags-Anstalt, 1988), pp. 709–715.

36. "Richtlinien für die Ausbildung der Sicherungsdivisionen," pp. 4, 6, OKH Ia, 3/21/41.

37. Ibid., pp. 3–5.

38. Hesse, *Sowjetrussische Partisanenkrieg*, pp. 81–82.

39. Bernhard Chiari, *Alltag hinter der Front: Besatzung, Kollaboration und Widerstand in Weißrußland 1941–1944* (Düsseldorf: Droste, 1998), pp. 96–159; Theo J. Schulte, *The German Army and Nazi Policies in Occupied Russia* (Oxford: Berg, 1989), pp. 150–179.

40. On the Secret Field Police, see Klaus Geßner, *Geheime Feldpolizei: Zur Funktion und Organisation der faschistischen Wehrmacht* (Berlin: Militärverlag der DDR, 1986).

41. Förster, "Die Sicherung des 'Lebensraumes,'" pp. 1253–1254.

42. Schulte, *German Army in Occupied Russia*, pp. 43–45.

43. Ibid., p. 47.

44. Cooper, *The Phantom War*, p. 89.

45. The full texts of the directives, along with the slight modifications Field Marshal von Brauchitsch inserted to guard against possible damage to discipline, are reproduced in Wolfram Wette and Gerd R. Ueberschär, eds., *Der deutsche Überfall auf die Sowjetunion 1941: Berichte, Analyse, Dokumente* (Frankfurt am Main: Fischer, 1991), pp. 251–254, 258–260.

46. On the leadership principle as applied to domestic policy, see Ian Kershaw, *The Nazi Dictatorship: Problems and Perspectives of Interpretation*, 4th ed.(London: Edward Arnold, 2000), chap. 4. On the nature of rear area security directives as guidelines rather than clear orders, see Hannes Heer, "The Logic of the War of Extermination: The Wehrmacht and the Anti-Partisan War," in Heer and Naumann, *War of Extermination*, pp. 99–103. Heer arguably overstates the actual degree to which "leadership principle"-type directives brutalized the Wehrmacht antipartisan campaign, but his observations as to *how* they worked are illuminating.

47. Geoffrey P. Megargee, *Inside Hitler's High Command* (Lawrence: University Press of Kansas, 2000), pp. 5–11.

48. Betr.: "Ausübung der Kriegsgerichtbarkeit im Gebiet 'Barbarossa' und besondere Maßnahmen der Truppe," 5/14/41, Abt. L (IV Qu.), OKW WFSt; reprinted in Wette and Ueberschär, *Überfall*, pp. 251–253.

49. Reprisals against civilians were not formally prohibited in warfare until the 1949 Geneva Convention. At the "Hostage Trial" of former German generals in Nuremberg, however, the Allies drew up criteria for "fair" reprisal taking which, the Allies claimed, German troops had consistently failed to observe. Reprisals, the Allies asserted, should be carried out only under the following conditions: (1) it had not proved possible to apprehend the actual perpetrators of an attack; (2) the population as a whole had been party to the offense; that is to say, that it had supported the partisans; (3) ideally, those selected for reprisal had actively assisted the attack; (4) those selected had been drawn from the area where the attack had taken place; (5) judicial proceedings had been carried out; (6) the reprisal was conducted as a last resort, after other measures such as curfews had failed; TWCNMT, 11: 1230–1317, IWM; Zentrale Stelle der Landesjustizverwaltungen, *Geisel- und Partisanentötungen im Zweiten Weltkrieg: Hinweise zur rechtlichen Beurteilung* (Ludwigsburg: Zentrale Stelle der Landesjustizverwaltungen, 1968), pp. 48–55.

50. Anlage, "Richtlinien für die Behandlung politischer Kommissare," 6/6/41, Abt. L (IV/Qu.), OKW WFSt; reprinted in Wette and Ueberschär, *Überfall*, pp. 259–260.

51. Förster, "Das Unternehmen 'Barbarossa,'" p. 525.

52. Anlage 3, "Richtlinien für das Verhalten der Truppe in Russland," 5/19/41, Abt. L (IV/Qu.), OKW WFSt; reprinted in Wette and Ueberschär, *Überfall*, pp. 258–259.

53. Timm C. Richter, "Die Wehrmacht und der Partisanenkrieg in den besetzten Gebieten der Sowjetunion," in Rolf-Dieter Müller and Hans-Erich Volkmann, eds., *Die Wehrmacht: Mythos und Realität* (Munich: Oldenbourg, 1999), p. 841. On the formation, movements, and activities of the Einsatzgruppen in 1941, see Helmut Krausnick and Hans-Heinrich Wilhelm, *Die Truppe des Weltanschauungskrieges: Die Einsatzgruppen der Sicherheitspolizei und des SD 1938–1942* (Stuttgart: Deutsche Verlags-Anstalt, 1981); Hans-Heinrich Wilhelm, *Die Einsatzgruppe A der Sicherheitspolizei und des SD 1941/42* (Frankfurt am Main: Lang, 1996); Ralf Ogorreck, *Die Einsatzgruppen und die "Genesis der Endlösung"* (Berlin: Metropol, 1996); Peter Klein, ed., *Die Einsatzgruppen in der besetzten Sowjetunion 1941/42: Die Tätigkeits- und Lageberichte des SD* (Berlin: Gedenk- und Bildungsstätte Haus der Wannsee Konferenz, 1997); Peter Longerich, *Politik der Vernichtung: Eine Gesamtdarstellung der nationalsozialistischen Judenverfolgung* (Munich: Piper, 1998); Klaus-Michael Mallmann, "Die Türöffner der "Endlösung,""

in Mallmann and Gerhard Paul, eds., *Die Gestapo im Zweiten Weltkrieg* (Darmstadt: Primus, 2000), pp. 437–463.

54. Reprinted in Wette and Ueberschär, *Überfall*, pp. 249–251.

55. On the Order Police, see Christopher Browning, *Ordinary Men: Reserve Police Battalion 101 and the Final Solution in Poland* (New York: Harper Collins, 1992); idem, *Nazi Policies, Jewish Workers, German Killers* (Cambridge: Cambridge University Press, 2000), pp. 116–169; Martin Dean, *Collaboration in the Holocaust* (Basingstoke: Macmillan, 2000), pp. 60–64, 78 ff.; Konrad Kwiet, "Auftakt zum Holocaust," in Wolfgang Benz, ed., *Der Nationalsozialismus: Studien zur Ideologie* (Frankfurt am Main: Fischer, 1993), pp. 191–208; Andrej Angrick, Martina Vogt, Silke Ammerschubert, and Peter Klein, "'Da hätte man schon ein Tagebuch führen müssen,'" in Helge Grabitz, Wolfgang Scheffler, Klaus Büstlein, and Johannes Tuchel, eds., *Die Normalität des Verbrechens* (Berlin: Edition Hentrich, 1994), pp. 325–385; Jürgen Matthäus, "What about the "Ordinary Men?": The German Order Police and the Holocaust in the Occupied Soviet Union," *Holocaust and Genocide Studies* 10 (1996), 134–150; Edward B. Westermann, "Himmler's Uniformed Police on the Eastern Front: The Reich's Secret Soldiers 1941–1942," *War in History* 3 (1996), 320–329; idem, "'Ordinary Men' or 'Ideological Soldiers'? Police Battalion 310 in Russia, 1942," *German Studies Review* 21 (1998), 41–68.

56. "Festlegung des Befehlshabers des rückwärtigen Heeresgebietes 102 (Mitte) über den Einsatz von Kräften der Ordnungspolizei und des SD im Heeresgebiet," 6/24/41, RHGeb. Mitte Ia; reprinted in Norbert Müller, ed., *Deutsche Besatzungspolitik in der UdSSR 1941–1944: Dokumente* (Cologne: Pahl-Rugenstein, 1980), pp. 68–69.

57. Manfred Messerschmidt, "Harte Sühne am Judentum. Befehlslage und Wissen in der deutschen Wehrmacht," in Jörg Wollenberg, ed., *"Niemand war dabei und keiner hat's gewußt": Die deutsche Öffentlichkeit und die Judenverfolgung 1933–1945* (Munich: Piper, 1989), p. 116.

58. Förster, "Das Unternehmen 'Barbarossa,'" pp. 501, 1235; idem, "Das nationalsozialistische Herrschaftssystem und der Krieg gegen die Sowjetunion," in Reinhard Rürup, ed., *Der Krieg gegen die Sowjetunion 1941–1945: Eine Dokumentation* (Berlin: Argon, 1991), p. 42.

59. Förster, "Das Unternehmen 'Barbarossa,'" p. 522.

60. Manfred Messerschmidt, *Die Wehrmacht im NS-Staat: Zeit der Indoktrination* (Hamburg: R. V. Decker's, 1969), pp. 326–328.

61. Förster, "Das nationalsozialistische Herrschaftssystem," p. 42.

62. Alexander B. Rossino, "Polish 'Neighbors' and German Invaders: Contextualizing Anti-Jewish Violence in the Bialystok District during the Opening Weeks of Operation Barbarossa," *Polin* 16 (2003), 431–452.

63. Idem, *Hitler Strikes Poland*, p. 234.

64. Christian Streit, *Keine Kameraden: Die Wehrmacht und die sowjetischen Kriegsgefangenen 1941–1945*, 4th ed. (Bonn: Dietz, 1997), pp. 50–61.

65. Kershaw, *Hitler, 1936–1945*, p. 359.

66. Jörg Friedrich, *Das Gesetz des Krieges: Das deutsche Heer in Rußland 1941 bis 1945. Der Prozeß gegen das Oberkommando der Wehrmacht* (Munich: Piper, 1993), pp. 412–444; Richter, "Die Wehrmacht und der Partisanenkrieg," p. 843.

67. Förster, "Die Sicherung des 'Lebensraumes,'" pp. 1234–35; idem, "The Relationship between Operation Barbarossa as an Ideological War of Extermination and the Final Solution," in David Cesarani, ed., *The Final Solution: Origins and Implementation* (London: Routledge, 1994), p. 94.

68. Helmut Krausnick, *Hitlers Einsatzgruppen: Die Truppe des Weltanschauungskrieges 1938–1942* (Frankfurt am Main: Fischer, 1985), pp. 179–183; Rossino, "Polish 'Neighbors.'"

2. "Jew-Bolsheviks," Civilians, and Partisans

1. For an introduction to the military campaign, see Alan Clark, *Barbarossa: The Russian-German Conflict, 1941–1945* (London: Hutchinson, 1965).

2. Sich.-Div. 221 Ia, 6/23/41, file 16748/7, T-315/1666, NA; KTB, 5/6–12/13/41, ibid.

3. EM Nr. 43, p. 7, Chef der Sipo etc., 8/5/41, T-175/233, NA.

4. KTB, 5/6–12/13/41, Sich.-Div. 221 Ia, 7/18/41, file 16748/7, T-315/1666, NA; RHGeb. Mitte Ia, 7/18/41, file 16748/9, T-315/1667, NA.

5. KTB, 5/6–12/13/41, Sich.-Div. 221 Ia, 7/20/41, file 16748/7, T-315/1666, NA; "Divisionsbefehl für die Übernahme des erweiterten Sicherungsraumes," Sich.-Div. 221 Ia, 7/20/41, file 16748/9, T-315/1667, NA; Jürgen Förster, "Die Sicherung des 'Lebensraumes,'" in Horst Boog et al., *Der Angriff auf die Sowjetunion* (Frankfurt am Main: Fischer, 1991), p. 1254.

6. EM Nr. 43, p. 8, Chef der Sipo etc., 8/5/41, T-175/233, NA.

7. Kenneth Slepyan, "The People's Avengers: Soviet Partisans, Stalinist Society and the Politics of Resistance, 1941–1944" (Ph.D. diss., University of Michigan, 1994), pp. 25–36.

8. Christian Gerlach, *Kalkulierte Morde: Die deutsche Wirtschafts- und Vernichtungspolitik in Weißrußland 1941 bis 1944* (Hamburg: Hamburger Edition, 1999), pp. 876–877.

9. Hannes Heer, "The Logic of the War of Extermination," in Heer and Klaus Naumann, eds., *War of Extermination: The German Military in World War II, 1941–1944* (Oxford: Berghahn, 2000), p. 96.

10. Omer Bartov, *Hitler's Army: Soldiers, Nazis, and War in the Third Reich* (New York: Oxford University Press, 1992), p. 84.

11. Förster, "Die Sicherung des 'Lebensraumes,'" p. 1235.

12. Ibid., pp. 1236–37.

13. Sich.-Div. 221 Ic, 12/14/41, file 16748/32, T-315/1673, NA; TB, 5/ 10–12/14/41, p. 5, ibid.

14. Christian Gerlach, "German Economic Interests, Occupation Policy, and the Murder of the Jews in Belorussia, 1941/43," in Ulrich Herbert, ed., *National Socialist Extermination Policies: Contemporary German Perspectives and Controversies* (Oxford: Berghahn, 2000), pp. 217–220; Rolf-Dieter Müller, "Das Scheitern der Wirtschaftlichen Blitzkriegstrategie," in Boog et al., *Der Angriff*, p. 1184; Hannes Heer, "Killing Fields: The Wehrmacht and the Holocaust in Belorussia, 1941–42," in Heer and Naumann, *War of Extermination*, pp. 56–59; Raul Hilberg, "Wehrmacht und Judenvernichtung," in Walter Manoschek, ed., *Die Wehrmacht im Rassenkrieg* (Vienna: Picus, 1996), pp. 26–28.

15. Heer, "Killing Fields," pp. 57–58.

16. "Geschäftsverteilung für Feldkommandantur 528 (V) für den Einsatz im Osten," Feldkommmandantur 528 (V), n.d., file 16748/18, T-315/1672, NA.

17. Anlage 278, Sich.-Div. 221 Ia, 7/4/41, file 16748/9, T-315/1667, NA.

18. Hinweis auf Verwaltungsanordnung Nr. 3, p. 3, Sich.-Div. 221 VII, 7/27/41, file 16748/13, T-315/1667, NA.

19. Captain Hermann Kremp, 2d Security Regiment, 7/17/41, Sammlung Sterz, BfZ. Not his real name.

20. Sich.-Div. 221 Ia, 7/8/41, RH 26-221/10, BA-MA.

21. Anlage 381, Sich.-Div. 221 Ia, 7/18/41, RH 26-221/12, BA-MA. It is not clear whether this order was written by Pflugbeil or Haupt, but given what else is known about them, it is virtually certain that both approved of it. There is no record of either the 286th or the 403d Security Divisions employing this measure. Given the incompleteness of these divisions' files, they may have done so.

22. The one possible exception in the division's files concerns an incident on 26 July. On this day, Army Group Center Rear Area command wrote to the 221st ordering the immediate transfer to the SS of twenty Communists who, contrary to instructions, were being held in prison by one of the division's units. The 221st's Operations Section explained that this had been merely a temporary measure until the Communists were handed over. No further paperwork on this incident was generated, so it seems, on balance, that it was not an act of "resistance" on the part of the unit in ques-

tion; Betr.: "Tagesmeldung vom 7/25/41," RHGeb. Mitte Ia, 7/26/41, file 16748/9, T-315/1667, NA.

23. Helmut Krausnick, *Hitlers Einsatzgruppen: Die Truppe des Weltanschauungskrieges 1938–1942* (Frankfurt am Main: Fischer, 1985), p. 207. While there is no thorough quantitative study on the extent to which the Commissar Order was implemented, it seems that security divisions implemented it thoroughly until it became clear that it was hardening Soviet resistance. On the conduct of the Commissar Order, see Förster, "Die Sicherung des 'Lebensraumes,'" pp. 1258–65; Horst Rohde, "Politische Indoktrination in höheren Stäben und in der Truppe—Untersucht am Beispiel des Kommissarbefehls," in Hans Poeppel, Wilhelm-Karl Prinz von Preußen, and Karl-Günther von Hase, eds., *Die Soldaten der Wehrmacht* (Munich: Herbig, 1998), pp. 124–158; Gerlach, *Kalkulierte Morde*, pp. 834–837.

24. An example from the 403d Security Division highlights this complexity. In November the 403d's intelligence officer, Lieutenant Scharfenroth, advocated widespread distribution of a rabidly malevolent anti-Semitic tract, "War Aims of the Global Plutocracy," in order to "clear away the [troops'] last vestiges of inappropriate sentimentality toward the 'chosen people.'" But his primary motive may have been pressure from above. Indeed, Scharfenroth himself made clear that he was responding to a higher-level order, issued by the Armed Forces High Command on 25 October, for the troops to be indoctrinated more rigorously; TB, November 1941, p. 3, Sich.-Div. 403 Ic, 11/22/41, file 15701/3, T-315/2206, NA.

25. Peter Longerich, *Politik der Vernichtung: Eine Gesamtdarstellung der nationalsozialistischen Judenverfolgung* (Munich: Piper, 1998), pp. 345–349, 309–310; Dieter Pohl, "Die Holocaust-Forschung und Goldhagens Thesen," *Vierteljahreshefte für Zeitgeschichte* 45 (1997), 26.

26. Longerich, *Politik der Vernichtung*, pp. 348–349.

27. Krausnick, *Hitlers Einsatzgruppen*, pp. 179–183.

28. KTB, 5/6–12/13/41, Sich.-Div. 221 Ia, 6/28/41, file 16748/7, T-315/1666, NA.

29. Hans Safrian, "Komplizen des Genozids. Zum Anteil der Heeresgruppe Süd an der Verfolgung und Ermordung der Juden in der Ukraine 1941," in Manoschek, *Die Wehrmacht im Rassenkrieg*, p. 104. See also Förster, "Die Sicherung des 'Lebensraumes,'" pp. 1244–46.

30. Longerich, *Politik der Vernichtung*, p. 303; Ruth Bettina Birn, *Die Höheren SS- und Polizei-Führer: Himmlers Vertreter im Reich und in den besetzten Ostgebieten* (Düsseldorf: Droste, 1986), pp. 220–221.

31. TB, 5/10–12/14/41, p. 5, Sich.-Div. 221 Ic, 12/14/41, file 16748/23, T-315/1673, NA; "Übergabebericht," p. 2, Sich.-Div. 221 Ic, 7/28/41, ibid.

32. "Eine schlesische Division erstürmt Bialystok," p. 2, Sich.-Div. 221, Ic, ibid.

33. KTB, 5/6–12/13/41, Sich.-Div. 221 Ia, 6/30/41, file 16748/7, T-315/1666, NA.

34. Gunner Heinz Backe, 291st Infantry Division, 7/10/41, Sammlung Sterz, BfZ. Not his real name.

35. Betr.: "Erfahrungen bei Säuberungsaktion," Inf.-Rgt. 350 Ia, 8/19/41, file 16748/18, T-315/1672, NA.

36. Jürgen Förster, "Wehrmacht, Krieg, und Holocaust," in Rolf-Dieter Müller and Hans-Erich Volkmann, eds., *Die Wehrmacht: Mythos und Realität* (Munich: Oldenbourg, 1999), p. 955, n. 36.

37. KTB, 5/6–12/13/41, Sich.-Div. 221 Ia, 6/23–7/10/41, file 16748/7, T-315/1666, NA. Establishing how many commissars were handed over to the SS is complicated by the fact that, after 16 July, the division was instructed by General von Schenckendorff to pass on instructions concerning the Commissar Order by word of mouth rather than in writing; Sich.-Div. 221 Ic, 7/16/41, file 16748/9, T-315/1667, NA. For further examples of commissars apparently being shot by Eastern Army units, see Streit, *Keine Kameraden*, pp. 88–89; TB, July 1941, p. 2, Sich.-Div. 403 Ic; TB, August 1941, p. 1, both file 15701/3, T-315/2206, NA.

38. Förster, "Die Sicherung des 'Lebensraumes,'" p. 1234.

39. Ibid., p. 1264.

40. Divisions-Befehl Nr. 16, p. 2, Sich.-Div. 286 Ia, 7/2/41, file 16182/2, T-315/1884, NA. At this time both divisions were still serving as front-line units.

41. Joachim Hoffmann, "Die Kriegführung aus der Sicht der Sowjetunion," in Boog et al., *Der Angriff*, pp. 925–928.

42. Egon Niemann, 6th Infantry Division, 8/5/41, Sammlung Sterz, BfZ. Not his real name.

43. Hoffmann, "Die Kriegführung," pp. 921–924. The NKVD, the People's Commissariat of Internal Affairs, was the successor to the GPU. It administered all regular and security police formations.

44. Heinz Hagemann, 6th Infantry Division, 7/7/41, Sammlung Sterz, BfZ. Not his real name.

45. "Rundfunkrede Stalins vom 7/3/41," XIX Gebirgskorps, file 15085/26, BA-MA; reprinted in Wolfram Wette and Gerd R. Ueberschär, eds., *Der deutsche Überfall auf die Sowjetunion 1941: Berichte, Analyse, Dokumente* (Frankfurt am Main: Fischer, 1991), pp. 273–275.

46. Förster, "Die Sicherung des 'Lebensraumes,'" p. 1233.

47. Ibid., pp. 1233–1235.

48. Bartov, *Hitler's Army*, p. 126.

49. Matthew Cooper, *The Phantom War: The German Struggle against Soviet Partisans, 1941–1944* (London: MacDonald and Jane's, 1979), p. 1; Theo J. Schulte, *The German Army and Nazi Policies in Occupied Russia* (Oxford: Berg, 1989), pp. 127, 266–267.

50. Hans Umbreit, "Das unbewältigte Problem. Der Partisanenkrieg im Rücken der Ostfront," in Jürgen Förster, ed., *Stalingrad: Ereignis—Wirkung—Symbol* (Zurich: Piper, 1992), pp. 130–150; idem, "Die Verantwortlichkeit der Wehrmacht als Okkupationsarmee," in Müller and Volkmann, *Die Wehrmacht*, p. 752.

51. Schulte, *German Army in Occupied Russia*, pp. 266–267.

52. Alexander Dallin, Ralph Mavrogordato, and Wilhelm Moll, "Partisan Psychological Warfare and Popular Attitudes," in John A. Armstrong, ed., *Soviet Partisans in World War II* (Madison: University of Wisconsin Press, 1964), pp. 219, 221.

53. Betr.: "Bericht über die Versorgungslage und den Einsatz der Versorgungstruppen seit Beginn der Operationen in Rußland," p. 8, Sich.-Div. 286 Ib, 8/3/41, file 16182/2, T-315/1884, NA.

54. The military value of this unit was clear to General von Schenckendorff also; Korpsbefehl Nr. 40, p. 1, RHGeb. Mitte Ia, 8/16/41, file 16748/10, T-315/1667, NA.

55. II/Inf.-Rgt. 350, 8/18/41, pp. 1–2, file 16748/18, T-315/1672, NA.

56. Erwin Jost, 4th company, Construction Battalion 44, 7/26/41; Major Hans von Schönerer, 7th Panzer Division, 8/18/41, both Sammlung Sterz, BfZ. Not their real names.

57. Corporal Hans Brüning, 269th Infantry Division, 7/2/41, ibid. Not his real name.

58. Förster, "Die Sicherung des 'Lebensraumes,'" p. 1232.

59. Betr.: "Zivilverkehr," Sich.-Div. 221 Ia, 7/14/41, file 16748/9, T-315/1667, NA.

60. "Divisionsbefehl für die Übernahme des erweiterten Sicherungsraumes," p. 1, Sich.-Div. 221 Ia, 7/19/41, ibid.

61. Whether the Army High Command deliberately designated mainly eastern German units as security divisions because of the "harshness" with which they were likely to treat the population is not clear. Almost certainly, however, a major reason for their selection was the assumption that they would have a greater understanding of the "eastern mentality," in much the same way that the overwhelmingly Austrian units selected for security duty in Yugoslavia had greater understanding, it was believed, of the "Balkan mentality." Walter Manoschek, "The Extermination of the Jews in Serbia," in Herbert, *National Socialist Extermination Policies*, pp. 164–165.

62. "Eine schlesische Division erstürmt Bialystok," p. 2, Sich.-Div. 221 Ic, file 16748/23, T-315/1673, NA.

63. Corporal Heinz Hagemann, 6th Infantry Division, 7/17/41; Major Hans Schär, Pioneer Battalion 652, 6/26/41, both Sammlung Sterz, BfZ. Not their real names.

64. Betr.: "Lagebericht an Sich.-Div. 221 VII," p. 3, Sich.-Div. 221 Ic, 8/18/41, file 16748/23, T-315/1673, NA.

65. "Divisionsbefehl für die Übernahme des erweiterten Sicherungsraumes," p. 1, Sich.-Div. 221 Ia, 7/19/41, file 16748/9, T-315/1667, NA.

66. KTB, 5/6–12/13/41, Sich.-Div. 221 Ia, 6/23/41, file 16748/7, T-315/1666, NA.

67. Anlage 266, p. 2, Sich.-Div. 221 Ia, 7/4/41, file 16748/9, T-315/1667, NA.

68. Anlage 392, p. 1, Sich.-Div. 221 Ia, 7/19/41, ibid.

69. Wirtschaftsinspektion Mitte Führungschef, 7/22/41, file 14768/3, T-501/2, NA.

70. Sich.-Div. 221 Ia, 8/13/41, file 16748/10, T-315/1667, NA.

71. Anlage 438, p. 2, Sich.-Div. 221 Ia, 7/26/41, file 16748/9, ibid.

72. Erfahrungen aus dem Osteinsatz, p. 3, Sich.-Div. 403 Ia, 8/6/41, file 15701/3, T-315/2206, NA. Not his real name.

73. TB, September 1941, p. 3, Sich.-Div. 403 Ic, ibid. Not his real name.

74. "Sonderbefehl über Befriedung des durch die Div. besetzten Raumes," p. 3, Sich.-Div. 403 Ia, 8/15/41, file 15701/3, ibid.

75. The extent to which antipartisan warfare was disparaged back in the Reich, and the negative effect of this upon antipartisan troops, were noted by the 203d Security Division in a February 1943 report; Monatsbericht, p. 4, Sich.-Div. 203 Ia, 2/5/43, file 39350/2, T-315/1586, NA.

76. Lieutenant Helmut Hahn, 258th Infantry Division, 7/15/41, Sammlung Sterz, BfZ. Not his real name.

77. File on Johann Pflugbeil, Heeresgeneralkartei, BA-MA. Of the other six, Ditfurth had been captured by the Soviets, Müller had died naturally, and three (Barton, Jacobi, and Lendle) had retired or had been put on the Wehrmacht's officer reserve list. Files on Alfred Jacobi and Hubert Lendle, Heeresgeneralkartei, BA-MA; Nachruf: Generalleutnant Kurt Müller. Heeres-Verordnungsblatt, 5/1/43, Teil C, p. 1, DDSt; entry for Gottfried Barton, pp. 210–211, Dermot Bradley, ed., *Die Generäle des Heeres*, vol. 1 (Osnabrück: Biblio Verlag, 1993); entry for Wolfgang von Ditfurth, pp. 150–151, idem, *Die Generäle des Heeres*, vol. 2 (Osnabrück: Biblio Verlag, 1994). On Richert (executed, like Ditfurth, by the Soviets in 1946), the personal sources are not clear. The final entry in his military record notes that he went on leave between April and May 1944. File on Johann-Georg Richert, Heeresgeneralkartei, BA-MA.

78. "Eine schlesische Division erstürmt Bialystok," Sich.-Div. 221 Ic, n.d., file 16748/23, T-315/1673, NA. This version of events is confirmed by

VII Corps, to which the 221st was subordinate at this point; KTB, 6/22–10/1/41, VII Armee-Korps, 6/27/41, file 17263/1, film 41703, NA.

3. Bloodshed Mushrooms

1. The 707th served along with two other infantry divisions, the 252d and 339th, in the central sector. Although these units were called infantry divisions, their fighting power was similar to that of security divisions.

2. Christian Gerlach, *Kalkulierte Morde: Die deutsche Wirtschafts- und Vernichtungspolitik in Weißrußland 1941 bis 1944* (Hamburg: Hamburger Edition, 1999), p. 619.

3. Jürgen Förster, "Die Sicherung des 'Lebensraumes,'" in Horst Boog et al., *Der Angriff auf die Sowjetunion* (Frankfurt am Main: Fischer, 1991), pp. 1253–54. For detailed treatment of the 707th's killings, which takes into account not only its commanders' extreme anti-Semitism but also the role of its particular circumstances, see Christian Gerlach, *Kalkulierte Morde*, pp. 609–628. See also Hannes Heer, "Killing Fields: The Wehrmacht and the Holocaust in Belorussia, 1941–42," in Heer and Klaus Naumann, eds., *War of Extermination: The German Military in World War II, 1941–1944* (Oxford: Berghahn, 2000), pp. 69–73; Raul Hilberg, "Wehrmacht und Judenvernichtung," in Walter Manoschek, ed., *Die Wehrmacht im Rassenkrieg* (Vienna: Picus, 1996), p. 34; Jürgen Förster, "Wehrmacht, Krieg, und Holocaust," in Rolf-Dieter Müller and Hans-Erich Volkmann, eds., *Die Wehrmacht: Mythos und Realität* (Munich: Oldenbourg, 1999), pp. 958–959; Peter Lieb, "Täter aus Überzeugung? Oberst Carl von Andrian und die Judenmorde der 707. Infanteriedivision 1941/42," *Vierteljahreshefte für Zeitgeschichte* 50 (2002), 523–557. Lieb's article suggests that not all this unit's officers followed their commanding officer's lead wholeheartedly.

4. KTB, 3/15–11/20/41, Sich.-Div. 403 Ia, 10/31/41, file 15701/1, T-315/2206, NA; Gerlach, *Kalkulierte Morde*, p. 604.

5. KTB, 3/15–12/31/41, Sich.-Div. 286 Ia, 9/16–11/30/41, file 16182/1, T-315/1884, NA.

6. For this reason, the 221st's figures are compiled from the division's daily communiqués to the Army Group Center Rear Area. The total figure of partisan dead in the divisional war diary is about 400 lower than the figure given in the daily communiqués.

7. Tagesmeldungen an RHGeb. Mitte, Sich.-Div. 221 Ia, 5/20–12/14/41, file 16748/16, T-315/1671, NA.

8. Gerlach, *Kalkulierte Morde*, p. 604.

9. For overviews of the debate, see Ian Kershaw, *The Nazi Dictatorship: Problems and Perspectives of Interpretation*, 4th ed. (London: Edward Arnold, 2000), chap. 5; Ulrich Herbert, "Extermination Policy: New Answers

and Questions about the History of the 'Holocaust' in German Historiography," in Herbert, ed., *National Socialist Extermination Policies: Contemporary German Perspectives and Controversies* (Oxford: Berghahn, 2000), pp. 1–52.

10. On the involvement of all three agencies in the unfolding of the Final Solution in the Soviet Union during 1941, see Peter Longerich, *Politik der Vernichtung: Eine Gesamtdarstellung der nationalsozialistischen Judenverfolgung* (Munich: Piper, 1998), pp. 293–418; Klaus-Michael Mallmann and Gerhard Paul, eds., *Die Gestapo im Zweiten Weltkrieg* (Darmstadt: Primus, 2000).

11. Hans Safrian, "Komplizen des Genozids. Zum Anteil der Heeresgruppe Süd an der Verfolgung und Ermordung der Juden in der Ukraine 1941," in Manoschek, *Die Wehrmacht im Rassenkrieg*, pp. 109–111; Förster, "Wehrmacht, Krieg, und Holocaust," pp. 956–957.

12. For further indications of the Eastern Army's state of knowledge about the Einsatzgruppe killings, and its collusion in them, see Helmut Krausnick, *Hitlers Einsatzgruppen: Die Truppe des Weltanschauungskrieges 1938–1942* (Frankfurt am Main: Fischer, 1985), pp. 195–214.

13. Jörg Friedrich, *Das Gesetz des Krieges: Das deutsche Heer in Rußland 1941 bis 1945. Der Prozeß gegen das Oberkommando der Wehrmacht* (Munich: Piper, 1993), p. 414.

14. EM Nr. 124, p. 2, Chef der Sipo etc., 10/25/41, T-175/234, NA; EM Nr. 133, pp. 24–25, Chef der Sipo etc., 11/14/41, ibid.

15. Christian Streit, "Ostkrieg, Antibolschewismus, und 'Endlösung,'" *Geschichte und Gesellschaft* 17 (1991), 251–252.

16. Gerlach, *Kalkulierte Morde*, p. 604.

17. Omer Bartov, *Hitler's Army: Soldiers, Nazis, and War in the Third Reich* (New York: Oxford University Press, 1992), p. 130.

18. "Der Partisan, seine Organisation und seine Bekämpfung," p. 14, RHGeb. Mitte Ia, 10/12/41, file 14684/3, T-501/2, NA.

19. Förster, "Die Sicherung des 'Lebensraumes,'" p. 1240.

20. Streit, "Ostkrieg, Antibolschewismus, und 'Endlösung,'" pp. 251 ff.; Andreas Hillgruber, "Die 'Endlösung' und das deutsche Ostimperium als Kernstück des rassenideologischen Regimes des Nationalsozialismus," *Vierteljahreshefte für Zeitgeschichte* 20 (1972), 133–153.

21. Jürgen Förster, "The Relationship between Operation Barbarossa as an Ideological War of Extermination and the Final Solution," in David Cesarani, ed., *The Final Solution: Origins and Implementation* (London: Routledge, 1994), pp. 96–98; Rolf-Dieter Müller, "Die Wehrmacht—Historische Last und Verantwortung. Die Historiographie im Spannungsfeld von Wissenschaft und Vergangenheitsbewältigung," in Müller and Volkmann, *Die Wehrmacht*, p. 23.

22. Betr.: "Partisanentätigkeit," Sich.-Div. 286 Ia, 7/11/41, file 16182/3, T-315/1884, NA.

23. KTB, 5/6–12/13/41, Sich.-Div. 221 Ia, 9/12/41, file 16748/7, T-315/1666, NA.

24. Betr.: "Tagesmeldung," LSR 45 Ia, 10/31/41, 11/2/41, 11/8/41, file 16748/19, T-315/1672, NA. For further examples, see Heer, "Killing Fields," p. 117.

25. Betr.: "Vorgänge in Boguschewskoye," Sich.-Div. 286 Ia, 9/7/41, file 16182/3, T-315/1884, NA; Lagebericht, 10/1–10/7/41, Inf.-Rgt. 691 Ia, 10/8/41, ibid.

26. Heer, "Killing Fields," p. 61.

27. Ibid., nn. 34–37.

28. In addition to the instances attributed to the 354th and 691st Security Regiments cited above, in which ninety-two Jews were killed, see Betr.: "Einsatz der Kompanie," 11/Inf.-Rgt. 354, 10/28/41, file 16182/3, T-315/1884, NA (Jewish partisan shot); Bericht, pp. 4–5, 8/Inf.-Rgt. 354, 11/5/41, ibid. (two Jews hanged for anti-German sedition).

29. On the 252d and 339th Infantry Divisions in this respect, see Gerlach, *Kalkulierte Morde*, pp. 602–606; Hannes Heer, "The Logic of the War of Extermination," in Heer and Naumann, *War of Extermination*, pp. 103–106.

30. EM Nr. 17, p. 8, Chef der Sipo etc., 9/7/41, T-175/233, NA.

31. EM Nr. 43, p. 8, Chef der Sipo etc., 8/5/41, ibid. On the Soviet authorities' evacuations and uprooting of industry in Belorussia, see Gerlach, *Kalkulierte Morde*, pp. 371–385.

32. In October, Einsatzgruppe B reported that the urban population perceived the Germans as caring markedly more about the rural population's situation; EM Nr. 106, p. 5, Chef der Sipo etc., 10/7/41, T-175/234, NA.

33. Betr.: "Lagebericht an Sich.-Div. 221 VII," p. 3, Sich.-Div. 221 Ic, 8/18/41, file 16748/23, T-315/1673, NA.

34. Rolf-Dieter Müller, "Das Scheitern der wirtschaftlichen "Blitzkriegstrategie," in Boog et al., *Der Angriff*, pp. 1168–1202; Gerlach, *Kalkulierte Morde*, pp. 265–292.

35. EM Nr. 43, p. 8, Chef der Sipo etc., 8/5/41, T-175/233, NA.

36. Leonid D. Grenkevich, *The Soviet Partisan Movement, 1941–1944: A Critical Historiographical Analysis* (London: Frank Cass, 1999), pp. 71–79.

37. Förster, "Die Sicherung des 'Lebensraumes,'" p. 1236.

38. KTB, 5/6–12/13/41, Sich.-Div. 221 Ia, 9/1–9/30/41, file 16748/7, T-315/1666, NA; KTB, 3/15–12/31/41, Sich.-Div. 286 Ia, 9/1–9/30/41, file 16182/1, T-315/1884, NA; KTB, 3/15–11/20/41, Sich.-Div. 403 Ia, 9/1–9/30/41, RH 26-403/1, BA-MA.

39. The only notable incident recorded in the jurisdiction of either the 286th or 403d around this time was the killing, in the 286th's jurisdiction, of one soldier in a partisan attack on 3 September; KTB, 3/15–12/31/41, Sich.-Div. 286 Ia, 9/3/41, file 16182/1, T-315/1884, NA.

40. KTB, 5/6–12/13/41, Sich.-Div. 221 Ia, 9/2/41, 9/3/41, file 16748/7, T-315/1666, NA.

41. Ibid., 9/6/41.

42. Tagesmeldungen an RHGeb. Mitte, Sich.-Div. 221 Ia, 8/23–9/7/41, file 16748/16, T-315/1671, NA.

43. RHGeb. Mitte Ia, 8/27/41, file 16182/3, T-315/1884, NA; "Sonder-Befehl über Aufgaben im neuen Divisions-Bereich," Sich.-Div. 403 Ia, 9/4/41, file 15701/3, T-315/2206, NA.

44. Betr.: "Kollektivmaßnahmen," Sich.-Div. 221 Ic, 8/31/41, file 16748/10, T-315/1667, NA. Though Pflugbeil signed this document, it may not originally have been written by him. If not, however, it is certainly clear that the Operations Section perceived the situation ruthlessly. Either way, the essential point about the role of ruthless division-level attitudes in fueling escalation is not disqualified.

45. Sich.-Div. 221 Ic, 9/6/41, RH 26-221/17, BA-MA.

46. "Divisionsbefehl für die am 9/6/41 erfolgende Übernahme des erweiterten Div-Bereiches," p. 6, Sich.-Div. 221 Ia, 9/6/41, file 16748/10, T-315/1667, NA.

47. Voraus-Abt. Inf.-Rgt. 350, 10/14/41, p. 2, file 16748/19, T-315/1672, NA. Not his real name.

48. Betr.: "Aufstellung eines Partisanen-Bekämpfungs-Bataillon," Sich.-Div. 221 Ia, 9/7/41, file 16748/10, T-315/1667, NA. The battalion was to be a motorized unit.

49. File on Hellmuth Koch, Heeresgeneralkartei, BA-MA.

50. "Anweisung für SS-Kav[allerie]. Brigade," RHGeb. Mitte Ia, 9/5/41, RH 22/225, BA-MA. See also Ruth Bettina Birn, "Zweierlei Wirklichkeit?" in Bernd Wegner, ed., Zwei Wege nach Moskau. Vom Hiter-Stalin Pakt zum Unternehmen "Barbarossa" (Munich: Piper, 1991), pp. 275–290.

51. Voraus-Abt. Inf.-Rgt. 350, 10/14/41, p. 1, file 16748/19, T-315/1672, NA.

52. "Bericht über das Sonderunternehmen im Raume nördlich des R3-Abschnittes Pogost-Woly," pp. 2–3, III/Inf.-Rgt. 354, 9/23/41, RH 26-286/3, BA-MA.

53. Truman O. Anderson, "Incident at Baranivka: German Reprisals and the Soviet Partisan Movement in Ukraine, October–December 1941," Journal of Modern History 71 (September 1999), 585–623.

54. "Tagebuch eines Partisanen," 9/10/41, 10/12/41, file 15954/4, T-

315/1870, NA. The fact that the partisan-population relationship described in this diary is nuanced indicates that the diary was not concocted by the 281st itself.

55. "Merkblatt für die Bürgermeister," pp. 2, 4, Feldkommandantur 551, 9/8/41, file 16748/18, T-315/1672, NA.

56. "Erfahrungen aus dem Osteinsatz," p. 3, Sich.-Div. 403 Ia, 8/6/41, file 15701/3, T-315/2206, NA; TB, September 1941, p. 3, Sich.-Div. 403 Ic, ibid.

57. TB, October 1941, p. 4, Sich.-Div. 403 Ic, ibid.; Divisionsbefehl Nr. 24, Sich.-Div. 403 Ia, 10/11/41, ibid.

58. TB, September, October 1941, Sich.-Div. 403 Ic, ibid.

59. Divisions-Befehl Nr. 24, p. 2, Sich.-Div. 403 Ia, 10/11/41, ibid.

60. KTB, 3/15–11/20/41, Sich.-Div. 403 Ia, 10/12, 10/18, 10/23, 10/27/ 41, RH 26-403/1, BA-MA.

61. Tagesmeldungen an RHGeb. Mitte, Sich.-Div. 221 Ia, 9/16–11/30/ 41, file 16748/16, T-315/1671, NA.

62. Gerlach, *Kalkulierte Morde*, pp. 882–884.

63. Betr.: "Partisanentätigkeit," p. 1, Sich.-Div. 286 Ia, 11/7/41, file 16182/3, T-315/1884, NA.

64. Gerlach, *Kalkulierte Morde*, pp. 877–878.

65. Betr.: "Erfahrungsbericht über den Transport von Kriegsgefangenen," LSR 45, 9/24/41, file 16748/18, T-315/1672, NA.

66. "Ausbildung der Truppen unter schwierigen Verhältnissen," RHGeb. Mitte Ia/IIa, 9/19/41, file 16748/11, T-315/1668, NA.

67. On overstretch and the understrength, poor-quality troops of the 286th and 403d Security Divisions, see Betr.: "Erfahrungsbericht," Sich.-Div. 286 Ia, 9/22/41, file 16182/3, T-315/1884, NA; Betr.: "Partisanentätigkeit," p. 2, Sich.-Div. 286 Ia, 11/7/41, ibid.; TB, November 1941, Sich.-Div. 403 IIb, file 15701/3, T-315/2206, NA; Betr.: "Lagebeurteilung, 11/4/41," pp. 3–4, Sich.-Div. 403 Ia, ibid.

68. Besondere Anordnungen für die Versorgung Nr. 140/41, Sich.-Div. 221 Ib, 10/9/41, file 16748/25, T-315/1673, NA.

69. Betr.: "Eisenbahnlage," Sich.-Div. 221 Ia, 10/11/41, 10/21/41, file 16748/11, T-315/1668, NA.

70. Anlage 715, LSR 45, 9/17/41, Sich.-Div. 221 Ia, file 16748/10, T-315/1667, NA. Complaints by subordinate units as specific as this are likely on balance to have described genuine grievances. Concocted stories of hardships risked being exposed as fabrication by division-level officers sent to inspect the unit. See, for example, Betr.: "Ständiges Überprüfen der Gefechtsstärken und Pferdebestände," 221 Div. Ia, 5/7/42, file 22639/2, T-315/1676, NA.

71. The great majority of the 350th Infantry Regiment and the 45th Se-

curity Regiment was tied up protecting the railways and roads; Anlage 854, Sich.-Div. 221 Ia, 10/12/41, file 16748/11, T-315/1668, NA.
  72. Betr.: "Lagebeurteilung," pp. 2, 3, Sich.-Div. 221 Ia, 11/4/41, file 16748/12, ibid.
  73. Not his real name. Haupt was transferred to the staff of XXIII Army Corps and promoted to major in January 1942; "Personal-Nachweis," Pers 6. Personal file on Karl Haupt, BA-MA; Betr.: "Übergabe des Raumes der. Sich.-Div. 221 an die Sich.-Div. 286," Sich.-Div. 221 Ia, 12/14/41, file 16748/12, T-315/1668, NA.
  74. Betr.: "Partisanentätigkeit," Sich.-Div. 286 Ia, 11/7/41, file 16182/3, T-315/1884, NA; Betr.: "Lagebeurteilung," p. 3, Sich.-Div. 403 Ia, 11/4/41, file 15701/3, T-315/2206, NA.
  75. Though the 707th also compares closely to Wehrmacht security policy in Serbia in 1941; Walter Manoschek, "The Extermination of the Jews in Serbia," in Herbert, *National Socialist Extermination Policies*, p. 173.
  76. EM Nr. 146, p. 9, Chef der Sipo etc., 12/15/41, T-175/234, NA.

4. The Rules Change

  1. On the "breakthrough" to establishing a significant partisan movement during the winter of 1941–42, see John A. Armstrong and Kurt De Witt, "Organization and Control of the Partisan Movement," in Armstrong, ed., *Soviet Partisans in World War II* (Madison: University of Wisconsin Press, 1964), pp. 79–80, 89–93; Erich Hesse, *Der Sowjetrussische Partisanenkrieg 1941–1944 im Spiegel deutscher Kampfanweisungen und Befehle*, 2d ed. (Göttingen: Muster-Schmidt Verlag, 1993), chap. 8; Bernd Bonwetsch, "Sowjetische Partisanen, 1941–1944. Legende und Wirklichkeit des 'allgemeinen Volkskrieges,'" in Gerhard Schulz, ed., *Partisanen und Volkskrieg—zur Revolutionierung des Krieges im 20. Jahrhundert* (Göttingen: Vandenhoek & Rupprecht, 1985), pp. 100–101; Leonid Grenkevich, *The Soviet Partisan Movement, 1941–1944* (London: Frank Cass, 1999), pp. 153–222. For developments in particular regions, see Gerhard L. Weinberg, "The Yelnya-Dorogobuzh Area of Smolensk Oblast," in Armstrong, *Soviet Partisans*, pp. 411–422; Kurt De Witt and Wilhelm Moll, "The Bryansk Area," ibid., pp. 461–462; Ralph Mavrogordato and Earl Ziemke, "The Polotsk Lowland," ibid., pp. 532–554.
  2. Alexander Dallin, Ralph Mavrogordato, and Wilhelm Moll, "Partisan Psychological Warfare and Popular Attitudes," in Armstrong, *Soviet Partisans*, p. 322; Theo J. Schulte, *The German Army and Nazi Policies in Occupied Russia* (Oxford: Berg, 1989), p. 123.
  3. Bernd Wegner, "Der Krieg gegen die Sowjetunion 1942/43," in Horst Boog, Werner Rahn, Reinhard Stumpf, and Bernd Wegner, *Das Deut-*

sche Reich und der Zweite Weltkrieg, vol. 6: *Der Globale Krieg: Die Ausweitung zum Weltkrieg und der Wechsel der Initiative 1941–1943* (Stuttgart: Deutsche Verlags-Anstalt, 1990), pp. 911–912.

4. Witalij Wilenchik, *Die Partisanenbewegung in Weißrußland 1941–1944*, special reprint from *Forschungen zur osteuropäischen Geschichte* 34 (1984), 209; Joachim Hoffmann, "Die Kriegführung aus der Sicht der Sowjetunion," in *Der Angriff auf die Sowjetunion* (Frankfurt am Main: Fischer, 1991), p. 893.

5. On formation and details of the Central Committee, see Kenneth Slepyan, "The People's Avengers: Soviet Partisans, Stalinist Society, and the Politics of Resistance, 1941–1944" (Ph.D. diss., University of Michigan, 1994), pp. 119–127, Grenkevich, *Soviet Partisan Movement*, pp. 91–95.

6. Armstrong and De Witt, "Organization and Control of Partisan Movement," p. 92; EM Nr. 194, pp. 6–7, Chef der Sipo etc., 4/21/42, T-175/235, NA.

7. Dallin, Mavrogordato, and Moll, "Psychological Warfare," p. 273.

8. Ibid., p. 266.

9. On partisan propaganda toward the population, including "action propaganda" such as reprivatization of state farms, see Dallin, Mavrogordato, and Moll, "Psychological Warfare," pp. 249–319.

10. Bonwetsch, "Sowjetische Partisanen," p. 104; Slepyan, "People's Avengers," pp. 153–159.

11. Grenkevich, *Soviet Partisan Movement*, p. 190. Western observers place considerable stress on the extent of collaboration in the German rear. Grenkevich estimates that about 5 percent of the occupied population were actually German informers, another that there were up to a million active collaborators in the occupied Soviet Union; ibid., p. 189.

12. On partisan treatment of collaborators, see Dallin, Mavrogordato, and Moll, "Psychological Warfare," pp. 227–249; Slepyan, "People's Avengers," pp. 281–288; Grenkevich, *Soviet Partisan Movement*, pp. 189–191.

13. Dallin, Mavrogordato, and Moll, "Psychological Warfare," p. 235.

14. On partisan recruitment and requisitioning, see Armstrong and De Witt, "Organization and Control of Partisan Movement," pp. 152–155; Grenkevich, *Soviet Partisan Movement*, pp. 191–192, 198–201.

15. Bonwetsch, "Sowjetische Partisanen," p. 110.

16. Dallin, Mavrogordato, and Moll, "Psychological Warfare," pp. 322–326; Grenkevich, *Soviet Partisan Movement*, pp. 107–121.

17. Grenkevich, *Soviet Partisan Movement*, p. 111.

18. Monatsberichte, April–August 1942, RHGeb. Mitte Ia, file 31491/6, T-501/27, NA.

19. "Beurteilung der Lage im Heeresgebiet Mitte," p. 1, RHGeb. Mitte Ia, 5/31/42, file 24693/3, T-501/15, NA.

20. MadbO Nr. 8, p. 8, Chef der Sipo etc., 6/19/42, T-175/235, NA.

21. Sich.-Div. 203 VII, 4/16/42, p. 3, Lagebericht, file 29186/3, T-315/1586, NA. "Bandit" was the official designation for partisans after July 1942.

22. Matthew Cooper, *The Phantom War: The German Struggle against Soviet Partisans, 1941–1944* (London: MacDonald and Jane's, 1979), pp. 144–146.

23. Hannes Heer, "The Logic of the War of Extermination," in Heer and Klaus Naumann, eds., *War of Extermination: The German Military in World War II, 1941–1944* (Oxford: Berghahn, 2000), p. 116. See also Schulte, *German Army and Nazi Policies*, p. 139; Christian Gerlach, *Kalkulierte Morde: Die deutsche Wirtschafts- und Vernichtungspolitik in Weißrußland 1941 bis 1944* (Hamburg: Hamburger Edition, 1999), p. 964.

24. Edward B. Westermann, "Himmler's Uniformed Police on the Eastern Front: The Reich's Secret Soldiers 1941–1942," *War in History* 3 (1996), 320–329; idem, "'Ordinary Men' or 'Ideological Soldiers'?: Police Battalion 310 in Russia, 1942," *German Studies Review* 21 (1998), 41–68.

25. Schulte, *German Army and Nazi Policies*, pp. 234–239; Gerlach, *Kalkulierte Morde*, pp. 959–963; Klaus-Michael Mallmann, "'Aufgeräumt und abgebrannt.' Sicherheitspolizei und 'Bandenkampf' in der besetzten Sowjetunion," in Mallmann and Gerhard Paul, eds., *Die Gestapo im Zweiten Weltkrieg* (Darmstadt: Primus, 2000), pp. 503–520.

26. Timothy P. Mulligan, *The Politics of Illusion and Empire: German Occupation Policy in the Soviet Union, 1942–1943* (New York: Praeger, 1988), p. 138; Gerlach, *Kalkulierte Morde*, pp. 921–930.

27. Westermann, "Himmler's Uniformed Police"; idem, "'Ordinary Men' or 'Ideological Soldiers'?"

28. In the civilian-administered Reich commissariats in the western regions of the occupied Soviet Union, many Jews had been unable to flee from the German advance in time during 1941, while others had been shipped from the east into ghettos in the Reich commissariats. In the areas administered by the Eastern Army, most of the Jews had been murdered or deported already. Cooper, *Phantom War*, pp. 82–88; Gerlach, *Kalkulierte Morde*, pp. 930–958; Mallmann, "'Aufgeräumt und abgebrannt,'" pp. 517–520.

29. Cooper, *Phantom War*, p. 87. A recent case study of an SS antipartisan operation in the occupied Soviet Union is Ruth Bettina Birn, "Zaunkönig an 'Uhrmacher'. Große Partisanenaktionen 1942/43 am Beispiel des 'Unternehmens Winterzauber,'" *Militärgeschichtliche Zeitschrift* 60 (2001), 99–118.

30. Cooper, *Phantom War*, pp. 82–83.

31. On the military counterproductiveness of brutal SS operations, see Ziemke, "Polotsk Lowland," pp. 537–539; Mulligan, *Politics of Illusion and Empire*, pp. 142–143.

32. Mulligan, *Politics of Illusion and Empire*, p. 143.

33. Wegner, "Krieg gegen die Sowjetunion," p. 916.

34. Grenkevich, *Soviet Partisan Movement*, p. 111.

35. Mulligan, *Politics of Illusion and Empire*, pp. 123–135; Jürgen Förster, "Zum Rußlandbild der Militärs 1941–1945," in Hans-Erich Volkmann, ed., *Das Rußlandbild im Dritten Reich* (Cologne: Böhlau, 1994), p. 153.

36. On formation of the OD and eastern battalions in 1941, see Jürgen Förster, "Die Sicherung des 'Lebensraumes,'" in Horst Boog et al., *Der Angriff auf die Sowjetunion* (Frankfurt am Main: Fischer, 1991), pp. 1253–58.

37. EM Nr. 189, pp. 12–17, Chef der Sipo etc., 4/3/42, T-175/235, NA. On agricultural reform and its Belorussian variant, see Wilenchik, *Partisanenbewegung in Weißrußland*, pp. 195–201; Mulligan, *Politics of Illusion and Empire*, pp. 93–105.

38. Mulligan, *Politics of Illusion and Empire*, p. 139.

39. Tätigkeitsberichte, July—December 1942, RHGeb. Mitte Ic, file 31491/4, T-501/27, NA. On German "cultural policy" in Belorussia, see Wilenchik, *Partisanenbewegung in Weißrußland*, pp. 215–219. On general Wehrmacht propaganda directed toward the Russian population, see Ortwin Buchbender, *Das tönende Erz: Deutsche Propaganda gegen die Rote Armee im Zweiten Weltkrieg* (Stuttgart: Seewald, 1978), pp. 272–284; Schulte, *German Army and Nazi Policies*, pp. 150–179.

40. Wegner, "Krieg gegen die Sowjetunion," p. 920.

41. Wilenchik, *Partisanenbewegung in Weißrußland*, pp. 197–198; Mulligan, *Politics of Illusion and Empire*, pp. 95–96.

42. MadbO Nr. 13, p. 2, Chef der Sipo etc., 7/24/42, T-175/235, NA.

43. Ulrich Herbert, *Hitler's Foreign Workers* (Cambridge: Cambridge University Press, 1997), p. 168.

44. Ibid., pp. 167–171. While from March 1942 Sauckel enjoyed theoretical power to enforce labor conscription, commanders in the sectors administered by the Eastern Army often prevented him from exercising it. Mindful of the likely effect on the mood of the population, and also anxious to retain native labor in their own jurisdictions, they often applied the "voluntary" principle into 1943. Mulligan, *Politics of Illusion and Empire*, pp. 111–116.

45. Mulligan, *Politics of Illusion and Empire*, pp. 111–116.

46. Dallin, Mavrogordato, and Moll, "Psychological Warfare," p. 280.

47. "Durchführungsbefehl des Kommandeurs der 207. Sicherungsdivision zur Anweisung des Befehlshabers des rückwärtigen Heeresgebietes Nord vom 3/29/42 über rücksichtslose Partisanenbekämpfung, 31. März

1942," reprinted in Norbert Müller, ed., *Deutsche Besatzungspolitik in der UdSSR 1941–1944: Dokumente* (Cologne: Pahl-Rugenstein, 1980), p. 120.

48. Gerlach, *Kalkulierte Morde*, p. 611.

49. Heer, "Logic of War of Extermination," pp. 107–110; Gerlach, *Kalkulierte Morde*, pp. 914–916.

50. A phrase the British coined in their operations against tribes on India's Northwest Frontier during the nineteenth century.

51. Gerlach, *Kalkulierte Morde*, pp. 898–913.

52. Cooper, *Phantom War*, pp. 90–91.

53. For a list of major antipartisan operations in the area of present-day Belarus from 1942 to 1944, see Gerlach, *Kalkulierte Morde*, pp. 899–906.

54. Ibid., pp. 85–86. The scene in the hut was relayed to Grigoriev by another eyewitness. Given the death tolls that so many German antipartisan operations inflicted, this is probably a fairly accurate depiction.

55. Betr.: "Erfahrungen bei Befriedung der Räume 'Viereck' und 'Eule' im August 1942," Sich.-Rgt. 45, 9/1/42, file 29380/5, T-315/1679, NA; Monatsbericht, 9/6/42, p. 2, Sich.-Div. 203 Ia, file 29186/2, T-315/1585, NA; Sich.-Div. 203 VII, 4/16/42, p. 3, file 29186/3, ibid.; Monatsbericht, p. 1, Sich.-Div. 201 Ia, 2/5/43, RH 26-201/5, BA-MA.

56. Gerlach, *Kalkulierte Morde*, pp. 898, 885–893, 899–901.

57. Gerlach, *Kalkulierte Morde*, pp. 971–972, 972–973. Gerlach argues that Schenckendorff's selectivity can be ascribed to his desire to ease his conscience.

58. Betr.: "Behandlung von Banditen, Überläufern usw.," Sich.-Div. 221 Ic, 9/12/42, file 29380/9, T-315/1680, NA.

59. On the partisan warfare directives of August–December 1942, see Cooper, *Phantom War*, pp. 79–81; Mulligan, *Politics of Illusion and Empire*, pp. 137–146; Wegner, "Krieg gegen die Sowjetunion," pp. 918–923.

60. Mulligan, *Politics of Illusion and Empire*, p. 139.

61. Ibid., pp. 139–140.

62. Reproduced in Müller, *Deutsche Besatzungspolitik*, pp. 139–140.

63. For extensive treatment of the "economic antipartisan warfare" prosecuted in Belorussia during 1942 and especially 1943, see Gerlach, *Kalkulierte Morde*, pp. 975–1036. On the organizational setup of economic exploitation in areas administered by the Eastern Army, see Rolf-Dieter Müller, ed., *Die deutsche Wirtschaftspolitik in den besetzten sowjetischen Gebieten 1941–1943* (Boppard am Rhein: Harald Boldt, 1991).

64. Gerlach, *Kalkulierte Morde*, p. 898.

65. "Der Reichsmarschall d. Großdeutschen Reiches, 18727/6/3, gezeichnet: Göring"; reprinted in Müller, *Deutsche Besatzungspolitik*, pp. 134–135.

66. Umbreit, "Das unbewältigte Problem," p. 144.

67. It has been claimed that the search for labor sometimes prompted more killing, with women and children being killed simply because of their unsuitability for hard labor; Gerlach, *Kalkulierte Morde*, pp. 996–1007. Much of the evidence indicates that this was widespread practice in SS-led operations. To what extent it was the case in operations led by the Eastern Army remains unclear.

68. Ibid., pp. 975–996, 1010–36.

5. More of the Sugar, Less of the Whip

1. "Gefechtsstärken," KTB, 12/14/41–3/19/42, 221 Inf.-Div. Ia, file 19344/1, T-315/1674, NA; Inf.-Rgt. 135 Ia/IIb, 2/28/42, file 19344/2, ibid.; Art.-Rgt. 98 Ia, 3/1/42, ibid. The 221st was temporarily redesignated an infantry division during its front-line service.

2. Betr.: "Behandlung von Kriegsgefangenen, Partisanen und Bevölkerung," p. 3, 221 Div. Ic, 4/8/42, file 22639/6, T-315/1677, NA.

3. Beilage zur Anlage 2, "Weisungen für die Kampfführung," 221 Div. Ia, 3/24/42, file 22639/2, T-315/1676, NA.

4. Anlage 201, pp. 1–2, 221 Div. Ia, 5/6/42, ibid.

5. Gerhard L. Weinberg, "The Yelnya-Dorogobuzh Area of Smolensk Oblast," in John A. Armstrong, ed., *Soviet Partisans in World War II* (Madison: University of Wisconsin Press, 1964), pp. 390–397.

6. Ibid., p. 423.

7. Ibid., pp. 395–396.

8. EM Nr. 194, p. 6, Chef der Sipo etc., 4/21/42, T-175/235, NA.

9. EM Nr. 189, p. 17, ibid.

10. After the operation the Germans continued to observe this distinction, and were thus able to deprive the partisans of civilian support. The result was that all meaningful partisan activity in the area ceased until 1943. Weinberg, "Yelnya-Dorogobuzh Area," p. 398.

11. Ic Befehle und Mitteilungen Nr. 11, RHGeb. Mitte Ic, 4/9/42, file 22639/6, T-315/1677, NA.

12. Betr.: "Verhalten der Truppe im besetzten Gebiet," 221 Div. Ic, 3/24/42, ibid.

13. Betr.: "Behandlung von Kriegsgefangenen, Partisanen u. Bevölkerung," p. 3, 221 Div. Ic, 4/8/42, file 22639/2, T-315/1677, NA.

14. Betr.: "Propagandamaterial, Ernennung von Bürgermeistern, Bildung von Ordnungsdienst," 221 Div. Ic, 3/30/42, RH 26-221/34, BA-MA.

15. Betr.: "Behandlung von Kriegsgefangenen, Partisanen und Bevölkerung," p. 3, 221 Div. Ic, 4/8/42, file 112639/6, T-315/1677, NA.

16. Ibid. On 13 April Beck threatened the full force of the division's

courts in the event of further transgressions. However, neither this nor the threat of 24 March was ever carried out. Given Beck's genuine concern about relations with the population, it is almost certain that he meant these threats but did not receive the divisional court's backing. On Eastern Army military justice, see Omer Bartov, *Hitler's Army: Soldiers, Nazis and War in the Third Reich* (New York: Harper Collins, 1992), pp. 59–105.

17. Betr.: "Behandlung von Kriegsgefangenen, Partisanen und Bevölkerung," p. 2, 221 Div. Ic, 4/8/42, RH 26-221/34, BA-MA.

18. By the terms of this directive, all captured partisans were to be treated as prisoners of war, but deserters were to receive better treatment still; Hans Umbreit, "Das unbewältigte Problem. Der Partisanenkrieg im Rücken der Ostfront," in Jürgen Förster, ed., *Stalingrad: Ereignis— Wirkung—Symbol* (Zurich: Piper, 1992), p. 145. While the Army High Command had for months already been urging similar measures, and units in the field had been pursuing it, the ploy of awarding deserters with even better treatment than they had received in the Red Army seems to have been particularly far-sighted, especially given the fact that it was made in early 1942.

19. Not his real name.

20. Betr.: "Unternehmen Dreieck," p. 2, Sich.-Div. 221 Ia, 7/12/42, file 35408/1, T-315/1681, NA.

21. "Monatsberichte, Politische Überwachung der Bevölkerung, Juni– Dezember 1942," Sich.-Div. 221 Ic, file 29380/9, T-315/1680, NA.

22. Betr.: "Lagebericht, Februar 1943," p. 3, 203 Sich.-Div. VII, 2/25/ 43, file 29186/3, T-315/1586, NA.

23. Betr.: "Politische Überwachung der Bevölkerung," p. 2, Sich.-Div. 221 Ic, 8/9/42, file 29380/9, T-315/1680, NA; Betr.: "Politsche Überwachung der Bevölkerung," p. 2, Sich.-Div. 221 Ic, 7/19/42, ibid.

24. Betr.: "Politische Überwachung der Bevölkerung," p. 2, Sich.-Div. 221 Ic, 10/3/42, ibid.

25. MadbO Nr. 16, pp. 13–14, Chef der Sipo etc., 8/14/42, T-175/236, NA; MadbO Nr. 8, pp. 10–11, Chef der Sipo etc., 6/19/42, T-175/235, NA. In December 1941 the Sixteenth Army, which operated in northern Russia, identified the following topics as being of interest to the population: the reasons for the German attack, German military successes, the exploitation of workers and farmers in the Soviet Union, and the following aspects of Germany and National Socialism: the situation of German workers and farmers, social provisions, the spending power of the German consumer, schools, the German family, and Hitler's personality. Ortwin Buchbender, *Das tönende Erz: Deutsche Propaganda gegen die Rote Armee im Zweiten Weltkrieg* (Stuttgart: Seewald, 1978), p. 274.

26. Betr.: "Politische Überwachung der Bevölkerung," p. 2, Sich.-Div.

221 Ic, 10/3/42, file 35408/1, T-315/1681, NA. On similar efforts made across the German-occupied Soviet Union, see Buchbender, *Das tönende Erz*, pp. 133–139, 274–275.

27. Monatsbericht, p. 2, Sich.-Div. 221 Ic, 10/2/42, file 29380/9, T-315/1680, NA.

28. Monatsbericht, p. 3, Sich.-Div. 221 Ic, 11/3/42, ibid. On attempts to "revitalize the cultural existence" of the population, see Witalij Wilenchik, *Die Partisanenbewegung in Weißrußland 1941–1944*, special reprint from *Forschungen zur osteuropäischen Geschichte* 34 (1984), pp. 215–219; Theo J. Schulte, *The German Army and Nazi Policies in Occupied Russia* (Oxford: Berg, 1989), pp. 156–157. Some of the measures described in these works, such as promotion of education policy, were in the sphere of the Administrative Section, the files for which in the 221st Security Division's case are largely unavailable.

29. Monatsbericht, Sich.-Div. 221 Ic, 8/5/42, file 35408/1, T-315/1681, NA. On general eastern worker propaganda efforts, in which measures utilized by the 221st Security Division were employed widely, see Buchbender, *Das tönende Erz*, pp. 280–281.

30. TB, 6/18–12/31/42, p. 13, Sich.-Div. 221 Ic, file 29380/8, T-315/1680, NA.

31. Other units, for example Feldkommandantur 550 in the 203d Security Division's jurisdiction, also saw the importance of a major propaganda effort in this department; Betr.: "Anwerbung von Arbeitskräften für Deutschland," Feldkommandantur Staryje Dorogi, 7/10/42, file 32104, T-315/1586, NA; An die Rayonleiter, Bürgermeister und Dorfältesten: Betr.: "Lagebericht, Februar 1943," p. 8, Sich.-Div. 203 VII, 2/25/43, file 36050, ibid.

32. TB, 6/18–12/31/42, p. 13, Sich.-Div. 221 Ic, RH 26-221/74, BA-MA.

33. Betr.: "Arbeitseinsatz in Deutschland," Sich.-Div. 221 Ic, 12/4/42, file 29380/9, T-315/1680, NA.

34. TB, 6/18–12/31/42, p. 12, Sich.-Div. 221 Ic, file 29380/8, ibid.

35. RHGeb. Mitte Ia, 7/5/42, file 29380/2, T-315/1678, NA.

36. Betr.: "Festnahme der wehrfähigen Männer südlich Nowosybkow," Sich.-Div. 221 Ic, 7/16/42, file 29380/9, T-315/1680, NA.

37. Betr.: "Unternehmen Ankara," Sich.-Rgt. 36, 12/10/42, file 36509/11, T-315/1685, NA.

38. Monatsbericht, pp. 1–2, Sich.-Div. 221 Ia, 2/5/43, file 36509/4, T-315/1682, NA; Sich.-Div. 221 Ia, 12/14/42, file 36509/11, T-315/1685, NA.

39. Betr.: "Unternehmen Ankara II," p. 3, Sich.-Div. 221 Ia, 1/7/43, ibid.

40. Betr.: "Unternehmen 'Peter' (Einsatzbefehl)," Sich.-Div. 203 Ia, 1/5/43, file 35950/2, T-501/1586, NA.

41. It is unclear whether the "two-thirds" seizure cited here was greater than or at the same level as the "seizure to quota level" that the 221st Security Division decreed for the Ankara operations. It is unlikely to have been lower.

42. Wiko Witebsk KTB, 1/1–2/26/43, pp. 2–3, RW 31/795, BA-MA; Timothy P. Mulligan, *The Politics of Illusion and Empire: German Occupation Policy in the Soviet Union, 1942–1943* (New York: Praeger, 1988), p. 141; Christian Gerlach, *Kalkulierte Morde: Die deutsche Wirtschafts- und Vernichtungspolitik in Weißrußland 1941 bis 1944* (Hamburg: Hamburger Edition, 1999), pp. 1007–1010.

43. Betr.: "Überläufer," p. 1, Sich.-Div. 221 Ic, 12/3/42, file 29380/9, T-315/1680, NA.

44. Mulligan, *Politics of Illusion and Empire*, pp. 139–140.

45. Umbreit, "Das unbewältigte Problem," p. 145. How far the 221st was "ahead of the game" in urging such a measure in December 1942 is unclear, but no major works on the partisan war mention any other Army Group Center unit urging such measures at this stage.

46. De Witt and Moll make the same point; Kurt De Witt and Wilhelm Moll, "The Bryansk Area," in Armstrong, *Soviet Partisans*, p. 513.

47. "Feindlage!," 221 Div. Ic, 3/24/42, RH 26-221/34, BA-MA.

48. Betr.: "Ausrüstungs- u. Ausbildungsstand der neu eingetroffenen LS Bataillone," 221 Div. Ia, 4/9/42, file 22639/2, T-315/1676, NA; Betr.: "Zustand der Landesschützen-Bataillone," p. 2, 221 Div. Ia, 5/3/42, ibid.

49. Schulte, *German Army and Nazi Policies*, p. 259.

50. "Übergabeverhandlung!," 221 Div. Ic, 6/16/42, file 22639/6, T-315/1677, NA.

51. Betr.: "Behandlung von Kriegsgefangenen, Partisanen und Bevölkerung," p. 3, 221 Div. Ic, RH 26-221/34, BA-MA.

52. 221 Div. Ic, 6/4/42, RH 26-221/73, ibid.

53. TB, 6/18–12/31/42, p. 1, Sich.-Div. 221 Ic, file 29380/8, T-315/1680, NA. Though this account almost certainly is exaggerated—the idea of a security division failing completely to build up an intelligence network is difficult to believe—it probably contained at least a significant degree of truth. There would have been nothing to gain from falsely and openly accusing another security division of incompetence. This would have invited damaging counterallegations.

54. Betr.: "V-Leute," p. 1, Sich.-Div. 221 Ic, 10/17/42, file 29380/9, ibid.

55. Betr.: "Bandenlage," p. 2, Sich.-Div. 221 Ic, 9/15/42, ibid.

56. Betr.: "Überläufer," p. 1, Sich.-Div. 221 Ic, 12/3/42, ibid. Certainly, the coordination and effectiveness of the partisans in the 221st's region were surpassed by those of their fellows elsewhere. See, for instance,

Monatsbericht, p. 1, Sich.-Div. 201 Ia, 8/6/42, file 29196/2, T-315/1583, NA; Monatsbericht, p. 1, Sich.-Div. 201 Ia, 1/6/43, ibid.

57. Betr.: "Bandenlage," pp. 2–4, Sich.-Div. 221 Ic, 10/28/42, file 29380/9, T-315/1680, NA; Betr.: "Bandenlage," p. 2, Sich.-Div. 221 Ic, 12/4/42, ibid.

58. De Witt and Moll, "Bryansk Area," pp. 466–467; Ralph Mavrogordato and Earl Ziemke, "The Polotsk Lowland," in Armstrong, *Soviet Partisans*, pp. 554–556.

59. Monatsberichte, Sich.-Div. 201 Ia, 8/6, 9/6, 10/6, 11/6, 12/6/42, file 29196/2, T-315/1583, NA.

60. "Kräfteübersicht des Kommandierenden Generals der Sicherungstruppen und Befehlshaber im Heeresgebiet Mitte," 10/15/42, file 31242/2, T-501/26, NA.

61. Monatsbericht, p. 1, Sich.-Div. 221 Ia, 8/5/42, file 29380/9, T-315/1681, NA.

62. "Gefechts- u. Verpflegungsstärken der Sich.-Div. 221," 6/18–12/31/42, file 29380/1, T-315/1678, NA; TB, 7/4–12/31/42, pp. 1–2, Sich.-Div. 221 VII, 1/1/43, file 28380/9, T-315/1680, NA.

63. On other units' reports of OD defects, see Sich.-Div. 203 VII, 10/29/42, pp. 6, 8, file 29186/3, T-315/1586, NA; Betr.: "Lage u. Tätigkeitsbericht, 6/24/6–7/24/42," p. 5, Feldkommandantur 550, Kriegsverwaltungsgruppe Staryje Dorogi, 7/24/42, file 32104, ibid.; Lagebericht, pp. 5, 10–12, Feldkommandantur 581 Verwaltungsgruppe, 8/19/42, ibid.

64. KTB, 6/18–12/31/41, Sich.-Div. 221 Ib, 8/20/42, file 29380/11, T-315/1680, NA.

65. Betr.: "Ausrüstung des Ost.-Batl. 604 (Pripjet)," Sich.-Div. 221 Ia, 11/13/42, file 35408/2, T-315/1681, NA.

66. Monatsbericht, p. 1, Sich.-Div. 221 Ia, 10/5/42, ibid.

67. Betr.: "Zusammenfassung des Ersatzes für Sich.-Btl. 230, 302 u. 701 in eine Ausbildungs-Kompanie," Sich.-Div. 221 Ia, 7/23/42, file 35408/1, ibid.

68. "Aktenvermerk! (Major Kriebel)," 8/26/42, file 33408/1, ibid.

69. Betr.: "Ausbau und Sicherung der Stützpunkte und Unterkünfte," Sich.-Div. 221 Ia, 10/30/42, file 35408/2, ibid.

70. Sich.-Div. 221 IIa TB, 6/17/42—3/15/43, RH 26-221/79, BA-MA.

71. Schulte, *German Army and Nazi Policies*, p. 261.

72. Corporal Otto Hirschfeld, 198th Infantry Division, 3/22/42, Sammlung Sterz, BfZ. Not his real name.

73. Betr.: "Bahnsicherung," p. 2, Sich.-Div. 221 Ia, 10/4/42, file 35408/2, T-315/1681, NA. Schulte cites a report to General von Schenckendorff from late 1942 making similar observations; *German Army and Nazi Policies*, p. 146.

74. Betr.: "Zustand der Landesschützenbataillone," Sich.-Div. 221 Ia, 5/ 3/42, RH 26-221/33, BA-MA. On health problems faced by rear-area troops, see Schulte, *German Army and Nazi Policies*, pp. 255–258.

75. Anthony Kellett, *Combat Motivation* (Boston: Kluwer Boston, 1982), p. 253.

76. "Beurteilung, Wehrersatzbezirk Stettin," 4/15/39, Pers. 6. File on Alfred Jacobi, BA-MA.

77. Monatsberichte, July–November 1942, Sich.-Div. 221 Ia, files 35408/1 and /2, T-315/1681, NA.

78. Anlage 1, "Abschlußbericht, Unternehmen Luchs," Sich.-Div. 201 Ia, 9/17/42, file 29196/2, T-315/1584, NA; Anlage 1, "Abschlußbericht, Unternehmen Blitz," Sich.-Div. 221 Ia, 10/5/42, ibid.

79. TB, 6/18–12/31/42, Sich.-Div. 221 Ic, file 29380/8, T-315/1680, NA; Monatsberichte, Sich.-Div. 201 Ia, 8/6, 9/6, 10/6, 11/6, 12/6/42, 1/6/ 43, file 29196/2, T-315/1584, NA.

80. Gerlach, *Kalkulierte Morde*, pp. 899–901.

81. That said, the 201st's files are much less comprehensive than the 221st's, and grave reservations (as opposed to outright protest, which would have been highly unlikely) may have been expressed in a document now missing from western archives.

82. Gerlach, *Kalkulierte Morde*, pp. 901, 904 (for qualification of the reliability of the figures), 1012–1015. Einsatzkommando 9's Surash Troop was under direct command of the Third Panzer Army; ibid., p. 960.

83. Ibid., pp. 899–902.

84. There is no record of Einsatzgruppe units having taken an active part in any of the 221st's mobile operations during the second half of 1942. The largest Secret Field Police commitment in a 221st mobile operation between mid-June 1942 and the end of January 1943 was three detachments involved in Operation Ankara II. The 201st committed eleven Secret Field Police detachments to Operation Lightning Ball; Betr.: "Unternehmen 'Ankara,'" p. 2, Sich.-Div. 221 Ia, 1/7/43, file 36509/11, T-315/1685, NA; "Gefechts-Bericht zum Unternehmen 'Kugelblitz,'" 2/22–3/8/43, Angriffsgruppe Jacobi Ia, 12/3/43, RH 26-201/11, BA-MA.

85. EM Nr. 107, p. 5, Chef der Sipo etc., 10/8/41, T-175/234, NA; EM Nr. 121, p. 7, 10/22/41, ibid.; EM Nr. 133, p. 8, 11/14/41, ibid.

86. Betr.: "Lagebeurteilung," p. 5, Sich.-Div. 221 Ia, 11/4/41, file 16748/ 12, T-315/1668, NA.

87. Betr.: "Politische Überwachung der Bevölkerung," p. 2, Sich.-Div. 221 Ic, 8/9/42, file 29380/9, T-315/1680, NA. Einsatzgruppe B called for similar efforts; MadbO Nr. 16, 8/14/42, pp. 13–17, T-175/236, NA.

88. Monatsbericht, p. 2, Sich.-Div. 221 Ic, 11/3/42, file 29380/9, T-315/ 1680, NA.

89. Ibid.

90. Betr.: "Politische Überwachung der Bevölkerung," p. 2, Sich.-Div. 221 Ic, 10/3/42, file 29380/9, ibid.

91. Betr.: "Politsche Überwachung der Bevölkerung," p. 2, Sich.-Div. 221 Ic, 7/19/42, ibid. It is also likely, even though the 221st's discipline reports fail to mention it, that the division's own troops behaved abominably also.

92. Betr.: "Politische Überwachung der Bevölkerung," p. 2, Sich.-Div. 221 Ic, 10/3/42, file 29380/9, ibid.

93. Lt. Emerich Pohl, Ortskommandantur (II) 351, 5/3/42, Sammlung Sterz, BfZ. Not his real name.

94. SS Color Sergeant Hellmut Prantl, Sonderkommando 7a, 6/29/42, Sammlung Sterz, BfZ. Not his real name.

95. Betr.: "Politische Überwachung der Bevölkerung," p. 1, Sich.-Div. 221 Ic, 10/3/42, file 29380/9, T-315/1680, NA.

96. Monatsbericht, p. 1, Sich.-Div. 221 Ic, 11/2/42, ibid.; Monatsbericht, p. 9, Sich.-Div. 221 Ia, 10/5/42, file 35408/2, T-315/1681, NA. Other units made similar reports; Betr.: "Lagebericht, August 1942," pp. 4–5, Sich.-Div. 203 VII, 9/1/42, file 29186/3, T-315/1586, NA; MadbO Nr. 16, pp. 11–12, Chef der Sipo etc., 8/14/42, T-175/236, NA; MadbO Nr. 22, pp. 14–15, Chef der Sipo etc., 9/25/42, ibid.

97. Betr.: "Politische Überwachung der Bevölkerung," p. 1, Sich.-Div. 221 Ic, 11/3/42, file 29380/9, T-315/1680, NA.

98. Betr.: "Monatsbericht," p. 1, Sich.-Div. 221 Ic, 12/2/42, ibid.; "Politische Überwachung der Bevölkerung," p. 1, Sich.-Div. 221 Ic, 12/3/42, 1/2/43, ibid.

99. Betr.: "Geplante Evakuierung," Der Kommandant der Feldkommandantur 528 (V), 10/20/42, file 29380/5, T-315/1679, NA.

100. Betr.: "Politische Überwachung der Bevölkerung," p. 2, Sich.-Div. 221 Ic, 12/3/42, file 29380/9, T-315/1680, NA.

101. Monatsbericht, p. 2, Sich.-Div. 221 Ic, 8/5/42, file 35408/1, T-315/1681, NA.

102. Betr.: "Politische Überwachung der Bevölkerung," p. 1, Sich.-Div. 221 Ic, 1/2/43, file 29380/9, T-315/1680, NA.

103. Alexander Dallin, Ralph Mavrogoradto, and Wilhelm Moll, "Partisan Psychological Warfare and Popular Attitudes," in Armstrong, *Soviet Partisans*, pp. 227–241; Kenneth Slepyan, "The People's Avengers: Soviet Partisans, Stalinist Society and the Politics of Resistance, 1941–1944" (Ph.D. diss., University of Michigan, 1994), pp. 281–288.

104. Betr.: "Politische Überwachung der Bevölkerung," Sich.-Rgt. 27 Ic, 11/29/42, file 29380/9, T-315/1680, NA.

105. Monatsbericht, pp. 1–2, Sich.-Div. 221 Ic, 1/2/43, ibid.

106. Betr.: "Politische Überwachung der Bevölkerung," p. 2, Sich.-Div. 221 Ic, 8/9/42, 10/3/42, ibid.

107. "Bericht des V-Mannes Loginow, Sachar, über Reise in den Bezirk Chotimsk von 10/1–10/10/42," Sich.-Div. 221 Ic, 10/22/42, ibid.

108. Betr.: "Politische Überwachung der Bevölkerung," p. 2, Sich.-Div. 221 Ic, 12/3/42, ibid.

109. "Berichte der V-Männer Wo. und Wa. über die Lage ostwärts Tschetschersk," Sich.-Div. 221 Ic, 10/24/42, ibid.

110. Betr.: "Politische Überwachung der Bevölkerung," p. 2, Sich.-Div. 221 Ic, 1/2/43.

111. MadbO Nr. 35, p. 8, Chef der Sipo etc., 12/23/42, T-175/236, NA.

112. KTB, 3/20–6/17/42, Sich.-Div. 203 Ia, 6/10/42, file 29186/1, T-315/1585, NA. The fact that this citation comes from the divisional war diary, not from a report intended for external use, makes it especially reliable.

113. KTB, 6/18–12/31/42, Sich.-Div. 203 Ia, 7/1/42, ibid. Not his real name.

114. Sich.-Div. 203 VII, 8/2/42, p. 4, file 29186/3, ibid.

115. Divisionsbefehl Nr. 69, Sich.-Div. 203 Ia, 11/14/42, file 29186/2, ibid.

116. Sich.-Div. 203 Ia, 10/6/42, ibid.

117. Monatsberichte, July—October 1942, Sich.-Div. 221 Ia, files 35408/1 and /2, T-315/1681, NA; Monatsberichte, July—October 1942, Sich.-Div. 203 Ia, file 29186/2, T-315/1585, NA.

118. Monatsbericht, p. 1, Sich.-Div. 203 Ia, 7/6/42, file 29186/2, T-315/1585, NA; Monatsbericht, pp. 2–4, Sich.-Div. 203 VII, 8/2/42, file 29186/3, T-315/1586, NA.

119. Monatsbericht, pp. 1–2, Sich.-Div. 203 VII, 11/28/42, ibid.

120. Monatsbericht, Sich.-Div. 221 Ic, 9/2/42, file 29380/9, T-315/1680, NA; Betr.: "Politische Überwachung der Bevölkerung," pp. 1–2, Sich.-Div. 221 Ic, 11/3/42, ibid.; Monatsbericht, p. 1, Sich.-Div. 221 Ic, 11/3/42, ibid. These appraisals seem sincere when one considers that the Einsatzgruppe reports, which can be considered more impartial, still displayed a similar degree of guarded optimism even by the end of 1942.

121. For detailed comparison of the two divisions' situations, see Ben Shepherd, "German Army Security Units in Russia, 1941–1943: A Case Study" (Ph.D. diss., University of Birmingham, 2000), pp. 148–153.

122. Lagebericht, July 1942, pp. 1–2, 707 Inf.-Div. Ic, 8/1/42, file 27797/3, T-315/2246, NA.

123. See, for instance, Hans Meier-Welcker, *Aufzeichnungen eines Generalstabsoffiziers 1939–1942* (Freiburg im Breisgau: Rombach, 1982).

124. Schulte makes a similar point; *German Army and Nazi Policies*, p. 290.
125. Ibid., p. 102.
126. Betr.: "Lagebericht," p. 2, Sich.-Div. 221 Ic, 8/18/41, file 16748/23, T-315/1673, NA.
127. TB, December 1941, RHGeb. Mitte Ic, 1/3/42, file 14684/4, T-501/1, NA.
128. TB, 5/10–12/31/41, p. 3, Sich.-Div. 221 Ic, 12/14/41, file 16748/23, T-315/1673, NA.
129. Betr.: "Lagebeurteilung," Sich.-Div. 221 Ia, 11/4/41, file 16748/12, T-315/1668, NA; Betr.: "Einsatz von aus der russischen Bevölkerung zusammengestellten Ordnungspolizei," Sich.-Div. 221 Ia, 10/15/41, file 16748/11, ibid.; Betr.: "Aufstellung einer Kosaken-Hundertschaft," Sich.-Div. 221 Ia, 10/27/41, ibid.
130. Jürgen Förster, "Die Sicherung des 'Lebensraumes,'" in Horst Boog et al., *Der Angriff auf die Sowjetunion* (Frankfurt am Main: Fischer, 1991), p. 256.
131. "Übergabeverhandlung," p. 1, 221 Div. Ic, 6/16/42, file 22639/6, T-315/1677, NA. The report's balanced judgment—it also conceded that the population of other areas had been hungry, despondent, and beyond effective mobilization—indicates that it reflects fairly the successes and failures of the hearts-and-minds effort; ibid., p. 2.
132. Weinberg, "Yelnya-Dorogobuzh Area," pp. 450–458.
133. Betr.: "Monatsbericht, August 1942," p. 2, Sich.-Div. 221 Ic, 9/2/42, file 29380/9, T-315/1680, NA.
134. Betr.: "Politische Überwachung der Bevölkerung," p. 1, Sich.-Div. 221 Ic, 7/19/42, ibid.
135. Further signs of the Gomel reports' reliability are that they, too, were open about the shortcomings of the hearts-and-minds campaign. On 29 July, for example, the Intelligence Section reported that printed propaganda material was not available in sufficient amounts; Betr.: "Politische Überwachung der Bevölkerung," Sich.-Div. 221 Ic, 7/29/42, ibid.
136. John Ellis, *From the Barrel of a Gun: A History of Guerrilla, Revolutionary, and Civil Warfare from the Romans to the Present* (London: Greenhill, 1995), p. 148.
137. Mulligan, *Politics of Illusion and Empire*, pp. 140–141.
138. Ellis, *From the Barrel of a Gun*, p. 148.
139. Gerlach, *Kalkulierte Morde*, p. 907.

6. Locusts in Field Gray

1. Alexander Dallin, Ralph Mavrogordato, and Wilhelm Moll, "Partisan Psychological Warfare and Popular Attitudes," in John A. Armstrong,

ed., *Soviet Partisans in World War II* (Madison: University of Wisconsin Press, 1964), pp. 328–329.

2. Erich Hesse, *Der Sowjetrussische Partisanenkrieg 1941–1944 im Spiegel deutscher Kampfanweisungen und Befehle,* 2d ed. (Göttingen: Muster-Schmidt Verlag, 1993), pp. 207–208; Leonid D. Grenkevich, *The Soviet Partisan Movement, 1941–1944: A Critical Historiographical Analysis* (London: Frank Cass, 1999), p. 299.

3. Dallin, Mavrogordato, and Moll, "Psychological Warfare," pp. 328–332.

4. Christian Gerlach, *Kalkulierte Morde: Die deutsche Wirtschafts- und Vernichtungspolitik in Weißrußland 1941 bis 1944* (Hamburg: Hamburger Edition, 1999), p. 1030.

5. Grenkevich, *Soviet Partisan Movement,* pp. 299 ff.

6. Betr.: "Bandenlage, 26 April—25 Mai 1943," p. 1, Sich.-Div. 221 Ic, 5/26/43, file 36509/24, T-315/1687, NA.

7. Monatsbericht, p. 1, Sich-Div. 221 Ia, 5/6/43, file 36509/5, T-315/1683, NA.

8. Betr.: "Bandenlage im Divisions-Bereich/Rückführung abgegebener Bataillone," pp. 3–4, Sich.-Div. 221 Ia, 6/11/43, ibid.

9. Monatsbericht, p. 5, Sich.-Div. 221 Ia, 6/7/43, ibid.

10. "Bericht über die Kontrolle der Dg VII im Abschnitt Dowsk-Tsecherikof am 4/7/43," Oberleutnant André, 4/8/43, RH 26-221/53, BA-MA.

11. Betr.: "Bewaffnung der Sich.-Truppen," Sich.-Rgt. 45, 5/31/43, file 36509/9, T-315/1684, NA. The direness of the regiment's own weaponry relative to that of the partisans may have been somewhat exaggerated.

12. Betr.: "Bandenlage im Divisions-Bereich, Februar 1943," p. 1, Sich.-Div. 221 Ic, 3/7/43, file 36509/24, T-315/1687, NA; "Bandenlage im Divisions-Bereich, März 1943," p. 1, Sich.-Div. 221 Ic, ibid.

13. Der Kommandant der Feldkommandantur 528 (V) Ia, 5/11/43, pp. 1–2, file 36509/8, T-315/1684, NA.

14. Meldung, 6/11/43, file 36509/9, ibid. In the spring of 1943 all police regiments were redesignated SS police regiments.

15. Monatsbericht, pp. 5–6, Sich.-Div. 221 Ia, 7/6/43, file 36509/5, T-315/1683, NA. In the case of Feldkommandantur Gomel this description applied only to the west of its area.

16. Betr.: "Bandenlage im Divisions-Bereich, insbesondere Dg VII und Pk-Straße. Rückführung abgegebener Bataillone," Sich.-Div. 221 Ia, 6/11/43, file 36509/5, T-315/1682, NA.

17. Monatsbericht, pp. 3–4, Sich.-Div. 221 Ia, 7/6/43, file 36509/5, T-315/1683, NA.

18. Timothy P. Mulligan, *The Politics of Illusion and Empire: German*

Occupation Policy in the Soviet Union, 1942–1943 (New York: Praeger, 1988), pp. 123–146; Hans Umbreit, "Das unbewältigte Problem." Der Partisanenkrieg im Rücken der Ostfront," in Jürgen Förster, ed., *Stalingrad: Ereignis—Wirkung—Symbol* (Zurich: Piper, 1992), pp. 138–142.

19. Mulligan, *Politics of Illusion and Empire*, pp. 141, 140; Bernd Wegner, "Der Krieg gegen die Sowjetunion 1942/43," in Horst Boog, Werner Rauhn, Reinhard Stumpf, and Bernd Wegner, *Das Deutsche Reich und der Zweite Weltkrieg*, vol. 6: *Der Globale Krieg: Die Ausweitung zum Weltkrieg und der Wechsel der Initiative, 1941–1943* (Stuttgart: Deutsche Verlags-Anstalt, 1990), p. 921; Betr.: "Lagebericht, Februar 1943," 203 Sich.-Div. VII/Mil. Verw., 2/25/43, file 35950/2, T-315/1586, NA.

20. Gerlach, *Kalkulierte Morde*, pp. 1036–52.

21. On distribution of Russian-language newspapers, OD cultivation, eastern worker propaganda, and other propaganda at this time, see Monatsbericht, p. 2, Sich.-Div. 221 Ic, 5/3/43, file 36509/24, T-315/1687, NA; Betr.: "Sicherung des Divisions-Bereiches," Sich.-Div. 221 Ia, 3/11/43, file 36509/4, T-315/1682, NA; Betr.: "Propagandistische Betreuung der Arbeitertransporte," Sich.-Div. 221 Ic, 6/26/43, file 36509/24, T-315/1687, NA; Betr.: "Beitrag zum Monatsbericht 221. Sich.-Division Ia, Mai 1943," p. 1, Sich.-Div. 221 Ic, 6/2/43, ibid.; "Besondere Anordnungen für die Versorgung Nr. 42/43," Sich.-Div. 221 Ib, 6/29/43, file 36509/27, ibid.

22. Betr.: "Beitrag zum Monatsbericht 221. Sich-Division Ia, Mai 1943," p. 1, Sich.-Div. 221 Ic, 6/2/43, file 36509/24, T-315/1687, NA.

23. Betr.: "Politische Überwachung der Bevölkerung," p. 3, Sich.-Div. 221 Ic, 6/30/43, ibid. On other pleas by officers for a more realistic approach to propaganda, see Jürgen Förster, "Zum Rußlandbild der Militärs 1941–1945," in Hans-Erich Volkmann, ed., *Das Rußlandbild im Dritten Reich* (Cologne: Böhlau, 1994), pp. 157–160.

24. Betr.: "Politische Überwachung der Bevölkerung," p. 2, Sich.-Div. 221 Ic, 5/31/43, file 36509/24, T-315/1687, NA.

25. Betr.: "Unternehmen des Kgl. ung. VII A. K. im Raum südlich Nowosybkoff, 7/2/43," Sich.-Div. 221 Ia/Ib, file 36509/19, T-315/1686, NA.

26. Betr.: "Unternehmen südl. Nowosybkoff," Sich.-Div. 221 Ia, ibid.

27. Betr.: "Umgruppierung der 102 le[ichte] ung[arische] Div[ision]," RHGeb. Mitte Ia, 7/16/43, file 36509/9, T-315/1684, NA.

28. Truman O. Anderson, "A Hungarian *Vernichtungskrieg?* Hungarian Troops and the Soviet Partisan War in Ukraine 1942," *Militärgeschichtliche Mitteilungen* 58 (1999), 345–366.

29. Betr.: "Unternehmen 'Csobo,'" 7/2/43, III/Sich.-Rgt. 45, file 36509/19, T-315/1686, NA.

30. KTB, 1/1–6/1/43, Sich.-Div. 221 Ia, 1/3–4/30/43, file 36509/1, T-315/1682, NA.

31. Betr.: "Unternehmen 'Osterhase,'" p. 2, Sich.-Div. 221 Ia, 4/6/43, file 36509/13, T-315/1685, NA.

32. See Appendix A.

33. Monatsbericht, p. 2, Sich.-Div. 221 Ic, 3/4/43, file 36509/24, T-315/1687, NA.

34. Betr.: "Politische Überwachung der Bevölkerung," p. 1, Sich.-Div. 221 Ic, 3/1/43, ibid.

35. Monatsbericht, Sich.-Div. 221 Ic, 2/2/43, ibid.; Betr.: "Politische Überwachung der Bevölkerung," p. 1, Sich.-Div. 221 Ic, 1/30/43, ibid.

36. Betr.: "Italienische 8. Armee im Bereich der Division; Gruppe Geheime Feldpolizei 729," 2/23/43, Sich.-Div. 221 Ic, 2/20/43, ibid.; Betr.: "Zersetzende Verhalten italienischer Soldaten. Bericht," ibid.; Betr.: "Politische Überwachung der Bevölkerung," p. 1, Sich.-Div. 221 Ic, 3/31/43, ibid.

37. Betr.: "Politische Überwachung der Bevölkerung," p. 1, Sich.-Div. 221 Ic, 4/30/43, ibid.

38. WiKo 212 (Mogilew), 5/18/43, RW 31/849, BA-MA; "Lage- und Tätigkeitsbericht Nr. 17, Gesamtüberblick," ibid.

39. Betr.: "Bandenlage im Divisions-Bereich, Januar 1943," p. 1, Sich.-Div. 221 Ic, 2/8/43, file 36509/24, T-315/1687, NA.

40. Betr.: "Vernehmung des Ogfr. Paul Meynecken von der Propaganda-Staffel Gomel, der aus Banditengefangenschaft befreit wurde," Sich.-Div. 221 Ic 6/8/43, ibid.

41. Monatsbericht, p. 4, Sich.-Div. 221 Ia, 6/7/43, file 36509/5, ibid. The precise wording was that partisan propaganda was taking effect in "only" the areas endangered by the partisans, but by this stage much of the division's jurisdiction fell into this category.

42. Monatsbericht, 6/20–7/20/43, p. 1, Prop.-Abt. W Staffel Gomel, 7/21/43, file 36509/24, ibid.

43. Monatsbericht, p. 6, Sich.-Div. 221 Ia, 7/6/43, file 36509/5, ibid.

44. TB, 1/1–8/31/43, p. 10, Sich.-Div. 221 Ic, 11/19/43, file 36509/24, ibid. Seventy-four OD men went "missing" in May 1943, compared with twenty-four during March; Monatsbericht, p. 2, Sich.-Div. 221 Ic, 4/2/43, ibid.; Monatsbericht, p. 2, Sich.-Div. 221 Ic, 6/2/43, ibid. Such increases were the norm across the Army Group Center Rear Area; Monatsbericht, p. 14, Sich.-Div. 203 Ia, 3/7/43, file 35950/2, T-315/1586, NA; Monatsbericht, p. 18, Sich.-Div., 203 Ia, 6/7/43, ibid. Redefecting collaborators accounted for a significant portion of new partisan recruits during 1943. In the Smolensk area from April to October 1943, for example, they made up 12

percent (723) of new recruits; Kenneth Slepyan, "The People's Avengers: Soviet Partisans, Stalinist Society and the Politics of Resistance, 1941–1944" (Ph.D. diss., University of Michigan, 1994), p. 205.

45. Betr.: "Politische Überwachung der Bevölkerung," p. 2, Sich.-Div. 221 Ic, 5/31/43, file 36509/24, T-315/1687, NA.

46. Betr.: "Abschliessender Bericht über Julikäfer II," p. 3, III/Sich.-Rgt. 930 Stab [HQ], 8/10/43, file 36509/9, T-315/1684, NA.

47. Betr.: "Politische Überwachung der Bevölkerung," p. 2, Sich.-Div. 221 Ic, 8/1/43, file 36509/24, T-315/1687, NA.

48. Monatsbericht, 1/20–2/20/43, p. 1, Prop.-Abt. W Staffel Gomel, 2/20/43, ibid.; Monatsbericht, 2/20–3/20/43, pp. 1–2, Prop.-Abt. W Staffel Gomel, 3/21/43, ibid.

49. Monatsbericht, 3/20–4/20/43, p. 1, Prop.-Abt. W Staffel Gomel, 4/20/43, ibid.

50. Betr.: "Beitrag zum Monatsbericht 221. Sich.-Div. Ia, Mai 1943," p. 2, Sich.-Div. 221 Ic, 6/2/43, ibid.; Betr.: "Einsatz der Prop.-Staffel Gomel," Sich.-Div. 221 Ic, 7/2/43, ibid.

51. Betr.: "Propagandistische Betreuung der Arbeitertransporte," p. 2, Sich.-Div. 221 Ic, 6/26/43, ibid.

52. Monatsbericht, 6/20–7/20/43, Prop.-Abt. W. Staffel Gomel, 7/21/43, ibid.

53. Betr.: "Wirkung der Propaganda des Generals Wlassow," Sich.-Div. 221 Ic, 6/20/43, ibid. This failure seems to have been widespread; Betr.: "Lagebericht, März 1943," p. 7, Sich.-Div. 203 VII, 3/26/43, file 36050, T-315/1586, NA.

54. Betr.: "Beitrag zu Monatsbericht 221. Sich-Division Ia, Juni 1943," p. 1, Sich.-Div. 221 Ic, 7/1/43, file 36509/24, T-315/1687, NA.

55. Sich.-Div. 221 Ic, 7/4/43, ibid. Though this document was signed by Major Kriebel, the fact that it was issued through the Intelligence Section strongly suggests that Beck wrote it. Even if Kriebel wrote it, the fact that the Intelligence Section was party to it without comment is significant.

56. Anlage 127 (no date): "Flugblatt Übersetzung aus den Russischen: 'Kameraden der Gruppe Fjodorow,'" n.d., Sich.-Div. 221 Ic, ibid.

57. Omer Bartov, *The Eastern Front, 1941–45: German Troops and the Barbarization of Warfare* (Basingstoke: Macmillan, 1985), pp. 147–148.

58. "Kriegstagebuch der Gruppe La Klinzy. Überblick, 4/1–7/1/43," p. 1, WiKo 210 (Klinzy), Gruppe Landwirtschaft, 7/11/43, file WiID/857, T-77/1147, NA.

59. Lagebericht Nr. 26, p. 5, Wirtschaftinspektion Mitte Stab I/Id, 4/2/43, file WiID/368, T-77/1099, NA. Given the particular concern of these units, these reports may have exaggerated economic problems somewhat.

60. Monatsüberblick, May 1943, WiKo Gomel 1–5/43, file WiID/864, T-77/1147, NA.

61. Monatsüberblick, March 1943, p. 2, WiKo Gomel 1–5/43, file WiID/863, ibid.

62. Monatsbericht, p. 13, Sich.-Div. 221 Ia, 6/7/43, file 36509/5, T-315/1683, NA.

63. "Besondere Anordnungen für die Versorgung," RHGeb. Mitte Quartiermiester, 4/25/43, RH 26-221/51b, BA-MA.

64. Betr.: "Verpflegung," Kommandeur Sich.-Rgt. 183, 7/13/43, file 36509/9, T-315/1684, NA.

65. TB, August 1943, p. 7, Sich.-Div. 221 Ic, 11/19/43, file 36509/24, T-315/1687, NA.

66. Kürzer Überblick über die Tätigkeit der Gruppe Landwirtschaft, 4/1–6/30/43, p. 1, WiKo Klinzy, file WiID/856, T-77/1147, NA.

67. Gerlach, *Kalkulierte Morde*, p. 999. There is no specific mention of what the 221st's portion of the quota constituted.

68. Betr.: "Bandenlage, 6/26–7/25/43," p. 1, Sich.-Div. 221 Ic, 7/27/43, file 36509/24, T-315/1687, NA.

69. Betr.: "Unternehmen der 102. le. ung. Div.," Sich.-Div. 221 Ia, 7/3/43, file 36509/5, T-315/1683, NA.

70. Betr.: "Aktivierung der Bandenbekämpfung," Sich.-Div. 221 Ia, 6/25/43, ibid.

71. Ibid., p. 2.

72. Sich.-Div. 221 Ia, 7/4/43, file 36509/9, T-315/1684, NA.

73. Monatsbericht, July 1943, Sich.-Div. 221 Ia, file 36509/5, T-315/1683, NA.

74. KTB, 7/1–7/11/43, p. 1, WiKo 210 (Klinzy), Gruppe Landwirtschaft, 7/11/43, file WiID/857, T-77/1147, NA.

75. Betr.: "Unternehmen 'Sommerfest,'" p. 2, Sich.-Div. 221 Ib, 6/27/43, file 36509/17, T-315/1686, NA.

7. Fear in the Forest

1. Corporal Erich Stahl, Guard Battalion 542, 10/20/41, Sammlung Sterz, BfZ. Not his real name.

2. Private Hans Schröder, 389th Infantry Division, 6/19/42, ibid. Not his real name.

3. Corporal Hans Waigel, 4th Panzer Division, 7/21/42, ibid.

4. Ibid., 6/9/42.

5. See, for instance, Hans Meier-Welcker, *Aufzeichnungen eines Generalstabsoffiziers 1939–1942* (Freiburg im Breisgau: Rombach, 1982).

6. Timothy P. Mulligan, *The Politics of Illusion and Empire: German Occupation Policy in the Soviet Union, 1942–1943* (New York: Praeger, 1988), pp. 124, 132, n. 6.

7. These can only be fairly initial observations; exploring exactly how extensive fraternization was, and what its patterns were, would require extensive further research.

8. On relations between German troops and civilians, see Theo J. Schulte, *The German Army and Nazi Policies in Occupied Russia, 1941–1943* (Oxford: Berg, 1989), chap. 7.

9. Betr.: "Unternehmen Ankara. Gefechtsbericht, 12/19–12/24/42," p. 1, Sich.-Rgt. 36 Ia, 12/26/42, file 36509/11, T-315/1685, NA.

10. Ibid., p. 2.

11. TB, 3/22–6/17/42, pp. 2–3, 221 Div. Ic, 6/18/42, file 22639/6, T-315/1677, NA. The same report claimed another 1,227 dead and wounded, according to captured papers and interrogations of prisoners and deserters.

12. See Appendix B.

13. Gerhard L. Weinberg, "The Yelnya-Dorogobuzh Area of Smolensk Oblast," in John A. Armstrong, ed., *Soviet Partisans in World War II* (Madison: University of Wisconsin Press 1964), pp. 430–433.

14. TB, May 1942, p. 4, RHGeb. Mitte Ia, 6/10/42, file 24693/3, T-501/15, NA.

15. Weinberg, "Yelnya-Dorogobuzh Area," pp. 434–437. Though currently the most complete western account of the attitude of the Yelnya-Dorogobuzh region's population before and during the operations, the limitations of a study relying almost exclusively upon German Army sources need to be borne in mind. Indeed, as Weinberg himself points out, the fact that the sources were generated by units operating at the edges of such a partisan-infested area arguably renders such sources even less useful than usual. For a similar reason the relevant files of the Einsatzgruppen and the Economic Detachment Smolensk, which was economically responsible for the Yelnya-Dorogobuzh area, cannot provide particular enlightenment either; the former also because the Yelnya-Dorogobuzh area was a "special case," which in terms of population mood was below the Einsatzgruppen reports' radar screen, the latter presumably because the partisan situation in the area precluded the possibility of access by economic agencies. That said, the economic detachment's general statements on the effects of the food situation upon the population's mood in its jurisdiction may apply to the Yelnya-Dorogobuzh area also.

16. Not its real name; it was named after the officer who commanded it.

17. KTB, 3/20–6/17/42, 221 Div. Ia, 5/24/42, file 22639/1, T-315/1676, NA.

18. "Zustand der Landesschützen-Bataillone," p. 2, 221 Div. Ia, 5/3/42, file 22639/2, ibid. This was one of the new, weak battalions that had come under the 221st's command upon its arrival in the region. Assessment of its fighting power on 3 May judged it fully fit for security duty only.

19. Between July and December 1941, a similar phenomenon seems to have ensured that the 221st's static security troops were "credited" with killing only 197 of the 1,095 partisans recorded as killed in the daily communiqués to the Army Group Center Rear Area; Tagesmeldungen, 8/17–12/14/41, Sich-Div. 221 Ia, file 16748/16, T-315/1670, NA.

20. KTB, 3/20–6/17/42, 221 Div. Ia, 5/30/42, file 22639/1, T-315/1676, NA.

21. Ibid., 4/8/42. See also Appendix B.

22. KTB, 3/20–6/17/42, 221 Div. Ia, 3/27, 3/28/42, file 22639/1, T-315/1676, NA.

23. Ibid., 5/12/42. See also Appendix B.

24. Two machine guns (no rifles) were reported captured; KTB, 3/20–6/17/42, 221 Div. Ia, 5/12/42, file 22639/1, T-315/1676, NA.

25. Ibid., 4/30–5/3/42.

26. KTB, 6/18–12/31/41, Sich.-Div. 221 Ia, 7/28–8/21/42, file 29380/1, T-315/1678, NA; KTB, 4/1–12/31/42, Sich.-Div. 203 Ia, 6/12, 7/13, 8/8/42, file 29186/1, T-315/1585, ibid.

27. See Appendix B.

28. Anlagen zum Monatsbericht, June—December 1942, January 1943, Sich.-Div. 221 Ia, files 35408/1 and /2, T-315/1678, NA.

29. Anlage 533, Sich.-Div. 221 Ia, 6/25/42, RH 26–221/38a, BA-MA.

30. Betr.: "4 Kp., Sich.-Btl. 706, Odessa," Sich.-Btl. 706, 7/2/42, file 29380/5, T-315/1679, NA.

31. RHGeb. Mitte, Chef des Generalstabes, 9/29/42, pp. 1–2, file 35408/1, T-315/1681, NA.

32. Kommandeur, 8/4/42, p. 1, Sich.-Div. 221, file 35408/1, ibid.

33. Tätigkeitsbericht, 6/17/42—3/15/43, p. 1, Sich.-Div. 221 IIa, RH 26–221/79, BA-MA; Gerald Reitlinger, *The House Built on Sand: The Conflicts of German Policy in Russia* (London: Cox and Wyman, 1961), p. 110.

34. Betr.: "Lage und Tätigkeitsbericht," 6/24–7/24/42, Feldkommandantur 550 Kr. Verwaltungsgruppe, Staryje Dorogi, 7/24/42, file 32104, T-315/1586, NA.

35. KTB, 6/18–12/31/42, Sich.-Div. 221 Ia, 9/6/42, file 29380/1, T-315/1678, NA.

36. Sich.-Rgt. 27, 7/7/42, file 29380/5, T-315/1679, NA.

37. Betr.: "Urlaubsscheine mit Hinweis auf bevorstehenden Waffenstillstand," Sich.-Div. 221 Ic, 11/21/42, file 29380/9, T-315/1680, NA.

38. See Appendix A. For more detail and tables on the operations, see Ben Shepherd, "Wehrmacht Security Regiments in the Soviet Partisan War, 1943," *European History Quarterly* 43 (2003), 493–529.

39. Betr.: "Unternehmen Klette II. Gefechtsbericht," Sich.-Rgt. 36 Ia, 2/9/43, file 36509/12, T-315/1685, NA.

40. Ibid., p. 15; Betr.: "Zersetsungserscheinungen in der franz. Legion," Sich.-Div. 221 Ic, 12/14/42, file 29380/9, T-315/1680, NA.

41. Betr.: "Unternehmen Klette II. Gefechtsbericht," p. 15, Sich.-Rgt. 36 Ia, 2/9/43.

42. "Besondere Anordnungen zum Divisions-Befehl für Unternehmen Klette II," p. 2, 707 Inf.-Div. Ia, 1/10/43, file 36509/4, T-315/1682, NA.

43. Betr.: "Überläufer," p. 1, Sich.-Div. 221 Ic, 12/3/42, file 29380/9, T-315/1680, NA.

44. "Besondere Anordnungen zum Divisions-Befehl für Unternehmen Klette II," p. 4.

45. See Appendix B.

46. See Appendix B.

47. "Zusatzbericht zur Meldung über das Unternehmen vom 1/17/1/18/43," 2/Sich.-Btl. 791, 1/23/43, file 36509/12, T-315/1685, NA; Betr.: "Tagesmeldung," 2./Sich.-Btl. 791, 1/18/43, ibid.; "Gefechtsbericht der Sicherungsbesatzung Mglin," 1/19–1/21/43, Sich.-Btl. 791, 1/25/43, ibid.

48. KTB, 5/1–8/31/43, Sich.-Div. 221 Ia, 5/17, 8/29/43, file 36509/1, T-315/1682, NA.

49. Ibid.

50. Betr.: "Tagesmeldungen," pp. 2–3, 3/Sich.-Btl. 242, 6/14/43, file 36509/9, T-315/1684, NA.

51. Ic Befehle und Mitteilungen Nr. 3, p. 2, Sich.-Div. 221 Ic, 2/13/43, RH 26-221/51b, BA-MA.

52. Ibid., p. 3.

53. Ic Befehle und Mitteliungen Nr. 7, p. 1, ibid.

54. Ibid., p. 2.

55. Betr.: "Bandenlage im Bereich des Sich.-Batl. 242," p. 2, Sich.-Btl. 242, 5/10/43, file 36509/8, T-315/1684, NA.

56. KTB, 5/17/43, Sich.-Div. 221 Ia, file 36509/2, ibid.

57. Betr.: "Lage im Bereich des Sich.-Btl. 242," Sich.-Btl. 242, 5/30/43, file 36509/9, ibid.

58. Corporal Ludwig Birkenfeld, 3d company, Supply Battalion 563, 7/8/41, Sammlung Sterz, BfZ. Not his real name.

59. Betr.: "Bandenmeldung im Gebiet Propoisk u. Korma," pp. 1–2, Sich.-Rgt. 183, 6/17/43, file 36509/9, T-315/1684, NA.

60. Betr.: "Meldung über Mannschaftslage der 2. Kp. in Stützpunkt

Krasnopolje," 2 Kp., Sich.-Btl. 242, 8/13/43, ibid. This report may well be exaggerated—a partisan group this strong could have overwhelmed the company whenever it wanted to—but almost certainly the company was in a very bad state.

61. For comparison between the two units, including tables, see also Shepherd, "Wehrmacht Security Regiments."

62. "Besetzung der Feldwachen und Stützpunkte," Sich.-Btl. 242, 4/25/43, file 36509/8, T-315/1684, NA; "Personelle Stärke der Stützpunkte und Wachen," Gren.-Rgt. 930, 4/24/43, ibid.; "Besetzung der Feldwachen und Stützpunkte," Sich.-Btl. 242, 5/25/43, file 36509/9, ibid.; "Personelle Stärke der Stützpunkte und Wachen," Sich.-Rgt. 930, 5/24/43, ibid.

63. Einsatz der Sich.-Div. 221, 5/1, 6/1/43, file 36509/5, T-315/1683, NA.

64. Betr.: "Bandenlage im Divisions-Bereich," Sich.-Div. 221 Ic, 4/4, 4/26, 6/27, 7/27/43, file 36509/24, T-315/1687, NA.

65. "Bericht über Verlauf und Ergebnis des Unternehmens 'Zugspitze,'" p. 2, Gren.-Rgt. 930 Ia, 2/8/43, file 36509/17, T-315/1686, NA.

66. Betr.: "Sprengungen im Abschnitt Belynkowitschi-Shurbin," p. 1, Gren.-Rgt. 930 Ia, 4/8/43, file 36509/8, T-315/1684, NA.

67. Betr.: "Evakuierung des Mamajewka-Gebietes," Sich.-Rgt. 930 Ia, 6/23/43, ibid. On the 930th's falling combat strength and increased problems along the railway lines, see "Gefechtsstärke der 930. Gren.-Rgt.," 2/1–5/11/43, ibid.; KTB, 1/1–6/1/43, Sich.-Div. 221 Ia, 4/1–5/31/43, file 36509/1, T-315/1682, NA.

68. Betr.: "Evakuierung des Mamajewka-Gebietes," Sich.-Rgt. 930 Ia, 6/26/43, file 36509/8, T-315/1684, NA.

69. File on Alfred Illig, Pers. 6, BA-MA. Not his real name.

70. Betr.: "Tagesmeldung," 4/21–4/30/42, p. 2, 221 Div. Ia, 5/1/42, file 22639/4, T-315/1677, NA.

71. An LSR 44, 221 Div. Ia, 4/27/42, file 22639/2, T-315/1676, NA; Tagesmeldung, 221 Div. Ia, 4/27/42, file 22639/4, T-315/1677, NA.

72. KTB, 3/20–6/17/42, 221 Div. Ia, 6/1/42, file 22639/1, T-315/1676, NA.

73. During the summer of 1942 all territorial regiments were redesignated security regiments. Territorial and guard battalions were redesignated security battalions.

74. "Befehl für die Sicherung und Aufklärung im Raum um Nowosybkoff," p. 2, Sich.-Rgt. 45, 6/23/42, file 29380/5, T-315/1679, NA.

75. KTB, 6/18–12/31/42, Sich.-Div. 221 Ia, 9/24/42, file 29380/1, T-315/1678, NA; Betr.: "Berichterstattung über Einsatz der Inf-Pi-Züge im Monat Oktober 1942," Sich.-Div. 221 Ia, 11/14/42, file 35408/2, T-315/1681, NA.

76. KTB, 6/18–12/31/42, Sich.-Div. 221 Ia, 10/21/42, file 29380/1, T-315/1678, NA.

77. Ibid., 9/12, 12/28/42.

78. Sich.-Div. 221 Ia, 4/29/43, file 36509/13, T-315/1685, NA; Sich.-Rgt. 45, 4/29/43, ibid.

79. Betr.: "Unternehmen 'Osterhase,'" p. 2, Sich.-Div. 221 Ia, 4/6/43, ibid.

80. "Erfahrungsbericht aus dem Unternehmen 'Osterhase,'" 4/27–4/30/43, pp. 1–2, Sich.-Btl. 242, 5/4/43, ibid.

81. Betr.: "Bericht über Unternehmen Osterhase," p. 5, Sich.-Div. 221 Ia, 5/2/43, ibid.

82. KTB, 12/22/42, Sich.-Div. 221 Ia, file 29380/1, T-315/1678, NA; KTB, 1/19/43, Sich.-Div. 221 Ia, file 36509/1, T-315/1682, NA; Betr.: "Unternehmen Ankara. Gefechtsbericht," 12/19–12/24/42, p. 1, Sich.-Rgt. 36 Ia, 12/26/42, file 36509/11, T-315/1685, NA; "Verlauf des Unternehmen Ankara I" (map, n.d.), ibid.; Betr.: "Unternehmen Ankara II," p. 1, Sich.-Div. 221 Ia, 1/16/43, ibid.; Sich.-Div. 221 Ia. "Geplanter Verlauf des Unternehmens Ankara II" (map, n.d.), ibid.; Betr.: "Unternehmen Ankara II. Gefechtsbericht," 1/17–1/21/43, Sich.-Rgt. 36 Ia, 1/25/43, file 36509/12, ibid.; Betr.: "Bericht über Unternehmen Osterhase," Sich.-Div. 221 Ia, 5/2/43, file 36509/13, ibid. See also Appendix A; Shepherd, "Wehrmacht Security Regiments."

83. Betr.: "Bericht über Unternehmen Osterhase," pp. 2–3, Sich.-Div. 221 Ia, 5/2/43, file 36509/13, T-315/1685, NA.

84. Ibid., p. 2.

85. Ibid.; Betr.: "Unternehmen Osterhase," Anlage 790, Sich.-Div. 221 Ib, 9/5/43, file 36504/27, T-315/1687, NA.

86. Corporal Werner Scheibe, 12th Panzer Division, 11/16/42, Sammlung Sterz, BfZ. Not his real name.

87. "Erfahrungen über den Kampf bei Kamenka und Lossow," Sich.-Rgt. 45, 5/1/43, file 36509/13, T-315/1685, NA. Lieutenant Meyer of the regimental Operations Section wrote the report on Wiemann's behalf.

88. Christian Streit, *Keine Kameraden: Die Wehrmacht und die sowjetischen Kriegsgefangenen 1941–1945*, 4th ed. (Bonn: Dietz, 1997), p. 84; Jürgen Förster, "Zum Rußlandbild der Militärs 1941–1945," in Hans-Erich Volkmann, ed., *Das Rußlandbild im Dritten Reich* (Cologne: Böhlau, 1994), p. 149.

89. Betr.: "Unternehmen 'Csobo,'" 7/2/43, III/Sich.-Rgt. 45, file 36509/19, T-315/1686, NA.

90. File on Hans Wiemann, Pers. 6, BA-MA.

91. "Lebenslauf," ibid.

92. File on Julius Lehmann, Heeresgeneralkartei, BA-MA. Not his real name.

93. Abw. IIIc, 5/3/35, file on Joachim von Geldern-Crispendorff, Pers. 6, BA-MA.

94. Beurteilung, 286 Sich.-Div., 3/1/43, BA-MA.

95. Betr.: "Tragen der Uniform," Der Chef des Generalstabes des Heeres, 3/1/39, BA-MA.

96. Kommando 221, Sich.-Div., 2/5/43, Beurteilung, file on Karl Hegedüs, BA-MA.

97. Zusatz zur Beurteilung vom 2/9/41 über Oberst Hegedüs, Kommandeur Inf.-Rgt. 279, 95 Infanterie-Division Kommandeur, 7/31/41, ibid.

98. 286 Sich.-Div., 3/1/43, file on Alois Luckmann, ibid.

99. Kommando, Sich.-Div. 221, 2/5/43, Beurteilung, file on Karl Hegedüs, ibid.; 286 Sich.-Div., 3/1/43, file on Alois Luckmann, ibid.; 286 Sich.-Div., 3/1/43, file on Joachim von Geldern-Crispendorff, ibid.; file on Julius Lehmann, RH7, Heeresgeneralkartei, BA-MA.

100. Sich.-Div. 221, 3/1/43, Pers 6. File on Hans Wiemann, BA-MA.

101. "Bericht über Erfahrungen in der Bandenbekämpfung (insbes. 'Nachbarhilfe' I u. II)," p. 2, Hauptm. Dresdner, 11/Sich.-Rgt. 45, 6/16/43, file 36509/5, T-315/1683, NA. Not his real name.

Conclusion

1. Erich Hesse, *Der Sowjetrussische Partisanenkrieg 1941–1944 im Spiegel deutscher Kampfanweisungen und Befehle*, 2d ed. (Göttingen: Muster-Schmidt Verlag, 1993), p. 270.

2. Timothy P. Mulligan, *The Politics of Illusion and Empire: German Occupation Policy in the Soviet Union, 1942–1943* (New York: Praeger, 1988), p. 144.

3. Hesse, *Sowjetrussische Partisanenkrieg*, pp. 264–268.

4. Christian Gerlach, *Kalkulierte Morde: Die deutsche Wirtschafts- und Vernichtungspolitik in Weißrußland 1941 bis 1944* (Hamburg: Hamburger Edition, 1999), p. 903.

5. Ibid., pp. 1045–47; Klaus-Michael Mallmann, "'Aufgeraümt und abgebrannt'. Sicherheitspolizei und 'Bandenkampf' in der besetzten Sowjetunion," in Mallmann and Gerhard Paul, eds., *Die Gestapo im Zweiten Weltkrieg* (Darmstadt: Primus, 2000), p. 512.

6. Theo J. Schulte, *The German Army and Nazi Policies in Occupied Russia, 1941–1943* (Oxford: Berg, 1989), p. 280.

7. For necessary qualifications of the partisans' military impact, see Gerlach, *Kalkulierte Morde*, pp. 864–869.

8. Geoffrey P. Megargee, *Inside Hitler's High Command* (Lawrence: University Press of Kansas, 2000), p. 198.

9. Hesse, *Sowjetrussische Partisanenkrieg*, pp. 260–263.

10. Schulte, *German Army in Occupied Russia*, p. 278.

11. Paul Kohl, *Der Krieg der deutschen Wehrmacht und der Polizei 1941–1944: Sowjetische Überlebende berichten* (Frankfurt am Main: Fischer, 1998), p. 272.

12. Hesse, *Sowjetrussische Partisanenkrieg*, pp. 253–254.

13. Ibid., pp. 271–275.

14. Ibid., pp. 274–275.

15. Schulte, *German Army in Occupied Russia*, p. 32.

16. No information in this respect could be found on Lieutenant-Colonel von der Groeben.

17. A study of officers in the interwar Austrian federal army awaits further research.

18. Joachim C. Fest, *The Face of the Third Reich* (London: Weidenfeld and Nicolson, 1970), p. 237.

19. File on Joachim von Geldern-Crispendorff, Abw. IIIc, 5/3/35, Pers. 6, BA-MA.

20. The restricted size of this sample necessarily brings with it caveats. A larger sample will be able to address the following issues: relationships between behavior patterns and other potentially important personal influences, such as experiences before and during World War I; personal characteristics common to "self-styled pragmatists" as well as to "fanatics" and "moderates"; and generational effects. The oldest officer of the eleven mentioned here was born in 1882 (Pflugbeil), the youngest in 1900 (Beck). Captain Haupt, a pivotal figure in the 221st's conduct during 1941, is the only Weimar generation officer (born 1908) of the 221st on whom personal details could be found. It will be possible to "fit" him into some kind of officer analysis only once a larger sample has unearthed comparable officers.

Bibliography of Primary Sources

Bibliothek für Zeitgeschichte (Library of Contemporary History), Stuttgart
    Soldiers' letters from Sammlung Sterz
Bundesarchiv-Militärarchiv (Federal Military Archive), Freiburg im
    Breisgau (BA-MA)
    Army Group files (RH 19 II)
    Army files (RH 20)
    Panzer Army files (RH 21)
    Army Group Rear Area/Army Rear Area files (RH 22)
    Army Corps files (RH 24)
    Infantry division files (RH 26)
    Economic Detachment/Economic Inspectorate files (RW 31)
    Officers' personal files (Pers 6 and RH 7)
U.S. National Archive, College Park, Maryland (NA)
    Army Group files (T-311)
    Army files (T-312)
    Panzer Army files (T-313)
    Army Group Rear Area/Army Rear Area files (T-501)
    Army Corps files (T-314)
    Infantry division files (T-315)
    Economic Detachment/Economic Inspectorate files (T-77)
    Einsatzgruppe reports from the Soviet Union (T-175)

Index

Anti-Bolshevism, 9, 12, 99, 224; and German collapse in 1918, 10; and Free Corps, 13; and Nazi aims for Soviet Union, 20–22; and anti-Semitism, 21–22, 24, 55, 90; and "criminal orders" of 1941, 23–24, 53, 55–56; and German middle class, 29; and Soviet brutality, 72–74; and "Jew equals Bolshevik equals partisan" equation, 90; in 221st Security Division's propaganda, 180; in 45th Security Regiment, 214. *See also* Commissars; Communists, treatment of

Anti-partisan warfare, conditions of, 76, 103–104, 106–107, 142, 161–165, 216–218, 226–230; terrain and environment, 51–52, 77–78, 146, 193, 195, 200; overstretch of German forces, 74–75, 105, 143–144, 146–147, 171, 193, 198, 199, 200, 203–207; inferior quality of German forces, 75, 105, 114, 140–141, 144–146, 170–171, 193, 195, 197–198, 201, 203–207; fear of partisan attack, 75–76, 77–78, 79; lack of mobility, 76–77, 97–98, 105; distrust of population, 78, 100–101, 194, 199; insufficient intelligence, 142–143; effect on efforts to engage population, 161–165, 185–187, 217–218; brutalizing effects on German soldiers' behavior, 76–77, 188–189. *See also* Anti-Slavism; Belorussia; Operations:

anti-partisan; Order Service; Wehrmacht: Feldkommandanturen; Wehrmacht: other units; Wehrmacht: Territorial and Security battalions; Wehrmacht: Territorial and Security regiments

Anti-Semitism, 9, 13, 29, 82, 224; in officer corps, 10–11, 19; and anti-Bolshevism, 12, 21–22, 74; and "criminal orders" of 1941, 23–24, 53, 55–56; toward Polish Jews in 1939, 46; Wehrmacht-SS cooperation over, 54–56; and divide and rule occupation policy, 56–57; in 221st Security Division, 66–72, 98–99, 158; "Jew equals Bolshevik equals partisan" equation, 88–94, 106–107; in 221st Security Division's propaganda, 180. *See also* Jews, treatment of

Anti-Slavism, 9, 10–11, 29, 76, 224; in officer corps, 10–12; and World War I, 11–12, 29, 213; and Free Corps, 12–13; and Nazi aims for Soviet Union, 21–22, 45–46, 116; and German perceptions of Soviet living conditions, 78–79; in 221st Security Division, 79–81, 83, 158, 208, 213, 217; in 403d Security Division, 83; in 203d Security Division, 156–157

Armed Forces High Command (OKW), 17, 172; issues security directives, 73–74, 88–89, 220; policy toward partisan deserters, 134, 140